W

ALSO BY DOMNICA RADULESCU

Feminist Activism in Academia:
Essays on Personal, Political and Professional Change
(McFarland, 2010)

Women's Comedic Art as Social Revolution

*Five Performers and the Lessons
of Their Subversive Humor*

DOMNICA RADULESCU

McFarland & Company, Inc., Publishers
Jefferson, North Carolina, and London

Portions of Chapter One originally appeared as "Isabella's Trick or What a Sixteenth-Century Comedienne Can Teach Us Today," in *The Theater of Teaching and the Teaching of Theater*, ed. Domnica Radulescu and Maria Stadter Fox (Lanham, Maryland: Lexington, 2005), 161–188.

LIBRARY OF CONGRESS CATALOGUING-IN-PUBLICATION DATA

Radulescu, Domnica, 1961–
    Women's comedic art as social revolution : five performers and the lessons of their subversive humor / Domnica Radulescu.
        p.   cm.
    Includes bibliographical references and index.

    ISBN 978-0-7864-6072-4
    softcover : acid free paper ∞

        1. Women comedians — Italy — History.   2. Women comedians — France — History.   3. Women comedians — United States — History.   4. Women in the theater — Italy — History.   5. Women in the theater — France — History. 6. Women in the theater — United States — History. 7. Feminism and theater — Italy — History.   8. Feminism and theater — France — History.   9. Feminism and theater — United States — History.   I. Title.
    PN1590.W64R34 2012
    792.702' 80922 — dc23
    [B]   2011043811

BRITISH LIBRARY CATALOGUING DATA ARE AVAILABLE

Front cover design by David K. Landis (Shake It Loose Graphics)

Manufactured in the United States of America

McFarland & Company, Inc., Publishers
  Box 611, Jefferson, North Carolina 28640
    www.mcfarlandpub.com

For my mother,
and for all the women who survive,
resist and thrive through laughter

Acknowledgments

I would like to acknowledge Washington and Lee University for support with research and travel funding and in particular for the Lenfest grants that have provided invaluable summer time for the completion of this manuscript.

I owe a large debt of gratitude to Shirley Richardson for her competent help with various logistical aspects of this project.

I am very thankful to Bess Ruff for the meticulous work in helping format the manuscript.

I am grateful to the staff of the Bibliothèque de l'Arsénal in Paris and the Newberry Library in Chicago for help with the study and research of archival documents. Deep thanks are owed to Traci Mierzwa for her superb help with indexing and other important editorial details.

I am grateful to all my funny, empowered and loving women friends who have inspired me and aided in the production of this book with their stories, sparkle, suggestions, and support.

Table of Contents

Preface

Women's Comedic Art as Social Revolution celebrates several exemplary women artists who created, each in a different historical period, revolutionary forms of comic performance and discourse, defying the flagrant prejudices about women being either incapable of creating humor other than as objects of male laughter, or being linked to humor other than laughing at the jokes of men. The works and modes of comic theatrical expression discussed in this book fall into the category designated by Jill Dolan as "utopian performatives,"[1] as they offer subversions of the status quo of patriarchal societies, communities and structures through laughter and in doing so they "describe or capture fleeting intimations of a better world."[2] These particular performances create communities through laughter and a comic response to the insults and injuries inflicted upon women through sexist humor and to various forms of gender inequity in society at large. The women artists who populate this book tell their stories in their own voices and through the lens of their own comedic imaginations and, as they do, so I wholeheartedly join with Jill Dolan in this statement: "To see women onstage, alone, telling stories is still, for me, a political moment, one I can't (or won't) take for granted."[3]

Several times while I was researching and writing this book, I was served by some of my male colleagues, both in the U.S. and in France (where I traveled quite often to engage in archival research for the book) with some of the following priceless attempts at a joke: "Women actually have humor?!" or "I didn't know women did comedy," or just simply a pretense of wonderment: "Women and comedy?!" For some reason these colleagues must have thought their joke was funny, for they laughed heartily at their lame attempts at humor, even though I stared at them without even a smile (on my most courageous days) or attempted a strained smile (on my more timid, reconciliatory "I don't want to embarrass the people who insult me" days). Invariably, a comment by a feminist humor critic would come to mind as I stood in front of the

1

colleague that was as intrigued by the idea that women engaged in the production of comedy as if I had told him that women possessed three rotating
heads that each spoke a different language. This critic says that often men
feel threatened by women's laughter because "they unconsciously are afraid
that the ultimate joke will be the size of their sexual apparatus."[4] I could have
served those unsupportive colleagues this line and most likely scored a victory,
but somehow I never mustered up enough courage to say it. Or almost never.
I thought it would be a cheap and unfair blow to allude to the man's virility
since the way he was endowed at birth was entirely beyond his control and I
would be doing unto others what women have had done unto them forever:
confuse biology with behavior.

But then as I thought of the countless times I had spent with my women
friends laughing until we couldn't breathe, I realized that quote was completely
true *and* fair: for what she means by "the size of their sexual apparatus" goes
beyond that literal size of male genitalia, which in all honesty has in all times
and all places produced great hilarity among women, and refers also to the
size of that symbol of power that is the phallus and that if allowed, would
express itself all the time with the irrepressible and shameless arrogance that
made my hundreds of hours of research and passionate writing about a subject
I loved seem insignificant and worthless. After I internalized that concept
deeply enough I realized that the men's attempted jokes about my research
in the area of women's comedy already expressed precisely that fear alluded
to by the feminist critic and that I didn't need to score another victory. The
very fact I was engaging in an intellectual exploration of the many ways in
which women's laughter has resisted, subverted, mocked or been victorious
over the real or imagined "size," the constructed power and arrogance of the
male phallus was victory enough. The next time a male colleague responded
with that same cynical line about women's humor being something of a puzzle
I actually found enough courage to respond in kind: "Believe it or not, we
do have humor, only you wouldn't understand it! You must be scared of it!"
I said, and actually winked. I rarely wink at people, but somehow that time
it seemed like the right thing to do, as if making an accomplice of the very
man who was trying to put me down while simultaneously hinting that I
knew why he might feel threatened by women's comedy and laughter: because
he might be undone and the phallus might actually prove to be in the inspired
words of another feminist humor theorist, a creature more akin to a sweet
benevolent creature. The colleague actually appeared embarrassed by my
response and asked me to elaborate on my book project. I was happy to oblige.

In a very primal and simple way this could be considered as the underlying motivation that runs through this book project: to counteract the phallic

arrogance of the men and the patriarchal institutions and ideologies that have failed to recognize women's equal contributions to the laughter of the world with an admittedly modest but passionately researched display of several funny, vibrant, giggling, ironic, sarcastic, mocking, laughing voices of women artists. And to say: "It's all right if you guys don't get it. What matters is that we women do and we are having a hell of a good time at it. However, feel free to join in the laughter any time, if you are man enough!"

These artists are the sixteenth century celebrated performer, poet, playwright, scholar, and improviser Isabella Andreini; the seventeenth century performer, improviser, creator of humor Catherine Biancolelli; the twentieth century Italian playwright, performer, feminist militant Franca Rame; and two contemporary playwright/performance artists working in the U.S. and exploding stereotypical representations of women through uncompromising irony and comedic virtuosity—Deb Margolin and Kimberly Dark. They all have in common the creation of a type of humor that subverts patriarchal modes of representation, conventional notions of gender roles and stereotypical images of women and that raises significant questions about the creativity of women and their condition in society. All performers discussed and/or interviewed in the first four chapters of my book are uniquely holistic in their approach to theater and have thus created a form of comic discourse and performance in which they are creators of their own comic roles, as well as directors and performers of these roles and/or improvisers of text and stage action.

In the fifth and last chapter of the book I create a practical guide for theater practitioners, teachers of theater and literature, and for all those who perform, teach theater or engage in both teaching and performance. The purpose of this last chapter is to inspire theater teachers and practitioners alike to the creation of shows, workshops, courses and a theatrical practice that makes use of feminist improvisational techniques, and of comedic strategies that empower women artists as well as women in society with the ability to create humor and subvert oppressive structures with laughter.

Women's Comedic Art as Social Revolution is the first extensive study of the comic and improvisational art of this particular set of female theater artists seen in relation to each other and to the tradition of the commedia dell'arte. While there is one doctoral dissertation[5] and one relatively recent study[6] that have treated at some length and devoted chapters to the performance art of Isabella Andreini and to her role in the creation of the "Renaissance woman," and while there is a handful of studies on the plays and performance art of Franca Rame, the only full-length article on the extraordinary contributions to Western comedy of the performer Catherine Biancolelli is one written by the author of this book.[7] There are no studies that explore in any depth the creation of humor, the improvisational comedy of all these artists, in comparison to each other and in relation to the theatrical tradition that has inspired them, as well as to the oppression of women in society in their respective times.

Furthermore, this is also the first study on female performers to offer a practical guide for theater practitioners and teachers, by taking the commedia dell'arte techniques used by Isabella Andreini, Catherine Biancolelli, and Franca Rame, linking them to contemporary performance artists and theater activists working in the United States and adjusting these techniques to the concerns of women and marginalized groups across different cultures today.

The texts used in the discussion of the comedy created by Catherine Biancolelli, from the collection of plays gathered by the seventeenth century actor Evaristo Gherardi, have never been analyzed or discussed at any length. There is one modern version of this six-volume collection,[8] but other than fleeting references to its existence in various studies about seventeenth century commedia dell'arte, this is the extent to which these texts have been explored. In my analysis, I have used one of the original seventeenth century editions. Therefore this book also holds an important historical value as it forges new ground in the rediscovery of archival texts and forgotten performers while connecting them with modern-day women performers and tracing the evolution of women's humor across historical periods and geographical areas. Finally, while there is a significant number of feminist studies about comic women writers and women's humor (such as Regina Barreca, Frances Gray, Judy Little, Philip Auslander, and Mahadev Apte) and an abundance of studies on commedia dell'arte in general, there are no studies that establish the links and similarities between the genre of the commedia dell'arte and modern feminist theater and performance. This gives a certain historical depth to the scholarship on feminist theater as well as to the emergence of modern theater in general.

Women's Comedic Art as Social Revolution is a necessary contribution to performance studies, women's studies and humor studies altogether, as it establishes a crucial missing link in the history of Western comedy and stresses the significant role that women have played in the development of Western theater. The book not only dispels misconceptions about women's inability to create humor but also traces the intricacies of the art of several pioneers of comic performance.

Introduction

Women's Humor Across the Ages

Myth has it that she lifted up her dress, revealed her naked vulva, made obscene gestures mocking the pains of birth and painted her body to suggest a face, with the breasts as eyes and the pubic area as the mouth. Performance art some three thousand years ago! Or *The Vagina Monologues* without the monologues! At the sight of this spectacle, the story goes, Demeter, the grieving goddess of the earth, mourning the loss of her daughter, laughed for the first time and allowed the earth to bloom and give harvest again, for the half a year when her daughter Persephone was back from her kingdom of death and doom.

Baubo, the old woman of Halimo, is the mythic figure who creates laughter and unabashedly sexual humor[1] and the only one who is capable of lifting the veil of mourning off Demeter's eyes as she grieves for Persephone. Demeter "laughs, relaxes and drinks the potion she had formerly refused" when Baubo shows "her organs lay bare all the parts veiled by shame." Iambe, daughter of Echo and Pan, is another mythological female clown who made Demeter laugh. She is talkative, joyous, unapologetically sexual in her funny chatter and acrobatic dances. "Through her mother Echo, 'a disembodied voice,' she is a babbler, a being who is all words, while Pan's paternity associates her with gestures that unite both music and dance with rude sexuality."[2]

Comic women and women who create laughter, or who entertain, have a long history; they have just been neglected. Women comedians have existed since antiquity, have crossed the Christian era, flourished with the commedia dell'arte and continue through the centuries to our days, when we are confronted with a significant rise in female writers and performers of comedy. Mary Unterbrink has remarked that "women have created their share of humor over the years, though they have not had an easy time presenting it to the public."[3]

5

The frescoes of Knossos present women acrobats; Horace refers to female entertainers, or "mimae." Though not allowed to perform speaking parts, in the mime performances of ancient Greece, women did play the women's parts.[4] Horace also mentions female comedians like Arbuscula of the first century B.C., whom he considered "magnificent and delightful." Cicero mentions the comedian Cytheris who was also the lover of the triumvir Anthony, and Dionysia, "the gesticularia and saltatricula," a famous female performer who apparently gained the impressive salary of two hundred thousand sesterces annually.[5]

According to Annette Lust, there were other famous women mimes such as Denisa, Valeria Cloppia, Lucilia, Hermione, Antiodemis and Julia Bassilla (237). In antiquity and in the early Christian era, "the mimic actress could appear as a dancer and as a gesticulator in precisely the same way as her male counterpart," notes Nicoll (85). "Was it not a mimic actress," he remarks, "who in later days, rose from the theater in which she had been reared to occupy the proudest throne in Christendom? Theodora, Empress of the Eastern Empire, was in her youth a mima" (85). Procopius notes about her, "Very clever and witty she was, and she gained great fame from her skill in her adopted profession. But as a woman, she had no sense of shame. No one ever saw her blushing" (98). It is said about Theodora that one of her acts was to lie naked on the stage, place grains on her body and let a flock of geese feed on the grain. Some food for thought for the fathers of the church! The female comedians or mimic actresses were as important artistically as men during the rule of Theodora and throughout some of the early Christian period, before the fathers of the church started in due manner to link them to Satan and consider them "children of Satan."[6]

Middle Ages documents attest to the presence of real women onstage, and the French *contes* or *fabliaux* were almost always recounted by women storytellers (*conteuses* or *fabulatrici*).[7] In Boccaccio's *Decameron* it is the women who lead the game of storytelling and who tell the funniest and bawdiest of the stories, as well as the stories in which the female characters are bold initiators of sexual activity. It is one of the reasons why Boccaccio is considered as one of the first humanist feminists.[8] Franca Rame talks about the women's peasant culture, where it is the women who tell the stories. Once the children are asleep, the stories are obscene and bawdy. Rame notes, "Obscenity has always been the most efficient weapon against the threat of instilling in the people's heads the feeling of guilt, shame, sin; combating this threat has been the principal task of comic actors and in particular of actresses."[9] Rame touches here upon the important issue of women's centuries-old comic oral culture which grew in parallel but separately from men's written and oral culture and which has quite often emerged as an alternative form of comic expression, subversive of both patriarchal social structures and canonical forms of literary representation.[10]

Out of Italy, in the second half of the sixteenth century, several troupes of actors *and* actresses made their glorious appearance onto the stages and streets of Europe. They were known by such names as I Gelosi, I Confidenti, Gli Uniti, and the last Italian troupe in France was actually called the Ancienne Troupe de la Comédie Italienne (The Ancient Troupe of the Italian Comedy). These troupes became a great sensation *because* of the presence of real flesh-and-blood women, particularly in France and England, where women's roles were still played by young boys. The age of the commedia dell'arte started and women finally had their day in the theater, not just as silent mimes or singers, but as improvisers, performers, role creators. According to modern scholarship, women had a crucial role in the development of comedy and in the art of improvisation in the commedia dell'arte, a "secret" so well kept for the last four centuries[11] that common knowledge and a large body of scholarship recognized for a long time mostly the male clowns, the likes of Arlecchino, Pulcinella, and Buratino as the great creators of burlesque and slapstick humor, hardly mentioning any women. Although the great commedia actresses have received throughout the centuries a certain amount of praise from commedia historians and critics, they are rarely presented as creators of humor in their own right. Since commedia dell'arte is generally believed to mark the beginning of modern theater in Europe[12] and since, according to recent scholarship, women had so important a role in its development, the truth is clear: women performers and improvisers had a crucial role in the development of modern Western theater.

This book tells the stories of several women clowns who bequeathed to us an important artistic heritage and who have carried on, each in a different way, the spirit and the laughter of Baubo. The first woman lived five centuries ago in Italy, became the main actress of the most famous traveling acting troupe of her time, I Gelosi, and dazzled princes and princesses, kings and queens, poets, artists and philosophers with her artistic talents. Her name was Isabella Andreini. The second was also of Italian origin, but lived in France during the reign of Louis XIV, the Sun King, started acting also around the age of fifteen, became the most famous comic performer of the acting troupes of her time, drew the attention of Louis the XIV, and for fifteen years, dazzled and entertained audiences of all walks of life. She was Caterina Biancolelli. The third one is still alive, was born and lived in Italy, started acting when she was eight days old in her mother's arms, *almost* received the Nobel Prize together with her husband and performing partner of many decades, Dario

Fo, outraged Italy's conservative right with her radically political shows for
women, delighted and satisfied with her revolutionary shows the marginalized
and the downtrodden, mainly women, and is still making audiences all over
the world laugh and think. She was a senator in Italy: Franca Rame. The few
others I discuss or have interviewed for this book are contemporary female
American comedians, performance artists or theater activists who write and
perform or direct their own plays and who tackle in their art modern issues
of gender and its intersections with class, ethnicity, and sexual orientation.
Such artists are Deb Margolin, Kimberly Dark, Joan Lipkin, and Norma
Bowles.

   This book focuses on a certain kind of female performer who at times
improvises, who always creates her own roles, and who produces a kind of
humor, which, like the act of Baubo, dispels the sadness of other women by
its bold sexual overtones and sense of shared experience. I highlight the contributions that actresses from different periods in the development of modern
theater and performance have made in the domain of comic performance and
in the creation of a humor that subverts patriarchal modes of representation
and stereotypical images of women and raises significant questions about the
creativity of women and their condition in society. Two of these performers,
Isabella Andreini and Catherine Biancolelli, lived and acted a century apart
from each other, during the golden age of the commedia dell'arte, which
stretched roughly from the mid-sixteenth century to the end of the seventeenth
century, started in Italy and was quickly adopted and emulated in France.
The third performer, Franca Rame, follows in that tradition, and as a modern-day actress, playwright, director draws from the commedia traditions of
her own family of performers. She revolutionized Italian theater in the 1970s
and '80s and created a unique form of performance for and about women.
The American performers and theater groups discussed in the book, though
not obviously connected to the tradition of the commedia dell'arte, share with
those first actresses a subversive and carnivalesque humor that challenges all
traditional gender roles and that is empowering to women of many walks of
life. They also share the fact that they are creators of the texts they perform
onstage: they tell their own or other women's stories and bring female voices
to center stage.

   I argue that the comedy that Isabella Andreini and Catherine Biancolelli
have created, as female pioneers on some of the most important stages of Italy
and France, is profoundly subversive and revolutionary for their respective
times and bears many of the signs of what today would be considered feminist
humor and feminist performance. I then explore the comic performance of
Franca Rame in light of the tradition of female comedians and in particular

of these two stellar ancestors, while delineating the most striking aspects of what I consider to be full-fledged feminist comedy. I then discuss the comic art created onstage by contemporary female artists such as Deb Margolin in light of feminist performance strategies and aesthetics but also by comparison with the commedia type of female humor. I argue that the achievements of these artists bear not only on the development of feminist performance today, not only on the development of theater in general, but have significant value for the lives of women outside literary texts and outside the realm of artistic performance, in society.

That which links these performers across the centuries and which is particularly original about their contributions is the totality of their art: they are not only actresses of comic parts, but they are also largely the creators of their own parts, and they are not just any creators of comic roles, but most have also distinguished themselves by their remarkable talent as improvisers, that is, as creators in performance. Finally, their humor exhibits the following traits: it explodes gender stereotypes, is critical of the condition of women in society, and is different from the humor created by their male counterparts in the profession or by male writers. It produces a laughter of recognition which is comforting for women and has the potential of being uncomfortable for men, and it has a profoundly carnivalesque dimension in its displacing of hierarchies and mixing up of aesthetic categories. For the commedia actresses as for Franca Rame, improvisation is the pivotal point in the delineation of their particular type of humor and performance because it contains the element of surprise and freedom, which is nonexistent or is present to a much smaller extent in the literary, text-based theater written by male authors and developed during the last several centuries on the Western stages.

According to Gustave Attinger, "the spirit of the commedia is the fruit of a fusion between popular traditions and the spirit of the Renaissance."[13] Robert Henke notes: "At the heart of the commedia dell'arte was the structural tension between the linear, well-constructed plot based on a literary model and the centrifugal improvisations of the stand-up performer."[14] Also known as *commedia all'improviso* (improvised comedy), *commedia delle maschere* (comedy of masks) and *commedia dei zanni* (comedy of servants), this new type of theater is exclusively an actors' theater. The term *arte* is used in its ancient meaning of skill and professionalism, calling to mind the medieval guilds of specialized groups of professionals. The complete definition of this theater is given by the very names it has acquired: it relies entirely on the actors' professionalism and imagination, it is largely based on improvisation, most of the characters wear masks and the characters who give it its very comic essence are servants (Molinari). Its origins are multiple:

1. The *commedia erudita* of the Renaissance

2. The clowns, mimes and jugglers entertaining the masses in the street and the nobles and princes at their courts

3. The comedies of Terence and Plautus

4. Atelan farces (rustic farces with masques, developed in the time of the Roman Empire)

5. Asiatic mimes[15]

6. The women's oral tradition and the performing art of courtesans.[16]

Though no women were recorded earlier than the second half of the sixteenth century as performing full-fledged stage parts, women entertainers were not at all rare during the Renaissance. In most cases they held the status of courtesans or of *oneste meretrice* (honest courtesans). Having a high level of education, unparalleled by women of other social classes among whom, during the Renaissance, illiteracy was rampant,[17] courtesans were usually expected to be able to perform and entertain and were often quite skilled at improvising.[18]

The first contract of a commedia dell'arte troupe dates in 1545 — a troupe constituted exclusively of men. The year 1564 marks the date when the first woman appears in a contract — a certain Lucrezia of Sienna. Three years later, a woman called Vincenza, probably Vincenza Armani, was the leader of a troupe from Mantua, while another company was led by a certain Flaminia. Even traditional historical scholarship of the commedia dell'arte acknowledges that it was the participation of women that largely explains the sudden and rapidly growing success of the commedia troupes outside of Italy. Known commedia critics such as Pierre-Louis Duchartre, Ferdinando Taviani, and Gustave Attinger acknowledge the crucial role of actresses in the development and success of this theatrical genre. Attinger points out that not only did women heighten the comic element of the commedia but comedy could not have achieved the level it reached by the eighteenth century, were it not for the presence of women (327). Taviani notes that

> the feminine face of the Commedia dell'arte, today the most forgotten, represents, with any probability, the determining factor in the process by which the theater of the companies from the end of the 16th century, are still remembered today as a special genre and almost as an archetype of theater. And in fact, in the beginning, it was them, the actresses, who incarnated the noblest level of that which became the symbol of the Commedia dell'arte: improvisation.[19]

The revolutionary studies by Kathleen McGill have shown that it was the women performers who introduced and developed the highest level of virtuosity in the art of improvisation that lies at the very foundation of the genre. According to McGill, the main reasons why the first commedia actresses were such virtuosos of improvisation is that they were the inheritors of a rich women's oral culture which extended from storytelling, to songs and anecdotes for special occasions, to the poems and improvised lyrics of the courtesans. Fernando Taviani has analyzed in detail the revolutionary dimensions of the women's presence and creativity in the development of the commedia, in his study *La Fleur et le guerrier*. However, even the most modern feminist studies do not engage to any significant extent in discussions of the role of these actresses and improvisational artists, in the creation and development of certain types of humor and comic performance. That is precisely the purpose of my study.

Although I focus my study of women's creation of humor in the commedia theaters on the two exemplary actresses already mentioned, Isabella Andreini and Catherine Biancolelli, it is noteworthy that many other actresses are known to have contributed and achieved world fame during this golden age of commedia dell'arte. At least some of them probably deserve studies in their own right: Vitoria Piissimi, Vincenza Armani, Brigita Bianchi, Ursula Cortesi. The reasons for my choice of Andreini and Biancolelli are the following: with regard to the creation of roles and the production of comedy, Isabella Andreini and Catherine Biancolelli are known to have created the two most important and influential female roles, which were later incorporated in the theater of Molière, Marivaux, Goldoni, Beaumarchais, and echoed all the way to the modern theater of Eugène Ionesco or Jean Giraudoux or even today's American performance artists: the role of the inamorata, the young, romantic, passionate lover, and Colombine, the witty and salacious maid-confidante, and, most importantly, the female clown or trickster. With regard to the documentation and the actual written traces, Isabella Andreini, having been both a performer and a writer and scholar in her own right, left a significant body of work from which we can infer a great many things about her creativity, her views and her importance in the context of her time.[20] As for the fame they achieved during their own lifetime, these two actresses were about as accomplished as an actor/actress would have possibly hoped to be in their time; the documents and reports of their contemporaries attest to their remarkable talents. Finally, I believe Isabella Andreini and Catherine Biancolelli are responsible for the creation of a kind of humor that displays many of the traits feminist theorists consider marks of a particularly emancipated or revolutionary kind of female humor: subversive of stereotypical images of women, reflective of a women's culture as separate from and often subversive of the mainstream patriarchal culture, critical or even mocking of male-created social structures, institutions or modes of behavior, with bursts of that unabashed, comforting Baubo big laughter.

The great Molière, Marivaux, Goldoni, and Beaumarchais owe important debts to the first actresses of the commedia who, far from being simple performers of memorized scripts, were creators of roles, dialogues, scenarios, and initiators of a line of female characters that extends all the way into the twentieth century. While the male parts which developed during the commedia and originate as far back as Greek and Atelan farces, such as the silly, bawdy servant, the lusty old man, the pompous doctor, and the violent, arrogant captain, inspired many of the characters of classical comedy, the commedia female parts, being a newer creation, developed beyond the boundaries of caricature and fixed types and offered rich inspiration for the authors of classical comedy in France and Italy. Dorine, Toinette, Silvie, Lisette, Suzanna, Marceline, characters of Molière, Goldoni, Marivaux or Beaumarchais, would simply not exist without the *innamorate* and the *fantesche* (female servant) of the commedia dell'arte. Furthermore, it is precisely these characters who move the plot in classical comedy, devise the most unexpected and comic tricks and always have the last laugh.

As already noted, the golden age of the commedia dell'arte stretched between the second half of the sixteenth century up to the historic date of 1697, when the Italian troupe in residence in Paris was forced out by the police, with special mandate from the king. The offense of this most celebrated commedia troupe of the Biancolelli family was that they had announced the performance of the comedy *The False Prude* which was, for good reasons, perceived as a mockery of the king's religious wife Madame de Maintenon.[21] This period of almost one and a half centuries was a period of true creative opportunities for female performers, who not only produced comedy as actresses, but created it side by side with male performers, led the companies they were part of and were often responsible for much of the fame that these companies achieved. Actresses such as Isabella Andreini, Vittoria Piissimi, Vincenza Armani, Diana Ponti, Catherine and Isabella Biancolelli, Flaminia Riccoboni, Brigita Bianchi, Orsola Cortesi, became famous for their art of improvisation and for the comic roles they created, which, for the most part, had no precedent in ancient or popular forms of entertainment. The actress improviser, creator of her own comedy, of her own scenes, lines, roles, was a phenomenon particular to the golden age of the commedia, and sadly almost disappeared for over two centuries, as female comic roles became almost entirely the creation of male authors, while actresses regressed more and more to the status of objects of the male gaze at best and courtesans at worst. The exceptions of such legendary actresses as Sarah Bernhardt only confirm the absence of women from the realm of the creation of humor in the authentic, professional manner of the early commedia dell'arte actresses.[22]

That women are funny, that they have, throughout the ages created laughter and a multitude of forms of humor — which is often a transgressive humor — has been fiercely kept a secret by writers, critics, philosophers, theater historians and anthropologists. In parallel with the silencing of women's humor, a long tradition of clichés with regard to women's "lack of humor" has been created.[23] In the twentieth century, the seventies gave rise to an outburst of clichés about the bra-burning humorless feminists whose "crime" was not to have the sense to roll and roar with laughter at the long array of bulb-screwing jokes or, as the *Feminist Encyclopedia* points out, to not find "rape and sex with little girls funny," while having the audacity to smile at the idea of "male impotence and vaginas with teeth."[24]

For the past four decades, a significant amount of scholarship mostly by feminist critics has attempted and largely succeeded at counteracting such clichés and disparaging attitudes and at bringing into the open the well-kept "secret" that women can actually be funny. This body of scholarship has helped legitimize the notion that not only do women have a sense of humor, but they have for millennia created humor in a variety of forms, and have woven, like the mythic Arachne, a multicolored tapestry of comic expression, largely transmitted via oral culture and revealed in performance or in a variety of literary forms which break with traditional norms.

As feminist scholars have shown,[25] women's humor has largely been left unrecognized at best and censured or crushed at worst, for two main reasons: being often a humor which subverts and mocks patriarchy, it has been perceived as threatening to men; secondly, being often different in nature, in the object of laughter and in the forms of expression from male humor, and therefore not meeting the canonical standards of male humor, it has been dismissed as non-humor. Philip Auslander has pointed out that "humor in women's writing has often gone unrecognized as such by male critics or has been dismissed as trivial in comparison with the comic efforts of male writers" and women have been "excluded from the comic tradition, except as the object of male humor and have been assigned the 'responsive behavior,' that is, smiling and laughing at men's jokes."[26]

In the words of Regina Barreca, "The history of comedy has in fact been the history of male comedy." This corresponds in large degree to the silencing of women's comedy and humor. Frances Gray justly remarks that "most feminist activity has been centrally concerned with silence, and with its breaking" (13) and that, since "the field of comic discourse is perhaps the most fiercely guarded of all against female clowns and female critics, ... it is for this reason that it is as important for women to assume these roles as it is for them to enter fields more apparently vital to the achievement of social change" (13).

In his anthropological study of humor, Mahadev Apte argues that "women's humor reflects the existing inequality between the sexes not so much in its substance as in the constraints imposed on its occurrence, on the techniques used, on the social settings in which it occurs, and on the kind of audience that appreciates it" (69). In tune with this view, though a notch more radical, is Barreca's notion that a significant part of women's comedy has often "been misread because the anger underlying the humor has disturbed the conservative conventions of comedy" (10). According to many theoreticians of humor, these conventions are supposed to exude joy and, in Hegelian terms, to reflect a consciousness free of contradictions and at peace with itself. At least as radical is Anne Beatt's remark that the hidden reason why men feel threatened by women's humor is that "they unconsciously are afraid that the ultimate joke will be the size of their sexual apparatus."[27] In more general terms, this "ultimate joke" may refer to anything that has to do with male sexual performance in a literal way, or symbolically, with the phallus as a sign of power and social omnipotence.

Although according to Apte, anthropological data seem to point to the contrary, namely that "women's humor generally lacks the aggressive and hostile qualities of men's humor" (70), this absence seems to be due to the fact that

> women's relative lack of freedom to engage in certain types of activities in the public domain seems closely related to their socially inferior status in that domain and to the emphasis that many societies place on such cultural values as modesty, politeness, and passivity in the context of female roles [73].

An important distinction must be made between women's humor in culture and society, which is the object of anthropological studies of humor such as the one by Apte, and the creation of humor by women writers, performers and artists which often incorporates and gives voice, at the aesthetic or performative level, to the silenced women in society, and which forms the object of study of feminist theoreticians and critics in the domain of literature and performance arts, as well as of this book. The fact that women in society have so often been silenced, and prevented from expressing themselves in ways which contradict the image of the modest, passive woman, is complemented by the fact that there have been women artists, creators, and storytellers who have broken this pattern and have created humor and laughter throughout the centuries and across different cultures. Apte's anthropological findings also point to the absence, in most cultures, of female clowns and tricksters. However, the history of performance, as well as myth itself, reveals examples of female tricksters and clowns, and moreover of a female humor which is transgressive and subversive. It is precisely because of this silencing of women's humor in society, that when it does burst out from its cage, it is often transgressive, angry, disruptive, and for these reasons threatening to those who hold the reins of power and of joking out loud.

Take myth, for example. The Baubo type of humor — obscene, unrestrained, physical — sharply contradicts the view of women as modest and passive. By the time of Empress Theodora, the open display of the female body and of sexual humor was as subversive to the teachings of the church as it was severely condemned by the fathers of the church. Apte has shown that in many societies, from Iraq to France, to Sicily, to Nepal, women — particularly in rural settings — create "female dramas" among themselves in which they mock, impersonate and ridicule men, going as far as tying large phalli around their waists, chasing after another woman and mimicking sexual intercourse and/or rape (76–77); men are not allowed to participate or watch these comic displays, and are afraid of becoming the subject of women's ridicule — which indeed they are. Arachne, the bold mythic weaver who competes with Athena herself, is punished to the crawl and silence of the spider by the goddess who, of all the Olympian female figures, most upholds the patriarchal values of her father, Zeus. The reason for this punishment? She mockingly depicted in her beautiful tapestry the sexual exploits, or otherwise bluntly put the sexual assaults, of the great Zeus upon mortal and immortal women. Arachne is indeed the angry woman artist or creator of transgressive humor. In the words of another feminist theoretician of humor, she "mocks the deepest possible norms, norms four thousand years old."[28] Certainly, such humor has not been appreciated in patriarchal cultures, as it denounces, shakes, and questions the very roots at the base of the tree.

Baubo, the mythic woman who breaks Demeter's mourning and thus gets the Eleusynian mysteries started, or Theodora performing naked to the great outrage of the church, can be seen as the first examples of performance art, and as the beginning of comedy itself.[29] While several critics consider, on the contrary, that it was the Dionysian rites and the unleashed cult of the phallus which account for the emergence of comedy, there is no reason to believe that the complementary rites in honor of Demeter could not also be accepted as sources of comedy. In the view of Rosalind Miles, the celebrations in honor of the goddess, commonly known as "fertility rituals," were not actually about the growing of crops, but about the sexual pleasure and power of the goddess. Gray notes:

> A comedy linked to this rite, rather than to the Phallus, could abandon its insistence on compulsory marriage and eternal Oedipal conflict for a concentration on the pleasure of the moment. The Phallus could abandon its lonely role as hero and become penis again, fallible, unpredictable, irritating and cherishable: a creature more akin to Sooty than to Dionysus in all his power [30].[30]

It is precisely the seriousness of the Phallus as lonely "hero" that female laughter deflates quite often. If men so often worry that when alone with each other women often make fun of men's sexuality and sexual organs, it is because indeed they do. Luce Irigaray poignantly asks: "Isn't laughter the first form of liberation from a secular oppression? Isn't the phallic tantamount to the seriousness of meaning? Perhaps woman, and the sexual relation, transcend it 'first' in laughter?"[31]

The Baubo type of humor is, according to Gray, reflective of "a lost matriarchal paradise, you might say, a rich female culture in which one woman heals another, and ultimately Nature itself, by inventing comedy, a comedy joyously and benevolently sexual without being sexist" (1, 2). Both the Baubo sexual humor and the Arachne angry humor form what Gray has referred to as "a distinctly female form of laughter." Most feminist critics seem to agree, however, with one important fact: that women's humor, even when silenced or not recognized as such by men, is understood and appreciated by other women, particularly in the absence of men.[32]

The word and the concept of "feminist" will be used here in its larger sense of someone or something who or which "wishes to transform the sex-gender system,"[33] who or which "pays attention to women"[34] or is "a critique of male supremacy, formed and offered in the light of a will to change it, which in turn assumes a conviction that it is changeable."[35] I position myself as a feminist critic sharing the common belief of other feminist critics who, although extremely varied in their approaches, do generally agree "that oppression of women is a fact of life, that gender leaves its traces in literary texts and on literary history, and that feminist literary criticism plays a worthwhile part in the struggle to end oppression in the world outside of texts."[36] Rather than relying exclusively on any one feminist approach or theory, I engage in an eclectic approach reflective of what some critics have called "quilting": the stitching together of several approaches and theories which I believe best apply to the subject matter. I use the theories of French feminists Hélène Cixous and Luce Irigaray in the discussion of the relations between the female body, female humor and creativity, and, respectively, in the discussion of mimicry and hysteria as dimensions of subversive forms of performance for women. When discussing aspects of cross-dressing and acting in disguise, Judith Butler's theory of the construction of gender are pertinent, as are those of feminist humor theorists such as Judy Little and Lesley Ferris. When dealing with aspects of women's performative humor as a catalyst for social justice and gender equity, the work of Jill Dolan informs my explorations and conclusions. I, like Dolan, have always "connected performance and the possibility for something better in the world" and believe that "live performance provides a place where people come together, embodied and passionate, to share experiences of meaning making and imagination that can describe or capture fleeting intimations of a better world."[37]

I use the term "performance" in its complete meaning, which involves equally the use of "verbal art as action" and "the artistic event — the performance situation, involving performer, art form, audience and setting."[38] I take my theoretical cues in the discussion of performance from feminist performance theorists like Jill Dolan, Elin Diamond and Lizbeth Goodman, from folklore specialists who have studied the art of improvisation such as Albert Lord, and from feminist commedia critics such as Kathleen McGill, Ferdinando Taviani, and Louise Clubb.

In defining the specific character of the comedy created by these performers, I have made use of Bakhtin's theory of the carnival and Henri Bergson's theory of the mechanical, in combination with feminist comic theories of Regina Barreca, Judy Little, Frances Gray, Mahadev Apte, and Gloria Kaufman. I will delineate that which distinguishes the comedy of women artists and writers from that of men, that which in the comedy of these performers both resists and combats sexist attitudes and social injustice for women, as well as, at the aesthetic level, the canon of classical comedy, as for instance the "happy ending" in marriage. These female comic improvisers subvert both traditional discursive and dramatic forms such as the fixed comic types, the authority of the text, linear Aristotelian logic and plot development, and, ideologically, the idealized representation of women which is often inscribed within and corresponds to these particular forms, such as the "virtuous" woman whose identity is complete only through the union with a man in marriage, or the traditional norms of "feminine" beauty and comportment which praise passivity, frailty, sweetness, lack of sexual initiative and which ultimately deprive women of a voice of their own. The main characteristic of the comedy of these artists is that they create characters and images of women which elude definition and fixity through the very nature of their creative process of improvisation, through an organic and holistic flow between the body in performance and the creative imagination as it makes itself manifest onstage through language, gesture, and movement.

Shoshana Felman, in her discussion of women and madness, poses some very provocative questions with regard to the theories of "essentialist" feminists such as Luce Irigaray:

"What does speaking *for* women" imply? What is to speak *in the name of* the woman? What, in general manner, does speech *in the name of* mean? Is it not a precise repetition of the oppressive gesture of representation by means of which, throughout the history of logos, man has reduced the woman to the status of a silent and subordinate object, to something inherently *spoken for*? [9].[39]

In a broader sense, it seems inevitable for most feminist criticism and scholarship to speak *for* and *in the name* of women to some extent, and to fall, by various degrees, into the fallacy of generalizing. Any kind of criticism which is more obviously political in its orientation than other forms of criticism, be it Marxist, queer, or feminist, will speak "in the name of" someone. It is these same questions that have prompted, during the past decade, the proliferation of feminist voices and the increasing acceptance of difference and pluralism among feminists: precisely because ultimately, no one feminist critic can assume and presume to speak truly, authentically, in the name of all women or even of large groups of women. Maybe only anthropological "anti-criticism" and feminist ethnographies such as Lila Abu Lughod's *Speaking Women's Lives* or *Veiled Sentiments* fully allow women to speak for themselves and allow readers to form their own opinions on the stories they hear. Felman's questions must, however, be consistently asked as we form theories, as we try to make the world a better place for women. Ultimately, some of the authentic voices that touch us the most are precisely the voices of women artists who speak for themselves, while simultaneously touching upon issues that concern women across various ethnic, social, cultural, or racial lines. Paradoxically, what these performance artists confirm time and again is that the more specific and personal their stories, the more they touch us and the more authentically can we connect to them.

The performers I present in the pages of this book not only speak directly for themselves but they present themselves in flesh and blood to the world, tell their stories, laugh their laughs, make us laugh, act and talk as they are prompted, mostly by their own experience, talent, and imagination. It is why I believe the examples of such artists are ultimately stronger voices than any amount of feminist criticism, and it is why I avoid with consistency seeing them for too long through the lens of any one single feminist theory. As they speak for themselves such feminist performance artists incite us to also think of that which is similar in our own experience, to rethink our own modes of thinking, and mostly, as they make us laugh, they make each of us in the audience feel bolder about confronting what is wrong in our own lives or in the world.

Following the cues of the feminist theoreticians of humor mentioned so far and of performance theorists such as Judith Butler, Elin Diamond, Jill Dolan or Luce Irigray, this book analyzes in its first two chapters a distinctly female form of laughter as expressed in performance by the first influential actresses and improvisational female artists during the first one hundred and fifty years of the commedia dell'arte. The first Western actresses managed to create onstage and within the dynamic of their theater groups something like a virtual universe in which women could achieve onstage through the parts they created, that which they were deprived of in society: freedom, equality with men, and being in the center rather than on the margins.

Curiously, feminist performance criticism and humor theory have neglected or avoided, other than in the form of passing comments, any in-depth explorations of the commedia dell'arte as a rich source of inspiration or possible heritage for modern feminist theater. In fact, not little were my outrage and shock when, reading Sue-Ellen Case's anthology *Split Britches: Lesbian Practice/Feminist Performance* I ran into the dismissive sentence: "Yet, even amidst poor theater traditions Split Britches makes a unique contribution. *Commedia* after all offers the stories of fathers and sons."[40] If a passionate and prestigious feminist theoretician dismisses in one quick stroke an entire tradition in which women had an essential role and whose actresses portrayed precisely the empowered, gutsy, desperate, poor, no-nonsense, irreverent female characters standing up to those "fathers and sons," while also cross-dressing, riding horses, taking justice in their own hands (that Case claims were the invention of the Split Britches theater group), then indeed why should we be surprised that admittedly and openly traditional male critics would dismiss women's contribution to humor and theater in general?

My discussion of the comedy and humor of these first full-fledged female artists and of the ramifications of their art into modern forms of women's comedic expression, is not based necessarily on the idea of direct influences which, after all, are hard to establish and ascertain, but rather on the idea of revealing and enlarging the field of women's forms of comic expression throughout the ages, thus giving modern feminist and women's theaters a historical depth, and the comfort of a women's tradition of humor from which we can continue to draw empowerment and inspiration.

Aristotle held the view that comedy is what happens when people who are "inferior," such as women and slaves, imitate the actions of others. This has had long and noxious ramifications throughout the history of literature and culture, particularly because his theory of comedy, is based, as is his theory of tragedy, on generalizing upon existing dramas, such as the plays of Aristophanes. Indeed, Aristophanes' "inferior" comic characters are foreigners, slaves and women. Theoreticians of humor have developed superiority or disparagement theories,[41] incongruity theories,[42] and liberation or relief theories.[43] But, as Gray rightly points out, "'Classic' theories of humor..., sometimes assume that social and class differences have a bearing on the subject, but gender is virtually never mentioned" (20). And when gender is mentioned,

theories of comedy have by and large disparaged women and placed them in
a zone of inferiority vis-à-vis men.[44]

Modern feminist theorists, however, have not only revealed gender differences, in terms of the creation and appreciation of humor (therefore in
terms of the distinctions between the comic stimulus and the actual laughter),
but also in the connections between sexuality, power and humor. The act of
making someone laugh has been compared to a symbolic seduction,[45] which
in turn reflects a relation of power — like sexuality. Gray points out, "Like
sexuality, laughter has been sometimes highly valued, sometimes denigrated;
but like sexuality — indeed with sexuality — laughter has been closely bound
up with power" (6). Not only do women have had to overcome that "priceless"
and all too daunting "penis envy" and their own identity as a mere "lack" in
a world where the Phallus rules, but they have also been silenced in that area
which all too often has been relegated to the distinctly human, to that which,
according to philosophers from Aristotle to Kant to Bergson, separates humans
from animals: laughter. Women are "natural," and "instinctive," therefore
"incapable" of producing or engaging in a good laugh, therefore less "human."
Like sex, notes Gray, laughter is "something that men do to women" (7).

Uncovering the history and tradition of women's humor is comforting
and an excellent antidote to the sadness and discouragement one may feel in
the face of millennia of silencing and derision. Imagine the unrepressed laughter of Baubo and Demeter, imagine "shameless" Theodora feeding the geese
off her own body, imagine sixteenth century courtesans turned soldiers, imagine sixteenth century actresses dressed in drag and, behind it all, in the space
of their homes, imagine women all the way from sunny Sicily to freezing
Alaska, telling stories and joking about the all-too-powerful Phallus, mimicing, mocking and laughing together, comforting each other and weaving an
enormous and ironic tapestry which mirrors and mocks, in thick caricatures,
across the centuries, the self-assuredness of male sexuality and power.

It is ultimately, the most profound goal of this book: to provide some
comfort and empowerment to the seriously bruised image of women's ability
to create and appreciate humor. To reaffirm that at one time in the history of
Western performance and theater, women held a privileged place, is reason
for rejoicing. Whether actual influences of commedia dell'arte female humor
and performance upon modern women's humor and performance are to be
inferred, is ultimately, of lesser importance. What really matters in terms of
the larger picture of women's history and of breaking the silence is the discovery that twentieth century women stand-up comedians, playwrights, directors and comic performers do not stand alone on the long and often hostile
stage of history and that in fact their humor and the characters they create

and represent have roots which spread as far back as five centuries ago. What really matters is to find as many links as possible in the concatenation of women's laughs across the centuries. It matters to recognize Arachne's tapestry and Baubo's irreverence at all levels of artistic expression as well as at the level of culture and society.

Theories of humor have proliferated like mushrooms over the centuries, and they tend to be on the tedious side. Furthermore, as the assumption of so many traditional theories of humor is that the experiences of both sexes are identical and are largely outlined in terms of the male experience, "to read many of the 'classic' texts concerning humor ... can be a depressing experience for a woman."[46] It would be an unfruitful endeavor to engage in a survey or a long-winded analysis of theories of humor from Aristotle to the present, or even to attempt to establish and/or follow a rigid set of theories about humor and the comic. My intention is to reveal certain aspects of women's creation of humor and to delineate the ways in which they subvert and destabilize — at the level of performance — the status quo of patriarchy.

While I have incorporated, and, where appropriate, used certain canonical comic theories which have proven helpful in the delineation of a particular type of humor, such as the theories of Bergson or Bakhtin, I rely mostly on the scholarship of modern feminist critics of humor and comedy. Unlike the majority of classical studies of humor, feminist works about humor do not usually attempt to establish rigid theories. Rather, they are more fluid and often take into consideration the multitude of experiences of humor and laughter as they relate to social and historical context. They almost invariably assert women's "right" over language, women's affirmation of their abilities to play with language and to "dislodge the idea of lack from language."[47]

The woman clown or trickster is the central figure of this book. Isabella Andreini, though idealized in her own time and throughout the centuries as the noble, virtuous ingénue, turns out to have created a kaleidoscope of funny appearances, disguises and mini-roles by which she seems to mock, not only her own overtly feminine part of the inamorata, but also the other male parts in the theater of her time. She tricks, she mocks, she speaks and acts in obscene ways, she cross-dresses, just like the buffoons do. As I will show in the first chapter, Isabella is the creator of the female version of Bakhtin's carnival, five centuries ago.

Caterina Biancolelli develops the role of Colombina and takes it even beyond the comic heights reached in the commedia dell'arte by the famous Arlecchino. She mocks men and suitors of all social strata and walks of life, is at war with Arlecchino, impersonates all the important male figures of her society, lies, steals, deceives, never gets caught, always comes out on top, and always has the last laugh, just like the tricksters do. Her humor is unpredictable and biting, her laugh often unforgiving. Combining the playful sensuousness of the coquette with the ingenuity of the trickster, Colombina often creates a comedy that lacks the integrative and peace-giving characteristics of classical comedy and that certainly defies any preconceived ideas about women's comedy as "sweet," delicate, reconciliatory.

The young daughters in love and the defiant maids that fill the theater of Molière, Marivaux, Beaumarchais — those sacred monsters of classical comedy — would not have been what they are without the commedia dell'arte characters and without the input of these remarkable female improvisers and comedians. Isabella's romantic penchant for love combined with her defiance of paternal authority has profound echoes in the Marianes, Valéries, and Silvies of seventeenth and eighteenth century comedy, as Caterina reverberates her sharp irony and funny tricks all throughout the Toinettes, Lisettes, Marceline, Rosines and Susannes of the same comedy. If anything, these actresses created roles and improvised dialogues and stage actions which are in fact quite a bit more subversive and transgressive than those of the characters of the male playwrights. For instance, both Isabella and Colombina go through an impressive array of disguises, cross-dressings and impersonations of men, which are conspicuously absent from the plays of the male authors of classical comedy. The comic of cross-dressing of these actresses attains at times a dizzying effect of destabilizing gender lines and of turning the tables on patriarchal institutions and conventional images of women, in ways which we may not see again until the emergence of some twentieth century comediennes. Even when they do create strong female characters and endow them with wit and with some power to destabilize the authority of tyrannical fathers or husbands, the great authors of comedy still create female roles within the boundaries of accepted gender lines, and do not allow for the radical explosion of such lines, which can be achieved through cross-dressing, for instance, or through complete reversals and the use of the "woman on top" motif.

Franca Rame, also called by critics a twentieth century "Giulliaresca," or clown-trickster figure, combines all of the above features of her female commedia ancestors and creates a powerful feminist performance whose crisp and uncompromising humor denounces most forms of oppression of women by the patriarchal Western capitalist society, explodes stereotypical representations of women and gives women from all walks of life the comfort of laughter. She has her own modern carnival, in which she incorporates a multitude of female voices, which indeed tear down "all possible norms," fly with language, and revive the ancient goddess of laughter. Her comedy speaks to women from factories and from universities alike, to housewives and working mothers, and often the female characters she creates, from the dazzlingly blonde diva, to the "fat woman," to the exhausted working mother, or to the more recent no-nonsense sarcastic wife who teaches women ways of faking an orgasm, walk that fine line discussed by feminist theoreticians, between anger and laughter or between tears and laughter which has at times been dismissed by men as not funny, but which women generally find not only comical but also comforting and empowering.

The women whose stories form the subject of this book are each in their own way models of comic creation in performance, and all explode the boundaries between real life and created personae. As they walk in and out of their roles, on and off stage, their own stories are blended in with the characters they create, and, inversely, the roles they create onstage follow them into the street. They illustrate at best the double-edged sword that performance can be for women, while simultaneously subverting the very idea of performance, as ultimately they defy the fixity of the roles expected of them by audiences of their times. Working within the aesthetic system of the commedia dell'arte, which was famous precisely for its fixed parts, or *tipi fissi*, and in which roles often became inseparable from the person of the performer her/himself, these women artists made creative use of the performative techniques of the genre and of the creative opportunities that it offered them, while simultaneously making their own rules of creation as they went along. As they are largely responsible for the development of improvisation within the genre and therefore for the commedia's growing success during the Renaissance, Isabella and Caterina fly with it and break through the very fixity of the genre they helped establish as the most respected form of theatrical artistry during the Renaissance.

Franca Rame, drawing from the commedia tradition of her own family, breaks through the fixed roles that her own husband and stage partner had created for her and which had projected her on the screens and stages of Italy as the "blonde bombshell" of the fifties, to create a kind of performance whose originality lies largely in the element of improvisation, in the fluidity of the female parts and voices she creates, in the way it too defies and resists the fixity of canonical modern and bourgeois drama, the authority of the text, the tight corsets of any fixed female parts.

The two American women performers portrayed and interviewed in Chapter Four, Deb Margolin and Kimberly Dark, do not necessarily follow in an obvious or deliberate manner the tradition of the commedia dell'arte the way their Italian counterpart Franca Rame does. However their theatrical modus operandi, their style of working and of using both their own bodies and the theatrical space at their disposal, the totality of their performative

and creative work in the theater as creators of roles and performers simultaneously, the nature of their particular kind of comedy that dismantles canonical modes of representation in order to make room for the real concerns and
the diverse voices of women today, renders them akin to the artists discussed
before them. Deb Margolin often prefaces her performances, her classes and
interviews with the line: "The presence of a woman onstage is already something radical." It is also this sense of "something radical" with regard to
women's presence, voice, and actions onstage that the explorations and interviews in this chapter will illuminate.

The last chapter of the book pulls together all the threads of the commedia and feminist humor strategies explored in the first four chapters into
a practical guide for students, teachers, theater practitioners and activists. It
offers suggestions for experimentation with comic and performative improvisational techniques that are meant to use humor as a revolutionary strategy
for fighting sexist and homophobic stereotypes, for advancing social justice,
raising awareness about gender and other social inequities and actually creating
not only "intimations of a better world" but spaces that contain a better world,
or that turn "utopian performatives" into actual realities. I have myself experimented successfully with some of the techniques described here, and therefore
there is a less theoretical and more practical and personal dimension to this
entire chapter. Ultimately in the spirit of the commedia women and of the
genre of the commedia itself, which aimed at entertaining while also transforming communities and emancipating women and servants, the "utopian"
goal of this book is also to initiate social change, emancipation and revolutionary transformations of communities through the sparkle and the intricacies
of feminist humor. An interview with Norma Bowles, artistic director and
founder of the theater for social justice group called Fringe Benefits reveals
the revolutionary potential of comedy and of the commedia techniques in
dealing productively with various forms of discrimination and empowering
the marginalized and the oppressed. An interview with feminist playwright
and the artistic director of That Uppity Theater Company, Joan Lipkin, will
illustrate strategies of dealing with taboo subjects such as reproductive freedom, illness and disability with humor and comedic boldness.

I have deliberately brought it all home in the last two chapters of the
book, so to speak, that is, in the contemporary United States in order to create
an artistic arc across centuries and cultures and to create a utopic joining of
hands of funny women across history and geographical space. Such an arc
illustrates as well the third wave feminist project of applying, exploring, and
living feminism internationally and locally, unfolding it and making it present
and real at the level of large and small communities alike.

The women whose stories form the subject of this book are each in their own way models of comic creation in performance, and all of them explode the boundaries between real life and imagined personae. As they walk in and out of life and art, on and off stage, Isabella, Caterina, Franca, Deb, and Kimberly also give women performers and women in general important clues about how to negotiate the various tensions of performance, how to resist the various forms of oppression and/or marginalization, how to take possession of their bodies, lives and language, and finally, how to have the last laugh.

ONE

Isabella's "Tricks"
Carnival and Mimicry
in Sixteenth Century Italy

Isabella Andreini in the Context of Her Time

Imagine her for a brief moment: more than four hundred years ago, a very young woman of only fifteen, thirsty for the knowledge and education largely denied to women of that period,[1] starting a lifelong career in the ill-famed world of theater, side by side with her husband, almost 15 years her senior. Isabella Andreini acted, improvised and wrote stage dialogues, full-fledged plays and poems. She acquired the degree of education and erudition that opened for her the doors of the academies of the time, such as Academia degli Intenti. In addition, she was the mother of seven children, and tragically died at the young age of forty-two from a miscarriage, at the height of her talents and world fame, admired by the greatest poets of the time, by kings and queens throughout Europe.[2]

Born Isabella Canali in 1562 in Padua, the Italian actress and writer left an indelible mark on the history of Western theater. As Isabella Andreini, she became part of the generation of actresses who joined and became the leading forces of the commedia dell'arte troupes in the middle of the sixteenth century, women such as Vittoria Piissimi and Vincenza Armani.[3] These women created the roles of the ingénue or the inamorata, and exceeded their male counterparts in the art of improvisation. They often became the leading forces of the commedia dell'arte troupes that traveled throughout Europe and entertained both royalty and the masses, all avid for new forms of entertainment. Isabella is equally a pioneer, at the beginning of an important line of actresses who throughout the seventeenth century created the female comic parts that have remained inscribed in Italian, French and European comedy all the way to the theater of Eugène Ionesco: actresses such as Brigida Bianchi, Orsola Cortesi, Françoise and Catherine Biancolelli.

Isabella Canali Andreini was considered one of the greatest actresses of her time, if not *the* greatest. The company she joined when she married her husband, Francesco Andreini, became the most famous company of the time and played at the court of Henry IV in France, and all throughout Italy for the noblest royal families, such as the Medicis. My intention is to reveal the modernity and the comic dimensions of Isabella's performative style, and to show that her stage creativity, the way in which she negotiated her social and stage image and in which she transcended gender stereotypes in her art, speak vibrantly to us today.

While the two most recent book-length studies devoted to her life, theatrical, musical and literary career, one by Anne McNeil and the other by Melissa Vickery-Bareford have done a superb job in outlining and analyzing her contributions to the theater profession, to the development of performance and to literature in general, as well as to the creation of the "Renaissance woman" (Vickery-Bareford), much remains to be said in terms of the originality of Isabella's performative and improvisatory techniques, as well as the vitality of her writings. Kathleen McGill, Cesare Molinari and Ferdinando Taviani have also brought to light with great finesse Isabella's contributions to the art of improvisation and performance. What still needs to be done with regard to this accomplished performer-writer-comedian is the study of Isabella's role in the creation of a kind of comedy which could qualify as feminist humor *avant la lettre,* in light of modern feminist performance theories. It is the main endeavor of this chapter.

This is a daunting but, I believe, worthwhile endeavor which goes against the grain of two different lines of thought: firstly, the notion that performance and orality, having an ephemeral quality, are lesser forms of art than that which remains on a page or a canvas; and secondly, the notion that Isabella Andreini's performance art owes part of its greatness to the staunch image of a virtuous, sweet and innocent woman she apparently created on and off stage.

Western thought and patriarchy have tended to favor the written over the oral. *Verba volant, scripta manent* goes the Latin proverb ("The word flies, the letter stays"). That which is written on a page, the inscriptions in stone, or the images on a canvas are generally believed to illustrate the very essence of art as a form of expression which is expected to withstand the passage of time. In sonnets, Shakespeare warns us against "Devouring Time" and "Swift-footed Time" and extols the virtues of that which has the endurance and solidity of stone, the resonance of the written word, the "verse" which will "ever live young" (XIX). In contrast, oral traditions and performances have been viewed as secondary forms of artistic expression, due to their transitory and fluctuating nature. But libraries are also known to have gone up in flames, priceless manuscripts disappeared with them, and entire cities have been swallowed up by natural or man-created disasters and have turned to dust. *Vanitas gloria mundi* goes another Latin proverb. That the beauty which is created and which shines in the moment is of less value than that which is left on a page or on the walls of a temple, is relative. Paper burns and temples collapse. And after all, life goes on and on.

So often excluded from the written tradition, women have developed throughout the centuries a rich oral and performative culture which until only very recently has been dismissed as irrelevant to the written traditions, largely male-created. Since they have so often been identified with nature and their identities measured in terms of their ability to produce and rear children, women have often turned their disadvantage into a form of creativity and have done that which Hélène Cixous has beautifully urged women to do: write the body, steal language, explode the written laws, make life into a work of art and endow the moment with beauty, song, laughter. "A woman who both writes and performs, as so many woman comedians do, is making this image concrete, flesh and blood as well as ink, a lived parable of possibilities," notes Frances Gray, and she continues to say that "Cixous envisages for the woman's text to 'shatter' the framework of institutions ... blow up the law ... break up the 'truth' with laughter" (36).

Isabella was a woman who both wrote and performed and, ironically, given the restrictions placed upon women during her time, she had to overcome her gender and to make herself invisible as a woman in order to be taken seriously as an artist. She was perfect, she was respectable, she was sweet, graceful, virtuous, she inspired love, created innumerable lovers, but gave herself to none other than her husband. So the story goes about her! In one effigy she is portrayed with wings, like an angel. What does that tell us about her as an artist, as a comedian, as a writer? Precious little.

I believe that, wrapped up in her invisible cloak of perfection, beauty, grace, angelic sweetness and irreproachable respectability, Isabella broke up "the truth with laughter," wrote with her body and performed with her mind, made the word flesh and blood and ink. She distilled herself socially into a perfect image of accepted femininity, so much so that she ended up being accepted by her society almost as a man would have, and as an exception to her gender. With great intelligence and meticulous care, Isabella "played" her gender. In light of Judith Butler's concept of gender as a social construct and as performance, Isabella could be said to have constructed herself socially in order to match the role of the ideal woman created by her society. As I will attempt to prove, she then deconstructed that role onstage into many different roles and/or masks.

I will undertake a reconstructive analysis of the performative art of Isabella Andreini, and advance the bold notion that the art of performance, fleeting and difficult to hold against the passage of time as it may be, is equally valuable and respectable as any form of art. As a superb celebration of the moment, performance should not and cannot be judged in terms of literary norms and standards. Its beauty and incandescence lie largely in its evanescent quality and in non-literary attributes such as gesture, movement, voice, expression, timing. This is much like life itself, for has not theater so often and in the words of some of the greatest poets been likened to life and the world itself to a stage?

Performance art reveals women's creativity, starting with the comic drama of the ancient Baubo and continuing with today's mimes, performance artists and stand-up comedians. Although prevented from fully expressing themselves throughout the centuries at the level of performance, women have managed to overcome and resist their marginalization and, as shown in the introductory chapter, have created an alternative tradition of performance art and of comic expression. Even when the traditional theaters were off limits to them as actresses, they did perform as mimes, singers, dancers, jugglers. When they could not get into the theaters, they performed in the streets. When the streets were hostile to them, they became courtesans and performed for their "bene-factors," in palaces and mansions. When the word was forbidden to them, they spoke with their bodies and with their hands. When their tongues were cut off like Philomela of the Greek myth, they wove their stories of violation on tapestries. When challenged like Arachne, they boldly wove their derision of "Big Daddy" in colorful images; and when seeing the mourning of other women, they made smutty jokes and laughed like Baubo. In the inspired words of a feminist critic, the women's resisting voice "cannot be silenced."[4]

The second important grain of thought against which I will trace my study of Isabella's performance art is that the "secret" or reason for her fame is her proverbial virtue and the image she created of herself socially, to match her stage image.[5] I advance the thesis that she "played" her respectability, that she "played" her gender and her much praised feminine charm, and that the stage was largely for Isabella the place where she could transgress the gender she played socially as well as the first layer of her stage persona, which sup-posedly matched her social persona, that of the ingénue or the inamorata. I will go as far as affirm that Isabella's life was not divided into "real" life and "fictive," theatrical life, but that she led a life that was performative through-out. While in her own life she played the respectability for which everybody until today's critics have so praised her, onstage she often mocked and transgressed those conventions she felt necessary to abide by at the social level, in order to be taken seriously as an artist. We can thus look at Isabella's life as a kind of hall of mirrors, where the performances of art and of life reflect each other. What transpires in this hall of mirrors is equally the wit, the humor, the comedy that Isabella created onstage, and which have been surprisingly overlooked throughout the centuries.

Within a genre that has flourished and acquired the value of a myth, largely due to its comic dimensions, the first and most remarkable actress who contributed significantly to the development of the genre is looked at mostly in terms of her grace, physical beauty, and virtue, but *not* in terms of her comedic talent. Once in a while, a contemporary might be in awe of her eloquence and of her improvisational genius but never of the comic and carnivalesque qualities of her performance.[6]

The difficulty of my undertaking is obvious: the scarcity of proof and documentation which attest to the improvisational and comic creativity of someone like Isabella Andreini make it relatively hard to prove that she was a comic genius and an improvisational wonder on the stages of her time. My argument is also based on the risky assumption that, while responding to Isabella's art with awe, her audiences lacked to a certain degree the terms and concepts necessary to understand what so moved them about her performances and that, therefore, Isabella's art situates itself ahead of her time. However, those audiences had a significant advantage over us: they saw her perform, whereas we can only imagine her perform. But it is also these risks which make my task more challenging and exciting. For while performance is so much harder to ascertain and evaluate over the centuries than, say, poetry or actual dramatic texts, the fragments, comments and bits of proof we have of Isabella's acting, seen in light of her own writings, do offer us significant material from where we can draw several conclusions about her art.

In trying to build my argument, I will make use of three kinds of documents: the scenarios collected by Flaminio Scala, Isabella's own writings, particularly her pastoral play *La Myrtilla*, and the reports of her contemporaries about her performative talent and about actual performances. A certain amount of inferring, guessing and presupposing is unavoidable in this kind of reconstructive work. The purpose of my endeavor is twofold: to illuminate an important link in the Western history of women's comic performance, which has thus far remained largely in the shadow; and, by doing this, to establish a connection between the first influential comic actresses of the Western theater and some of today's women performers who are also creators of comedy.

The theoretical framework of my argument will consist of a combination of two main theories: Luce Irigaray's theory of mimesis-mimicry and "hystera theater"; and a modified version of Mikhail Bakhtin's idea of the carnival, seen through a feminist perspective. According to Luce Irigaray, since the mimetic tradition of Western forms of representation starting with Plato and Aristotle, have enclosed women within the discourse of lack and presented them as objects of the male desire and gaze, one way for women to resist and escape from this fatal enclosure is to mimic the mimetic modes of representation imposed upon them and by doing so to subvert them. This can be done through exaggerated thickening or caricaturing of the very norms and forms of femininity imposed upon women socially, culturally and aesthetically, or, in the extreme form, of hysteria. Through hysteria, or "hystera theater," women performers break up all recognizable referents and modes of mimetic representation, mix up the accepted conventions of inner and outer, the created and the real, and explode conventional notions of identity.[7] As Meaghan Morris has pointed out, despite the criticism of essentialism and biologism that has been brought at times against Irigaray, she "is very far from confusing the anatomical and the social, but she works with a deadly deliberation on the point of the confusion of the anatomical and cultural," continuously and deliberately resisting "definition as feminine."[8]

Bakhtin's idea of the carnival filtered through feminist thought can also prove a productive way of looking at Isabella's performances and discovering their modernity. The carnival, a form of celebration of the people, allowed the masses, according to Bakhtin, a "temporary suspension, both ideal and real, of hierarchical rank," and "a special type of communication impossible in everyday life," as well as a form of "liberating from norms of etiquette and decency imposed at other times." The language of the carnival is impregnated, according to Bakhtin, by the logic of things à l'envers, of the world "upside down," of "constant permutations between up and down, face and back, and by the most diverse forms of parodies, travesties, profanations and buffooneries."[9] From a feminist perspective, there are problems with Bakhtin's theory, although in appearance it is not a gender-specific theory of laughter and comedy. As Gray points out,

> The carnival world is one of material pleasures, of food and drink, song and dance and sport, and, inevitably, sexuality. But for the last three and a half thousand years, sexuality has meant male sexuality. Women's right to pleasure has certainly been from time to time envisaged; but I can't help wondering what it was like for a lone woman to walk the streets at carnival, and whether in this free communion she had the right to say no; and who looked after the subsequent babies if she didn't [31–32].

However, feminist studies have also shown that often in performance, visual representations, farces or stories, the carnivalesque reversals were often envisaging the "woman on top" motif, and therefore suggesting the possibility of gender reversals and of women who not only said no but who had the lead and the initiative. Judy Little notes that, throughout the centuries, women, whose position in society has been a liminal one, have also continued to develop forms of comedy which have threatened the established social order and have presented at least the subversive potentials of what she calls "liminality." She makes the point that, precisely in the fifteenth and sixteenth centuries, the "topos of the 'world upside down' was extremely popular" and that the "motif of the 'woman on top,' politically and domestically, a motif frequent in festive celebrations and in popular iconography, may have encouraged women to join the riots of laborers in pre-industrial Europe" (5–6). In the domain of literature, for instance, Boccaccio's *Decameron* is a superb illustration of the "woman on top" motif and offers an invigorating representation of women's intelligence, creativity, and sexuality, precisely in the mode of what Bakhtin has called "grotesque realism" and in the joyous, festive manner of what he has labeled as the "banquet:" the celebration of carnality in all its forms and colors. The laughter of the carnival, says Bakthin, is not the superior, sarcastic, distanced laughter of the modern period, but a laughter which brings together and blurs differences. Furthermore, it is a laughter which brings people and things down to earth and materializes the world, in the sense of a celebration of that which is closer to the earth, which comes and goes into the earth, which is connected to sexual pleasure, conception and birth and which ultimately points toward new beginnings (28–30). The idea of the carnival and of "the woman on top," which has since medieval farce been a source of laughter and comedy, is well in tune with that of the mockery of mimesis and the hystera theater, as they both are based on the reversal of known and accepted social and aesthetic conventions, both present alternatives to known modes of expression, and both suggest that laughter is a powerful social force which can shake the world and bring about freedom to those who suffer from lack of it.

As for the role of women in the creation of laughter, the mimicry of mimesis and the carnival theories represent helpful strategies in illuminating the distinctive form of subversive, transgressive and/or angry female humor which "mocks all possible norms." A feminist version of the carnival theory is also in tune with Cixous' notion of the Medusa laughter which "destroys all hierarchies." By doing so, "It will remove all difference between margin and the center."[10] Furthermore, the carnival theory blends well with that of mimesis mimicry in light of the rapport between the real and the imagined, between art and life. Though from different perspectives, as one takes into account gender primarily, both Irigaray's and Bakhtin's theories point toward the blurring of distinctions between art and life, or the real and the imaginary. Carnival, according to Bakhtin, situates itself on the border between life and art (16), and Irigaray's "hystera theater" breaks the boundaries between margin and center simultaneously with those between the created and the real.

Finally, the theoretical framework I have chosen for my study of Isabella Andreini's performance style and achievements is in harmony with the very theatrical genre of the commedia dell'arte. Isabella was already working within a revolutionary theatrical mode that contained a carnivalesque dimension. Some of the commedia characters and the burlesque forms of humor originated precisely with the street performers during the Middle Ages and the Renaissance in particular, as part of carnivals, celebrations and festivities.[11] Furthermore, the very characters who are supposed to have been at the basis of the creation of this genre, the *zannis*, or servants, engage in burlesque humor which can already be seen as subversive of patriarchy since the butt of their jokes is most often old men who lust after young women, authoritarian fathers who force their daughters into unwanted marriages, pretentious doctors avid for money — the many varieties of the *pater familia* figure. Bakhtin notes precisely the fact that the carnivalesque characters such as the buffoons, who will become the *zannis* in the commedia, remained buffoons in all the circumstances of their lives. The blurring of the distinctions between the stage and the social persona of the commedia actors is also considered by Taviani and Schino as fundamental to the development of the commedia.

The interesting fact about Isabella is that she was perceived to have been an ingénue onstage and in real life, while there is evidence that even if she may have been an ingénue in real life, she very often was a buffoon onstage. For Isabella, the stage is her carnival and her banquet, while real life have been for her what Bakhtin has called "the official feast" which "validates the stability, the immobility and the perennial nature of the rules which govern the world: hierarchy, values, religious norms and taboos, politics and morals" (18). Isabella was, so to speak, at the right moment at the right time, and she developed her stage roles to a degree of excellence which at least equaled those of the male actors, if not exceeded them. Playing in drag, in disguise, and mimicking other parts were already part of the arte of the commedia. The theatrical genre within which Isabella flourished as an artist was the ideal medium within which to weave and construct modern forms of humor that subverted, transgressed and exploded gender stereotypes.

In the anonymous Renaissance painting exhibited in the Musée Carnavalet, in Paris, Isabella Andreini appears richly attired in a white dress, blonde, exquisite, center stage, surrounded by the stylized figures of Pantalone, Arlecchino, several *zannis* (the clownish servants) and the chivalrous figure of the inamorato kneeling to her right side. Her contemporaries and critics through-out the centuries extolled her beauty, her virtue, her charismatic stage presence, her talents as a poet and writer. The descriptions of her acting and perform-ances, though, are more often than not eroticized and/or highly idealized.[12] Others are downright out of place, such as those of the famous commedia scholar Pierre-Louis Duchartre, who extols her beauty and talents one moment, and the next describes her face in a sixteenth century reproduction as "bovine."

At the other end of such uncouth comments are the inflamed verses of admiring contemporaries, who invariably describe her in terms of her physical presence and the erotic feelings it inspired. Amidst the many exuberant lines written in her honor, one can nevertheless get an idea of her performative versatility which, unlike the other actors in the commedia troupes who spe-cialized in acting one character almost exclusively, moved through a much wider range of impersonations and comedic roles.

Kathleen McGill has justly noted, "Fortunately, the fascination of con-temporary audiences with the women's bodies also produced other, more detailed commentary on the capabilities these bodies demonstrated in per-formance."[13] For instance, Gabriello Chiabrera wrote a poem in her honor. He gave an eroticized image of the actress — who as soon as she opened her voice *creasse amanti* (created lovers) — yet suggests that her stage presence had the capacity of awakening a variety of feelings in her audience. The poem also points out her capacity to produce laughter and exuberance: "No laughter did she awaken without blessing a heart."[14] Two centuries later, Francesco Zanetti notes that "having studied in depth the human heart, she knew how to touch the most hidden chords and awaken upon her will, love, pity, ten-derness, rage, despair, horror, fear, joy and exuberance."[15] Idealized and eroti-cized as they may be, these lines are more helpful in ascertaining Isabella's mode of performance than the really out of place comment about her sup-posedly "bovine" expression by Duchartre, a twentieth century critic.

Modern critics have compared her to Eleonora Duse (Taviani and Schino) and even to Marilyn Monroe (Gray). I would take the comparison a notch higher. Voluptuous and sensuous in her Renaissance corseted attire, with innocent blue eyes and blonde curly hair framing her face, Isabella could be seen as a Renaissance Marilyn. The French even cast coins with Isabella's image, and on one of the coins she is portrayed bare-breasted, though, iron-ically, with wings on her back, thus both eroticized and idealized into an angelic figure. Analogously, American billboards once loomed large above highways with Marilyn's pouting face and alluring cleavage, no wings attached, but an innocent expression which could almost look angelic if it wasn't for the heavy lipstick on the pouting, slightly open lips. Isabella was a Renaissance construct, as Marilyn was a Hollywood construct. Her contemporaries praised her to no end for her virtue and her sweetness — qualities highly appreciated in women during the Renaissance. The words *virtue, virtuous* and *honest* appear in virtually every description and commentary about her, including the two doctoral theses published in the past decade. Nobody ever worried about the virtue and honesty of any male commedia performers and improvisers, or about the virtue of any male writer, painter, or artist of any kind, for that matter. Ultimately, the Renaissance obsession with Isabella's presumed virtue and chastity is only the other side of the twentieth century obsession with Marilyn's potential promiscuity and explosive sexuality. Both are male constructs which, in McGill's felicitous phrase, "collapse the real distinction between the actual status of women and the range of male desires."[16]

Certainly Isabella's merits as a performer and writer stand in and of themselves, irrespective of her private and social image and reputation. I find the very notion of her "virtue" to be irrelevant to her artistic legacy, particularly since the whole idea of female virtue is a male invention (etymologically, the very word *virtue* derives from the Latin *vir*, meaning man) meant primarily to lock women within an idealized and usually unrealistic vision of sexuality.

Isabella's "virtue" as a faithful wife and mother of seven children combined with the allure of a beautiful physique radiating innocence and serenity must have been the sixteenth century version of Marilyn's famous "combination of sexuality and innocence" (Gray 10). In a sixteenth century painting of the Gelosi troupe at the Musée Carnavalet, Isabella's face indeed radiates sweetness and feminine charm, while the almost ballet-like posture of her body, richly attired in a Renaissance lavish dress, gives an idea of the grace that so enamored her contemporaries. Like Marilyn in many photographs, posters or movie images, Isabella is center stage, flanked by men on both sides, blonde, blue-eyed and with a slight air of vulnerability in her fragile beauty, as right in front of her stands Pantalone, the old man, with his male organ clearly and formidably shaped under his red Renaissance tights. Unlike Marilyn, Isabella was more attentive in crafting her own image for posterity, for in addition to her public appearances as an actress, she left a prolific body of written work that was taken seriously by the most important men of letters of her time. Celebrated as she was during her lifetime for her acting, Isabella must have understood that the transitory art of performance alone would not suffice to ensure her a stable place throughout the centuries, and that if anything, her stage presence, was going to be misconstrued and idealized, and ultimately her creativity and spark buried under piles of empty epithets. The most precious documents testifying to her theatrical talents are in fact not so much the awed descriptions of her contemporaries (though they do help in ascertaining her importance as an actress during her lifetime), but the collection of fifty scenarios of original theatrical pieces collected by Flaminio Scala (the leader of the commedia company that she joined with her husband in the latter half of the fifteen hundreds) and her own pastoral play entitled *La Mirtilla*.

Having to contend with a twenty-century-old tradition of theater created, acted, and produced by men, women invigorated and changed the nature of theater both at the level of text and performance[17] as they brought to the female roles created by male actors and writers, the authenticity and sparkle of their own identities and experiences[18] and the richness of a long, though largely unnoticed oral tradition of female creativity.[19] Furthermore, since the arte of the Italian commedia required the same degree of professionalism from actors and actresses alike, women were equally trained to perform both male and female parts, just as their male counterparts were. Playing in drag was one of the tricks of the trade for both actors and actresses.

The fact that the second half of the sixteenth century and most of the seventeenth century were also known as the golden age of the commedia dell'arte reflects not only the great success and the rapid flourishing of this theatrical genre which started in Italy and spread throughout Europe, but is also indicative of the democratic forms of production and creation that characterized this form of theater and the troupes who engaged in it. The shows were largely the product of collaborative work.[20] Roles were relatively equal to each other in length and importance and generally did not contend for primacy over other parts.[21] Not only were men and women within a company equal in terms of their creative input and leadership roles, but once women became generally accepted as intrinsic constituents of the commedia troupes, they often became its leaders. As Kathleen McGill notes, "When women began to perform on the stage, they immediately assumed the direction of the troupes, ... and companies became known in reference to their female stars, such as 'Piissimi and her troupe.'" The company called the Desirosi "were known as 'those of Diana,'" Marie de Medici wrote to her sister of "the actress Isabella and her company" ("Women and Performance," 68).

While Isabella Andreini was not altogether an exception among the actresses of her time in terms of performative talent and versatility, the general view of the critics is that she was exceptional for having created a perfectly well-rounded image of herself both as a private and public figure. Furthermore, she doubled the ephemeral success of her stage presence with the enduring marks of an accomplished writer and scholar. Thus, she not only brought the part of the inamorata to a degree of originality which awed princes, kings and queens, but she wrote poems, plays, stage dialogues and a large body of epistolary essays. These earned her the admiration of such famous authors as

Torquato Tasso, literary prizes (second to Tasso in a poetry contest), and a place in the famous *Academia degli Intenti*, next to the greatest and most erudite personalities of her time.

A year older than Shakespeare, she was often compared to him in terms of her varied accomplishments in the profession of theater and literature. Louise Clubb notes that "like Shakespeare her contemporary, Isabella was called the wonder of her profession and her age, but unlike him, she was called so in her own time by a vast international audience."[22] Unlike any other actresses of the commedia Isabella Andreini has, over the centuries, received a relatively high amount of recognition by male critics and scholars.[23] In her own writings, Isabella speaks modestly and almost apologetically of her thirst for knowledge and the pursuit of a profession in theater and literature. While calling herself "Cittadina del Mondo" in a letter to the duke of Savoy, Isabella attributes her desire for knowledge and for the immortality usually achieved by male writers to hazard and fortune. She dissociates herself from other women of her time, and speaks of herself as an exception to her gender: "having by chance been driven by a more ardent desire for knowledge, than most women of my status."[24]

While this is far from a feminist *avant la lettre* kind of statement, in a man's world, Isabella had to negotiate her place among writers and theater people more as a man than as an ordinary woman, while at the same time establishing for herself a perfect reputation as a virtuous woman. Because she was seen as an impeccable woman in a profession frequently associated with the life-style of courtesans, Isabella could hope to claim a place next to the important men of her time. It was Isabella who, for the first time liberated the image of the actress from its previous associations with the *onesta meretrice*[25] and who complemented her stage persona with an impressive social persona. Isabella was successful at both and, by not attracting any criticism to her private and social life, she could afford to attract attention to her artistic and intellectual endeavors. She understood that, in her world, a woman's most important assets were considered to be, as Zanetti does not let us forget, *l'onesta ed il candore* ("honesty and candor," 246). She also knew that the only way for her art to be taken seriously was to not give in to the desires of her adoring audience who, if we are to trust Zanetti, not only admired her but, once they saw her, instantaneously fell in love with her (245). On the contrary, someone like Marilyn Monroe erred precisely in the direction of allowing too much of her presence and private life be cannibalized and extended into the realm of her art, thus minimizing its importance and value.

Women continue to be, though in a lesser degree, as they were in Isabella's time, looked at, judged and appraised in light of their physical appearance on the one hand, and their private life on the other hand, while their intrinsic

Compagnia dei Comici Gelosi with Isabella Andreini (1562–1604) in the center depicted giving a performance in Paris. The individual with the large sword to her right is believed to be her husband, Francesco Andreini, in the role of Capitano. Oil on canvas to be found at the Musée Carnavalet. Anonymous artist.

intellectual or artistic merits and achievements are much too often neglected and mixed in with personal elements. Isabella Andreini achieved world fame and published her works during her lifetime, sparkled as an actress on numerous stages of Europe and in front of royalty and famous artists, maintained, at least in appearance, an exemplary marriage and work partnership with her husband, and mothered no less than seven children.

Though we should not fall into the same fallacy as the other critics have done, of judging her artistic accomplishments in terms of her private life, the fact itself of her private life having become known and subject of so much discussion cannot be overlooked. Whether she was a happy and willing mother of seven children or not, or whether she was happily married or not, or whether she was truly faithful to her husband or not, is hard to ascertain, nor is it my intention to do so, nor should we care. But, as feminist theoreticians have pointed out, the private is also political and McNeil and Vickery-Bareford do have a point in ascertaining that Isabella did a brilliant job at collapsing her private and social image into one glorious image of virtue, which in turn gave her, in the context of her time, the leverage to develop and express her art at a variety of levels: written, oral, performative. Isabella Andreini is truly a most empowering model for women of all ages and certainly a beautiful example of that which feminist theory and criticism of the past decades have been struggling for and urging women to have the courage to be: fully accomplished human beings. This is the first movement of Isabella's trick. Let us discover the next.

The Many Faces of Isabella — Creation of Humor — A Historical Perspective

When the public identified the actors playing Arlecchino or Pantalone or Capitan Spaventa with their stage personae to the point where they were called in real life by their stage names,[26] it was understood that they were above all, funny. As already noted earlier, one of the ideas Bakhtin advances with regard to the carnival is that the buffoons, whom he considers as essential to the laughter of the carnival, remain buffoons in real life. He does not mention, though, any women as creators of comedy and laughter.

The humor of the male commedia characters is generally bawdy, sexual, scatological, fitting precisely Bakhtin's notion of "grotesque realism." The ability to produce obscene humor was part of the trade, and the masses respected and adored these actors because of how funny they were and how well they could entertain. However, when it comes to women, scatological, sexual and risqué humor has been much too often associated with sexual promiscuity. Chaste, honest, candid and virtuous women would not speak and act in ways which would suggest the idea of sexual freedom and enjoyment of sexuality. To this day, there are critics who consider that "sex" is the purest theme for jokes for any entertainer.[27] When the entertainer is a man, we might add. One does not need to read any amount of comic theory to know that little girls have been invariably taught, throughout the centuries, that they should not speak and act in bold, obscene, improper ways — namely, like boys. Robin Lakoff and Deborah Tannen have done a significant amount of work in analyzing the linguistic gender differences with regard to what is culturally considered appropriate and what is not. "Woman's place" is to be demure, occasionally smile or blush at men's jokes, and have good knowledge of colors.[28] During the Renaissance, it was the jugglers, street performers, and courtesans who performed and who were bawdy and sexual in their humor. Therefore, by a simple syllogism, it is easy to see that women who were funny, therefore sexual or bawdy, would have been associated with prostitutes. It makes a lot of sense that the first commedia actresses, if they wanted to be taken seriously and escape these associations, had to stay away from the overtly funny roles and function artistically and socially at a level which allowed only for an idealized form of femininity to be exhibited.

Most studies or pages devoted to Isabella Andreini, from her own time to the present, cast her in a generally serious light. She seems to have a mythic persona. The attributes of "virtuous," "divine," "immortal," "sublime," "muse," "sweet," "lovely," occur time and again in reference to Isabella Andreini. For the most part, these attributes have been handed down from her contemporaries, actors and writers such as Pietro Mattei, Antonio Maria Spelta,[29] Nicoló Barbieri, Giuseppe Pavoni, who wrote accounts of her performances (Pavoni) or devoted significant space to her in their histories of Italian and/or French literature (Mattei, Spelta). The highly emotional and adoring epitaph written by her grief-stricken husband, Francesco, in which he identifies her to the nymph Fillide, one of the roles she had played, have also contributed to the seriousness and the idealized image of Isabella Andreini as angelic.[30]

What mostly interests me in terms of Isabella's achievements at the theatrical, literary and historical level are the ways in which she transgressed from the serious, the "sublime," the "divine" into the comic, the grotesque, the profoundly human. The scarcity of contemporary material describing actual performances makes the work of performance critics challenging and sometimes discouraging. Collections of scenarios do exist, like the one compiled by Flaminio Scala, who was also the director of the company of the Gelosi for a while. But these do not give much detail concerning the actual performances, nor do they give full accounts of the improvisational work that went on during the performances. Isabella's greatness as an actress is also known to us by accounts and diaries of her contemporaries, such as the ones mentioned earlier, and in little bits and pieces from the collections of scenarios which she created and acted in. The task I am setting for myself, that of bringing to light Isabella's greatness as a creator of humor, is daunting, to say the least. Based on the few accounts of her performances and of her role in the improvisation and creation of her roles, I will attempt, however, to bring to light those aspects of her artistic achievements which have been thus far overlooked.

The performance and role which brought Isabella the most acclaim and worldwide fame is *La Pazzia d'Isabella* (1589), in which she acted at the wedding festivities of the duke Fernando de Medici and his bride Christine de Lorraine. While Isabella's performance and in particular her famous *scena della pazzia* (mad scene), impressed all who saw it, the role and the scene were in fact profoundly transgressive of the persona that Isabella had created for herself onstage and in society. Specifically, her performances contrast with the image of the "sublime," "sweet," "lovely" Isabella. As critics have noted, mad scenes were an opportunity for actresses to exhibit the versatility of their talents.[31] And according to the sexist cynical views of some of her male contemporaries, mad scenes gave actresses "a chance to take off their clothes" in front of an audience.[32] But Isabella's scene offers something unique. Indeed, I venture to state that it heralds some of the acting and theatrical techniques characteristic of feminist performers, theater practitioners and performance artists of the twentieth century.

I will have to ask the reader to perform a leap of faith and a stretch of the imagination in order to visualize and imagine Isabella's creativity. After all, historical performance studies are in and of themselves something of an impossibility, as they are based on a foolish presumption: that of immortalizing, in a retroactive manner, the ephemeral, the forever lost gesture, voice, expression and spark of life that, once gone, is no more. Precious little is known about the performance, dialogues and actual exchanges performed onstage during the early commedia shows. Several critics agree that the scenarios of the early commedia have little or no literary value and they represent simply "working documents" of the troupes.[33] As Richard Andrews points out, "Dramatic artifacts differ substantially from literary ones in their compositional technique" (xii). The heart of the commedia dell'arte was its theatricality, "the exercise of interplay among the actors, as they improvised the dialogue to suit each occasion" (McKee, xv). We have little actual knowledge about this theatricality, except from the accounts of contemporaries, theater reviews of the time and several paintings whose artists tried to capture certain troupes in action. In a very profound way, the commedia dell'arte was maybe the purest form of theater, based not on textual and literary virtuosity but developing at its highest form the very essence of theater: space, movement, gesture, ritual, and the comic at its rawest form.

However, in reading the scenarios, non-literary and incomplete as they may be, it may in fact be easier to imagine flesh-and-blood characters moving onstage than in reading a traditional dramatic text, for the possibilities of dialogue are practically unlimited, and the potential for comedy immense. It is easy to understand how, once the basic plotlines are assimilated by the actors, the interplay between them, the dialogues and the stage movements would emerge in colorful trills. Not enough attention has been given to these scenarios, I believe, in the reconstructive attempts of early commedia performances.

The art of improvisation of the commedia has been likened by some critics to the improvisations of the jazz musicians, "performing 'solos' against a given rhythmic base in a manner that became automatic."[34] Isabella Andreini and a few other famous actresses such as Vittoria Piissimi and Vincenza Armani were known to have been virtuosos of improvisation, so much so that they were said to have been better at improvising onstage than some poets were at writing poetry. McGill notes, "Adriano Valerini wrote on the death of Vincenza Armani in 1568 that she succeeded better speaking improvisationally than the most consummate authors do upon contemplation." And Tommaso Garzoni wrote that "the women, imitating the Ciceronian art, made the comic art like oratory." McGill concludes that "women appeared to spectators as poets in action, professionals in the art of improvising words ("Women and Performance," 64).

As for Isabella's performances, improvisatory skills, and the roles she created, she inspired maybe more praises and poems during her lifetime than most other actors or actresses, her own husband, Francesco, included, but very few offer actual descriptions of her stage presence other than the awed general comments on how beautiful and talented she was. For instance, Tomasso Garzoni refers to Isabella as "decoration of the stage, ornament of the theaters, superb spectacle not in the least of virtue as of beauty" (4). Nicolo Barbieri, referring to Isabella as one of "the moderns of my time," notes that she was "honored" with "loving and decent praise for any gentlewoman, by the great Henry the IV of France" (22). And Gabriello Chiabrera, in the poem in which he sings her praises, calls her "most sweet Siren of the stage."[35]

On the contrary, the scenarios gathered by Flaminio Scala do attest to the many dimensions of her role as Isabella, although they rarely give any lines or bits of dialogue. An exception is made with the mad scene, in the scenario of *La pazzia d'Isabella*, where more detailed accounts of Isabella's stage movements and gestures as well as many of her lines are given in some detail.

The role that Isabella brought to unprecedented and unmatched heights, that of the inamorata, was not one of the comic parts like those of *Arlechino* or *Pantalone*, but was considered one of the *parti gravi*, the serious roles, whose lyricism established a contrast of theatrical mood and technique with the burlesque tone of the other masks. Furthermore, the inamorati were the only characters who did not wear masks, and this feature, as Vickery-Bareford so astutely noted, gave them an "intersocial dimension, meaning that the image created on-stage easily transferred to the off-stage world" (37). In terms of Isabella's creativity, Vickery-Bareford claims, she was able more than other actresses of her time, to "build her image first on the stage, and then encourage her audience to associate this image with her real person" (38). Her stage name was her real name and the lyrical, dignified dimension of her character was matched to some extent by her real-life proverbial virtue and romantic love of her husband. Poets such as Tasso praised this and she extended it into her own "rime," poems and letters on love. By taking a close look at Flaminio Scala's collection of scenarios and working one's way to the climactic one of the *Pazzia d'Isabella*, one starts to notice transgressions into the carnivalesque, leaps into the comic, and moments of "grotesque realism," which Isabella performs with panache.

Isabella's Comedy of Disguise

I will now proceed to a brief review of Isabella's many roles and disguises as seen in Scala's scenarios, in order to build my argument toward the mad scene and prove, in a progressive manner, that she was a powerful comic actress, very much in the tradition of the carnavelesque buffoons discussed by Bakhtin. In Scala's scenarios, Isabella is most always in love, often cries and is in distress because of various mishaps which prevent her from being with or marrying the man she loves, or because she is forced into marriages she does not want; these aspects do account for the role of the inamorata as a serious part. But that is only one facet of her role.

Even within her role of inamorata, Isabella laughs or produces laughter. She is often seen from a balcony[36] plotting or laughing with Flaminia (*Isabella's Trick*, 34), laughing and plotting with Arlechino, the overtly comic mask of the commedia (*Isabella's Trick*, 35); she is called "an insatiable slut"(44) by Flavio, the inamorato in the scenario *Flavio Betrayed*, to which she responds by slapping his face; she "shamefacedly caresses her husband"(51) in *The Jealous Old Man*; in this same play, in love with a young man, Oratio, Isabella plays a trick on her old and impotent husband. Telling him in the middle of a party "that she has to take care of her needs," she makes love with Oratio right behind the door guarded by the jealous Pantalone, after which she comes out onto the stage perspiring from "her exertion." In *La finta pazzia*, or *The Fake Madwoman*, Isabella, pretending to be insane, chases after Bigolo and Pantalone and "goes through the antics of a lunatic," but when Oratio, the man she loves, whispers something in her ear, she instantaneously "regains her sanity" (62). In *The Captain* she appears dressed up as a soldier running away with Capitan Spavento (the role made famous by her husband, Francesco).

In *The Faithful Pilgrim Lover*, Isabella plays the role of Fabritio, Oratio's page, entirely in drag; she/he "laughingly speaks of the misery of lovers," "draws her/his sword and chases" Arlechino (101). In *The Mirror*, Isabella again cross-dresses as Fabritio, and then plays a man "dressed in woman's clothes, pretending to weep" (117), speaking out oracles as he/she is looking into a mirror, and "sees Arlechino making soup for Pantalone" or "a young man like Pantalone, in a city that looks like Naples, make love to a woman, enjoy her, and the young woman is left pregnant by him" (119–20). In *The Tragic Events*, Isabella yet once again "enters dressed in man's clothes" and "is looking for horses to take her and her servant to Rome" (131). In *The Fake Tofano*, Isabella dresses up as her own father, Tofano, and utters "fatherly" words as "Here I am, my dear child" (176). In *The Jealousy of Isabella*, she utters such vulgar lines, when speaking of her rival, Franceschina: "There is that whore who is the cause of everything" (177), and yet again she "enters, dressed as a man, having found the occasion to get the clothes in a performance of a play given by the servants" (180) in order to prove her lover's faithlessness. In *The Faithless One*, she "enters dressed in man's clothes," for "she has fled from Bologna to avoid marrying Oratio and to follow Flavio, her lover, who was to wait for her in Ferrara" (194). In *The Hunt*, Isabella, angry that Pedroline is lying to her, "beats him," then when Franceschina tells her she is wrong to do so, "Isabella threatens to hit Franceschina too," and when Flavio tries to excuse Oratio, Isabella says "she is going to hit him with a club" (278).

From all her movements, disguises, chases, and arguments, it is hard to imagine that Isabella's part was very "serious," and we would be deeply misled to take a description of Isabella's acting talents such as the one by Tommaso Garzoni at face value: "The gracious Isabella, dignity of the scene, ornament of the stage, a superb spectacle no less of *virtu* than of beauty, has so illuminated the style of her profession, that while the world lasts, while the centuries endure, while time and seasons have life, every voice, every language, every cry, will echo the celebrated Isabella."[37] Enthusiastic as this account may be, its exuberance is largely reflective of a certain view of the actress which takes into account her physical beauty, her lyrical penchant and her proverbial virtue. But it altogether misses her comic genius, her versatility and her improvisational virtuosity.

While most actresses cross-dressed at times, Isabella did so more than any of her peer actresses, say, more than the ones playing the roles of Flaminia or Franceschina. In fact she cross-dresses in almost half of the commedia shows whose scenarios are collected by Scala. Cross-dressing of women was considered highly scandalous for the time. In fact, the sight of women dressed in men's attire was considered to be more indecent than actual nudity[38] and was directly associated with middle-class women who became prostitutes.[39] Even more scandalous, Isabella often played soldiers, and so invited comparisons with prostitutes who serviced the military. For the audiences of the end of the sixteenth century, a woman dressed as a soldier must have also brought to mind another Isabella: the famous prostitute Isabella de Luna, who had acquired world fame and became the protagonist of two Renaissance novellas by the time Andreini was acquiring her own fame as an actress.[40]

Isabella Andreini consistently moves into the realm of the risqué, the scandalous, and the forbidden. As Vickery-Bareford notes, "the provocative nature of a woman in man's clothing in Cinquecento Italy often has the practical and mercenary function of attracting customers" (52). In the article "La fleur et le guerrier," Taviani notes that "long culottes" were indicative of the dress of prostitutes. Furthermore, cross-dressing is usually a simple and obvious theatrical means of creating humor, and for each gender, the comedy derived from cross-dressing is complementary to each other. Men dressed in women's clothes are funny because they simultaneously mimic stereotypically "feminine" traits and caricature the male under the dress. During the Renaissance, "for a man, wearing women's dress undermined the authority inherently belonging to the superior sex and placed him in a position of shame."[41]

Women dressed in men's clothes are often a masquerade of stereotypically "masculine traits," while also contradicting the traditional feminine traits of grace, passivity and delicacy of features, speech or behavior. However, cross-dressing for women has also had, both historically and in theater, the added dimension of a liberation from the constraints imposed by patriarchal societies upon women and has given birth to "the disturbing concept that a woman might turn herself into a man and appropriate 'male' duties and prerogatives."[42] According to Jean Howard, "When women took men's clothes, they symbolically left their subordinate positions. They became master-less women, and this threatened overthrow of hierarchy was discursively read as the eruption of uncontrolled sexuality."[43] Cross-dressing is also a form of mimicry of both genders, or rather of the traditional constructs of both genders. Today, a woman dressed in pants is nothing like a novelty, yet in sixteenth century Europe, women dressed in the tights specific to masculine dress were something of a provocative sight. In the majority of Shakespeare's comedies, women characters disguise themselves as men in order to move the development of the plot in their favor and in order to achieve the freedom of movement, expression and action only available to men. One must keep in mind that in Shakespeare's plays, women's parts were played by boys, and therefore cross-dressing of women was in fact canceled out onstage, as boy actors returned to male attire in order to suggest a woman cross-dressed as a man.

Jean Howard rightly cautions us to not get too optimistic with regard to the subversive powers of women cross-dressing during the Elizabethan era in England (contemporaneous with Isabella's time in Italy), for although a cause of controversy and anxieties, cross-dressing by women may not have necessarily always challenged patriarchy and may have even helped serve its ends. In Shakespeare's plays, women who cross-dress, such as Viola in *Twelfth Night*, often do so from the vantage point of a "properly feminine subjectivity" (33) and ultimately in order to re-inscribe themselves, through marriage to the man of their choice, within the larger scheme of patriarchy. However, whether onstage or in the street, Howard points out, "female cross-dressing in any context had the potential to raise fears about women wearing the breeches and undermining the hierarchical social order" (29). And Elaine Aston notes that:

Cross-dressing, cross-gendering techniques represent a theatrically exciting way of demonstrating and de-automatising our perception of "naturalized" gender sign-systems. Crossing the gender divide may expose the way in which gender is organized as an arbitrary, artificial sign-system, which, like all such systems, it is possible to disturb and to deconstruct [74].

Isabella Andreini, though described by her contemporaries in lofty terms depicting an idealized vision of femininity, in fact played about half of her performances in male attire, mimicking male behavior. This is puzzling. All the descriptions of Isabella, including that of her grieving husband and the poems or lines written in her honor by Nicolo Barbieri, Torquato Tasso and Paolo Fabri, extol her beauty, her virtue, her grace, some her erudition and talent, presenting her as an exception to her gender, but none mention her comic versatility or her talent as a creator of humor. It is hard to believe that she was not as brilliant a comic actress and improviser as she was a lyric and serious actress. Chiabrera's poem mentioned earlier does give a slight sugges-tion of Isabella's ability to produce laughter, *riso*, and awaken hilarity in her audience. It was also, after all, part of the trade of the commedia actors to be comical and act in a variety of disguises, as Isabella herself notes in her *Rime*.

Isabella must have been primarily a superb comic actress who cunningly negotiated a respectable place for herself in the world of theater and in society at large by exploiting that aspect of her craft and persona which allowed her to be taken seriously in the world of men, and gave her the freedom to explore those areas of creation less reputable or less accepted for women, onstage. Ultimately, Isabella seems to have done a superb job at achieving what Deanna Shemek has called the "blurring of the given (or 'the natural') with the cre-ated," a process by which, she adds, "gender (the social understanding of what it means to be male or female) takes on its smudgy contours" (2). This also takes us back to Bakhtin's idea that the buffoons, of whom I believe Isabella is a feminine version, were poised on the border between art and life. The Isabella in real life maintained such a perfect reputation that she could onstage transgress most acceptable norms of femininity. Furthermore, her transgressive way of life, that of a "lady errant," or of a woman who left her house,[44] crossing Europe with an actors' troupe, was, to her own benefit, neglected.

I therefore disagree with the general views that Isabella matched her stage persona entirely to her real life persona and vice versa, and I maintain that she skillfully negotiated the space between an acceptable and a transgressive persona. She did so by creating at both the level of her life and that of the stage a first layer of acceptability, beneath which she could build deeper layers of rebellion.

Most of the cues in Flaminio Scala's scenarios referring to Isabella's dress-ing as a man are illustrative of the typical comic quid-pro-quos which the commedia dell'arte brought to such unmatched heights and which inspired the most famous playwrights of comedy: Shakespeare, Molière, Marivaux or Goldoni. Vickery-Bareford does a superb job in analyzing the functions and effects of Isabella's cross-dressing, noting that

> The completeness of the disguise to the characters, coupled with the audience's awareness of dual sexuality, created an unstable and fluctuating image of gender. This instability allowed Isabella to negotiate predetermined boundaries onstage and was the key to her ability to negotiate those same boundaries off stage" [53].

But not even she mentions anything with regard to Isabella's comic abilities.

As discussed earlier, women's humor has been consistently dismissed, marginalized and neglected over the centuries, and women have been recognized only as objects of humor and laughter, not as creators of comedy. In the nineteenth century, the French actor Constant Coquelin made the remark, in discussing the gender differences in the creation and appreciation of humor, that "woman does not try to be funny, she leaves that to man." He also said, "The masculine perception of humor is largely the enjoyment of buffoonery," while "women's appreciation of humor is far more refined."[45] And most feminist studies of humor mention in outrage Reginald Blyth's commentary that "women have not only no humor in themselves, but are the cause of the extinction of it in others," as well as Congreve's claims of the absence and incapacity of wit and humor in women. It is undoubtedly the same perception of women as incapable of producing humor, which must have rendered Isabella's contemporaries oblivious to her comic strategies and penchant for "buffoonery." That fine gauzy veil of idealizing praise they wove around her was, in some profound way, the kiss of death for a comedian.

There is significant evidence that Isabella had a profound ability to create comedy in improvisation. Kathleen McGill's study "Improvisatory Competence and the Cueing of Performance" analyzes with great detail the stage techniques and timing which commedia actors developed. She uses, as a model, one of Isabella Andreini's dialogues from the collection of writings gathered after her death by Francesco Andreini. Isabella herself wrote on the creation and rules governing comedy in her *Lettere* in the form of an *amoroso contrasto sopra la comedia* (lovers' quarrel about comedy). It is a dialogue between two characters, Erfilia and Diomede, which voices in revised manner, some of the Aristotelian theories of comedy, such as the necessity that comedy be "*tutta favola nulla prendendo dall'historia*" (all invention, fiction and nothing from history), that it have *il mezzo turbolento, & il fine lieto, e giocondo, senza ornamenti* ("the middle turbulent and the end happy, joyous, with no ornaments," 361–62). Erfilia recommends as best examples of comedy the works of such ancient authors as Plautus, Terence, and Aristophanes, whose funniest characters are irreverent buffoons.

The word *favola*, fiction, invention, referred to as the opposite of history or historical reality, is used many times in the dialogue on comedy and is the main concept discussed over and over again by the two lovers in their *amoroso contrasto*. It was in the fictive realm of her roles, in her many disguises and tricks that Isabella would have most intensely transcended her "given" persona into a "created" persona and thus would have displayed most comic versatility. Both the actors playing the serious parts, that is, the inamorati, and those playing the comic roles, such as Arlecchino, Pantalone and the *zanni*, had a certain set of memorized texts, or what Molinari has called "moving blocks," and a set of learned techniques with which they could build up their improvisations. Besides playing the role of the inamorata, Isabella also mimiced many other parts, from astrologers (*Isabella the Astrologer*), to Gypsies (*The Two Disguised Gypsies*), to soldiers, to old fathers, to young pages. Someone like her must have mastered and been able to use with panache the techniques and skills of all the other characters besides her own.

Is Isabella funny in all her disguises, her cross-dressing and her transgressive stage moments? Throughout so much of theatrical history, men played both male and female parts, yet when women entered the theatrical world, cross-dressing for both genders acquired a comic dimension, being mostly encountered in comedies. Shakespeare's comedies, for instance, are replete with women in male attire, but there are none in the tragedies. I am not referring to a woman playing a man's part in earnest, as for instance Isabella playing a man's part in Tasso's pastoral play *Aminta*. I am referring to cross-dressing as a form of disguise or of masquerade. Is there something intrinsically funny about disguise or masquerade? According to Henri Bergson, disguise or that which may be perceived as disguise in a certain society or fashion generally produces laughter. Bergson notes "how easy it is for a garment to become ridiculous." We grow accustomed to associating a certain form of "covering" with "the covered," so if there is a discrepancy between the "covering" and "the covered," we see the new and surprising garment as ridiculous, laughable.[46] Bergson's analysis of disguise then merges with the development of his theory of the mechanical overlapping the human. According to Bergson, whenever the pulsation, the "elasticity of life," is joined with or overlapped by rigidity or lack of elasticity, by movements or repetitions which resemble the mechanical more than the human, laughter ensues.

There is a profound difference between a woman or a man playing a man or, respectively, a woman's part (which has been abundantly done in tragedy), and between a woman or a man *disguised* as the other gender. The garment appears as separate from the person and therefore reflective of a certain mechanical rigidity which contrasts with the life of the person under the garment. The instances when Isabella enters "dressed as a man" are often accompanied by commentaries as to her pretending to cry or lament, or make fun or mock another character, as when she "laughingly speaks of the misery of lovers." The lines she may have uttered, once in a while quoted in the scenarios, also have a false, mocking ring, as for instance when she is dressed up as her own father and says, "Here I am, my dear child." We can imagine graceful, feminine Isabella thicken her voice to mimic an old father's manners, gestures, and tone. In short, Isabella both disguises herself and mimics the person whose disguise she has taken, thus establishing, for the audience members who know she is in disguise, a funny contrast between the expected allure of the feminine inamorata and the character she is imitating. The overlap between her usual feminine, alluring stage persona as the inamorata and the caricatured portrait of the father, the soldier, or the page that she represents in disguise, illustrate simultaneously Bergson's theory of the humor of disguise and that of the mechanical rigidity.

In addition to Bergson's comic theory, when discussing Isabella's comedy of cross-dressing, we also need to take into account the feminist interpretation that women's cross-dressing is more often than not a way of acquiring men's prerogatives. Furthermore, if we add to all of the above Irigaray's idea of the necessity for woman to mimic patriarchal modes and structures imposed upon her as well as to "play with mimesis" in order to recover "the place of her exploitation by discourse,"[47] we would arrive at the provocative conclusion that Isabella Andreini was creating a kind of humor that turned the signs of patriarchal power and authority into a masquerade. Isabella's humor, however, was possible and found fertile ground precisely within the genre of the commedia, which more than other forms of expression allowed for a constant and explosive destabilizing of identities and for democratic modes of interaction between men and women. As Isabella herself pointed out in her *Rime*, cross-dressing was part of the trade of acting, and furthermore, the Renaissance was a period which did encourage a certain fluidity and ambiguity of genders.

The fact that Isabella Andreini, whose fame as a graceful and virtuous woman were so great as to ensure her an important place among the literati of her time, acted numerous times in drag, caricaturing males in their most obvious postures of authority, the fact that she made mocking use of the sword, the phallic symbol par excellence, against male characters who stood in the way of her happiness, is revolutionary. I believe that her contemporaries and those who continued to extol her virtues long after her death were simply not getting the full extent of Isabella's humor. Were they to pay attention to it and take it seriously, they would have seen themselves as the very target of her humor. In all the scenarios in Flaminio Scala's collection, Isabella always comes out on top at the end of the play, after she has tricked fathers, lovers, males of all professions and social standings. She acts at times in complicity with Arlecchino, as in *Isabella's Trick*, or she creates moments of pure slapstick by chasing and drawing her/his sword against him as in *The Faithful Pilgrim Lover*. If we gave Bergson's theory of the comedy of disguise a feminist twist, we could reach the conclusion that Isabella's disguises must have been even funnier *because* they appeared in such contradiction with that which was perceived to be her "nature," and that her garments produced a strident clash with the image of a gracious, nymphlike, virtuous woman.

As has been pointed out by medieval and Renaissance scholars, "chastity, modesty, silence and obedience" were largely seen "as desirable and necessary female traits" by a large number of philosophers, writers and society at large.[48] Not only did Isabella explode this notion in many of the parts she played, but it seems she was poking fun at the very men who would be the advocates of such expectations and views of women: the quick-tempered soldier, the authoritarian father, the unstable lover. It is true that, again, these reversals, caricatures, mimicry, can all be seen as part of the carnival reversals so common in the Renaissance spectacle and in the culture of the carnival itself.[49] But a female buffoon was still something of a novelty, even for carnival culture. That which is most intriguing with regard to Isabella's comedy and which cannot be explained by carnival theory is the discrepancy between the highly idealized reports about her performances and her actual carnivalesque acting style. It is as if even her contemporaries did not actually notice the carnivalesque reversals she was performing under their very eyes and chose to look always in the direction of her lyrical portrayal of the inamorata, with some concession made to the madness scene which represented a known stepping-stone for all actresses of the commedia.

It may just be that it is only in our times that Isabella's subversive humor and transgressive performances can be fully appreciated and her comedy fully tasted. The ironic appropriation by a woman of male poses, gestures, dress and authority appears in a way even more transgressive and ironic in view of Freudian and Lacanian theories of woman as a lack and, in Irigaray's critical analysis of Freudian theory, of woman as "a disadvantaged little man," a "little man with a smaller penis."[50] Moreover, even in her roles as a woman, as Isabella the inamorata, Andreini quite often transgressed her image of virtue, modesty and chastity in language, gesture and action. For instance, in *The Jealous Husband*, she projects the image of a sexually independent woman and contradicts such common sense views of the "modest woman" who "seldom desires any sexual gratification for herself."[51] In *The Jealousy of Isabella*, she uses lewd language and slapstick humor when she beats up Pedrolino, chases after Arlechino and threatens to beat up everyone who stands in her way.

Other than the humor of disguise, Isabella also produced other types of humor: slapstick and burlesque, as in the scenes mentioned above, which has been relegated by some humor theoreticians to the category of humor of superiority (Freud, Aristotle); sexual humor, which has been associated by theoreticians of humor with an overcoming of embarrassment or has been seen as a form of liberation (Pavis, Freud, Kant). Of course in this area, Isabella is doubly a transgressor, as lewd language and explicitly sexual behavior have a long tradition of being associated with prostitution when spoken or performed by women — a grave offense — while socially acceptable and even appreciated when spoken or performed by men. Isabella acting the role of a young wife who has sexual intercourse with a young lover behind the door guarded by her gullible, old and jealous husband and who comes onstage suggesting the "exertion" of her enjoyment, is in sharp contrast with the image of Isabella seen by Garzoni, Barberi, Pavoni, Chiabrera, her own husband Francesco and largely by all her critics until today. Indeed, even Taviani and Schino's assumption that Isabella was such an excellent example of that well-kept "secret" of the commedia, according to which the stage image matched the social and private image of the actor, seems farfetched and not altogether realistic.

Rather, I believe that, by carefully weaving a perfect image of herself as a "virtuous" woman in the world, Isabella in fact turned her own private and social life into a performance. In its turn, the performance of the "virtuous," angelic Isabella in real life gave her the freedom to transgress this very image onstage. Isabella moved from performance to performance, and blurred the distinctions between her real life and her stage life, but not in the way in which her contemporaries and later critics have seen this blurring. It was under the guise of the character of Isabella the chaste, the virtuous, the eternal inamorata, that Isabella Andreini created a comic persona which subverted both her real-life persona and the first layer of her character as Isabella.

As Anne Ubersfeld has remarked, one of the jobs of an actor is to turn the involuntary signs into voluntary theatrical signs with meaning. She gives the example of "the homeliness, that is the non-conformity to the accepted code of the beautiful, which certain actress uses, not only as a sign of a violence that her femininity has been subjected to, but also as a revolt against all accepted norms of femininity."[52] Isabella's many disguises, particularly the cross-dressing, illustrate precisely the "revolt against all accepted norms of femininity," but also a double transformation of the involuntary signs into voluntary ones: the involuntary sign being her own beauty, she downplays it and covers it up, reverses the accepted norms of her own femininity, into that which is conventionally considered a lack thereof, and by doing this she destabilizes and de-centers the gaze of the audience so enamored of her feminine beauty and expecting to see her in what Duchartre calls ad nauseam the "delicious" feminine clothes of the commedia actresses.

It is also important to stress that Isabella, like all the other commedia performers, male and female, was operating in a theatrical system in which actors were, to use Ubersfeld terminology, creators of their own signs, and not the director's "semiotic objects of representation, like any of the other objects onstage" (139). But in either of the two systems, whether actors are the creators of their own signs or subjected to the vision of a director, actresses are, invariably more than the actors, objects of the male gaze. The Renaissance was a time in which the culture of the gaze and of the visual seems to have its roots.[53] This is when the female body started to be represented in two fundamental modes: saintly, dressed, desexualized, as the images of the Virgin, or eroticized, naked, provocatively dressed and thus implicitly demonic and linked to Eve, the "cause of all troubles."[54] Women dressed as men subvert both of these images and destabilize the dichotomic modes of the representations of women. Simultaneously, particularly if the cross-dressing is a form of disguise, they subvert the very signs of patriarchy, which requires, for its own survival, the existence of those two antithetic forms of femininity.

Isabella mocks men in their most self-important poses: the warrior pose of the soldier ready to kill, his sword drawn and pointed toward the enemy; the confident lover sure that no woman can resist him; the authoritarian father arbitrarily deciding the destiny of his children, particularly daughters. McGill makes the very interesting point that one of the reasons women changed the face of theater once they became part of the commedia troupes is that they were the carriers of a rich oral culture which endowed them with particular skills and ease in the art of improvisation. Judy Little argues that a significant amount of the comedy created by women derives from the liminality of women in society and is largely a comedy which "mocks the deepest possible norms, norms four thousand years old." And Mahadev Apte demonstrates with a variety of cross-cultural examples that women throughout history and in many cultures, from French and Italian to Nepalese and American Indian, have developed a collective humor which engages in "mock imitations of men" by "satire, teasing, joking, ridicule, and impersonation" (76–78). Courtesans, female street mimes and jugglers often cross-dressed, as did nuns in sixteenth century convents when they produced and performed convent drama.[55] Thus we can also see Isabella's frequent cross-dressing as reflecting the oral female tradition of impersonation, mockery and irony.

In trying to imagine Isabella in her many disguises, from Gypsy to astrologer to page to soldier, Judith Williamson's remarks about the relation between attire and identity seem appropriate, even though they pertain, not to her in particular, but to the general relation between women's identity and the clothes they wear:

> When I rummage through my wardrobe in the morning I am not merely faced with a choice of what to wear. I am faced with a choice of image. ... You know perfectly well that you will be seen differently for the whole day, depending on what you put on. ... The black leather skirt rules out girlish innocence, oily overalls tend to exclude sophistication, ditto smart suit and radical feminism. Often I have wished I could put them all on together, or appear simultaneously in every possible outfit, just to say, Fuck you for thinking any of these is *me*. But also, See, I can be all of them [102].

In the fifty scenarios of Scala's collection, out of which a little more than thirty have Isabella as a character, she acts in disguise in sixteen, and out of the sixteen, thirteen of the disguises involve cross-dressing. Therefore in almost half of the scenarios, Isabella appears, not as Isabella, but as a man, as a male servant, as a page, as a soldier, as a father, as a Turkish astrologer, as a Gypsy, as a madwoman. It is disconcerting when a feminist critic such as Lesley Ferris overlooks such crucial data and says the following about Isabella: "Her energetic, comic performance exudes style, wit, charisma. But she is maskless. She is merely playing herself" (46). Not only is she not "merely playing herself," but she rides a roller coaster of disguises and changed identities. Furthermore, such a statement is basically incorrect, for *both* the male and female roles of the lovers were maskless in the commedia, therefore the distinction between masked and maskless was based not on gender but on the nature of the characters.

There is something disturbing in the consistent amount of negation of Isabella's comic and fictional abilities as a performer and improviser and in the almost unanimous emphasis on her virtuous social persona matching her stage persona, even among the most radical of feminist critics. If anything, Isabella's many faces, the panorama of masquerades and disguises of her performances, strengthened by the abundant stage dialogues of all tones and on all topics, the famous *contrasti*, published posthumously by her husband, are a superb model for modern feminist performers and performance theoreticians of destabilizing the male gaze, of decentralizing accepted stereotypes about women and the very effigies in which her contemporaries coined her.

Isabella in fact does manage to some extent to do just that: offer her audience a kaleidoscope of images and identities of herself, almost simultaneously. The Gypsy's dress excludes her aristocratic inamorata dress, the Turkish astrologer's dress excludes the innocent inamorata dress, the soldier's clothes exclude all of these, the madwoman's disguise seems to echo Williamson: "Fuck you for believing any of these is *me*. But also, See, I can be all of them."

Although Isabella presented herself and was considered by her contemporaries to be something of an exception to her gender, her performative creativity was subversive as it also incorporated aspects of the "liminal" women's tradition. Having come from a modest environment, being of Venetian origins, she must have been well in tune with the women's oral traditions.[56] Of most Italian cities, the Venetian courtesans were the most famous in the Renaissance for their performing talents and education. As McGill has tried to argue, it is possible Isabella may have been trained for the profession of a courtesan, which was the profession that then allowed women the most education and most freedom vis-à-vis men. Isabella's trick is that the first layer of the image she created for herself was that of an exception to her gender. Paradoxically, she did this by illustrating a perfect image of her gender. This way, she could be more easily accepted and taken seriously, for being an exception to the female gender, or a perfect female, meant being somewhat like a man. It would have been much more threatening to patriarchy to consider Isabella as a superb *illustration* of her gender, for that would have meant acknowledging the power, creativity, and intelligence of women at a universal scale. Thus it is more revolutionary to see Isabella, as McGill does, as highly in tune with and representative of the women's culture of her time, than as an exception to her gender.

Isabella's comedy both as the inamorata and in her many disguises is doubly subversive, for it mocks the various symbols of patriarchy, while subtly bringing to the foreground and giving voice to an existing tradition of women's transgressive humor.

Isabella Gone Wild!

The famous "mad scene" of Isabella is the culmination of everything that has been said thus far. The description by Giuseppe Pavoni of Isabella's mad scene may be the closest we have to a real account of one of her performances. Cesare Molinari argues that this famous performance (1589) is in fact "the fullest result of Italian scenic art of the Renaissance and the sum, not only of theatrical modes, but of a complex and well-articulated vision of the world."[57]

While, as critics have noted, "mad scenes" were a stepping-stone for actresses of the commedia, what makes Isabella's scene a splendid illustration of subversive humor is that a) she starts speaking in a variety of languages as well as in a bawdy brand of Italian; b) she impersonates all the other male roles or masks in the play; c) she acts and speaks in nonsensical ways which break the coherence of mimetic representation.

The mad scenes had a long-standing tradition in the history of theater. Isabella's specific type of madness was called *sproposito* and was used by the inamorati as a last resort in desperate situations" (Vickery-Bareford). In Scala's scenario, entire paragraphs of Isabella's lines during the mad scene are quoted, and after each quotation, a note about how she "raves on," or "babbles on" or "improvises other such nonsense" is given. It is more obvious in this scenario than in any of the other ones that Isabella was a brilliant improviser, and that her comic skills combined a high level of professionalism, erudition and spontaneous expression. The scholars who discuss this famous scene point out the disruption and fluctuation of identities that Isabella's scene achieves. "She dismantled the boundaries that held the action of the serious characters distinct from that of the ridiculous ones, as well as the boundary that separated the male from the female characters" (Vickery-Bareford, 49). In his article "L'altra faccia del 1589: Isabella Andreini e la sua pazzia," Molinari points out that Isabella's mimicry of the other comic masks and her loss of identity as inamorata are even more poignantly comic as it is a *serious* character who imitates the already crazy and ridiculous characters (571).

I will take all of these arguments further and discuss Isabella's madness as an excellent example of what, centuries later, the feminist theoretician Luce Irigaray would call the woman's "mimesis-mimicry" and "hystera theater." As with so much of performance feminist theory, the practice often precedes the theory only to melt back into more practice.[58] The fact that women performers and women in general, across many cultures, historical periods and geographical areas, have been engaging for millennia in the mockery, mimicry and subversion of patriarchal structures and symbols, only strengthens the theories of modern feminists. In the words of Regina Barreca, "comedy by women is about de-centering, dis-locating and de-stabilizing the world" (15). Barreca also mentions "the figure of the hysteric" as "the paradigmatic rebel against reality-testing" who "refuses to acknowledge what others construct as reality" (16). In her madness, or in her moment of hysteria, Isabella does precisely this: de-centers and destabilizes the world, explodes mimesis and the traditional representation of femininity, blurs the boundaries "between inner and outer, depth and surface, truth and falsehood that consolidate identity for the Western subject."[59] By moving fluidly from one language to the other, Spanish, French, Greek, and, in Pavoni's description, in "many other languages," Isabella disrupts the carefully constructed stability of language, and, to use Diamond's felicitous phrase, undermines "the ideality of logos as truth" (370). It is not simply to show off her erudition, as critics have noted (Vickery-Bareford, Molinari) that Isabella starts to ramble, in front of a most aristocratic audience, in many of the European languages and, according to Pavoni's description, even in made-up languages. Could it be that the graceful, virtuous, sweet Isabella, performing at a royal wedding which is also the ultimate happy ending of traditional comedy, was in fact tearing through the very tapestry of humanist self-assurance, logocentrism and reliance on identity? And all this at an occasion where the woman's identity is sealed by the definitive "yes" of an imposed marriage? Catherine Gallagher remarks that the "unreserved giving of the woman's self to her husband is the act that keeps her whole. Only in this singular and total alienation does the woman maintain her complete self-identity."[60]

There is impressive evidence that through most of the medieval period and Renaissance marriage was, for women, largely a matter of exchange and economic dealings among families.[61] The year 1589, the year of the French princess's marriage, was still marked by the rule of the rebellious queen Margot who, through her unconventional personal choices and her writings, defied as much as she could the oppressive nature of marriage, and inspired women of her time to follow in her footsteps.[62] As for the potentialities of language for women creators of comedy, Barreca notes that "language also takes it upon itself for women writers to create the world; with no authority in an 'otherly created universe,' without faith in a reality that reality-testing can verify, language returns to the boundary of the imaginary and the symbolic and appears as magical thinking, as creation itself" (17). Isabella's linguistic delirium at the occasion of a royal wedding illuminates the potential relation between the disruption of language and the affirmation of marriage which contains in itself, particularly in the case of imposed marriages, the negation of the woman as an independent self. Isabella's comedy and madness — are they not also forms of rebellion against such unwanted marriages? And her carnival of multilingualism, is it not a cunning way of exploding that all too definitive "si" expected of her in the play, and imposed upon the bride in the audience of the play?

We must not forget as we explore the many layers of Isabella's performance, that she was equally an accomplished writer in her own time, and it was due to her skills as a poet and playwright that she was admired by her male contemporaries. As she improvises onstage, Isabella is also creating language, exploding language, playing with language and pushing the limits of language precisely into that region of "magical thinking." As Robert Henke has noted, Isabella "performed literature by the rhapsodic, combinatory method characteristic of (residually) oral performance traditions" and "her deservedly praised art was forged from a generative synthesis of literature and oral performance traditions" (105). He also notes that in her mad scene, Isabella departs from the "aesthetic of mimesis that the actress was largely responsible in bringing to the professional theater," as well as from her

> fictional "*primo essere*" ["first self," with the connotation of "essential" self], but also from her linguistic self to imitate, as the Venetian *buffoni* would, the dialects and probably gestures of the various *parti ridicule*. Suspending the fictional frame of the comedy, she presents a buffoonish stand-up or revue-style performance [104].

Isabella's comedy disrupts language, mimetic modes of representation, traditional images of femininity, accepted symbols and institutionalized structures of patriarchy, as well as her own accepted social and stage persona, that "essential self" which is the apparent self, the modest, virtuous woman prescribed by male writers in Renaissance treatises, and creates what Elin Diamond has called "a funnyhouse [sic] concatenation of irreconcilable 'selves'" (376). At an occasion so solemn, and so reinforcing the status quo of patriarchy as the marriage of a Medici with a French princess, Isabella's madness subverts the accepted wisdom and tells the "non-truth of truth-reality ... constructed as a shadow-and-mirror play" (Diamond, 371). It is important to keep in mind that the reason why, in the play, Isabella performs such an awe-inspiring mad scene is to obtain the man of her choice for a husband, and also to punish her fiancée for his unfaithful behavior. It is for similar reasons that she so often cross-dresses in the other plays.

The power of the Medicis during sixteenth century Renaissance is a well-known fact, as is the fact that women, particularly women of such noble birth as the French princess Christine de Lorraine, were more often than not objects of trade meant to ensure economic and political stability or to reinforce the power of a given family. Pavoni underlines the pleasure that Isabella's use of French and of French songs in her madness scene gave to the French bride. It must have alleviated by just a little bit the feeling of estrangement she must have felt amidst the all-powerful Italian aristocrats, away from her native country and tongue.

Could it be that maybe Isabella performs partly for the French bride as she gives this comedic tour de force which veers into hysteria, into masquerade, into a blurring of all accepted linguistic and behavioral norms? Could it be that Isabella, married to a man quite a bit older than herself, given away in marriage at the age of only fifteen by her needy family (Zannetti), possibly to avoid the life of a courtesan (McGill), is having a private conversation with the French bride, telling the truth in codified, burlesque manner, just like the Shakespearian clowns at the kings' courts? Could it be that in her revue-style masquerade of language and of all the different faces of masculinity represented by the male masks she impersonates, Isabella is simultaneously masquerading the very signs of femininity imposed upon women and especially upon women of her condition and of the condition of the French bride, that is, women who were expected to uphold an ideal image of virtuous femininity?

The widespread idea of Isabella Andreini having created a stage image to match her social image seems in fact something of a glaring misconception. How does the image of a "raving" (Scala's stage direction) "madwoman" speaking in tongues, sprinkling her rantings with one obscenity after another, changing her voice, her manner, her gestures to impersonate the bawdiest and most comical male characters in the cast, match that of a "virtuous," "sweet," "gracious" devoted wife and mother? I believe that the critics' failure to notice Isabella's remarkable comic and subversive acting and improvisatory style, is part of the same age-old "women have no sense of humor" cliché, which according to Barreca "is applied by men to every threatening woman ... and causes female energy to be directed 'against the Self while remaining disguised'" (20).

McGill's strong argument in the article "Women and Performance," that it was largely the actresses of the commedia, as carriers of a rich oral women's tradition, "who introduced, developed, and excelled at the practice of comic repertory improvisation" (65), forms a good basis for my own argument, that Isabella Andreini was at least as resourceful a creator of humor as any of the male actors of her time, her own husband included. At the same time, Isabella inscribes herself at the beginning of a long line of women performers and creators of humor who in fact, despite common belief, may have used conventional signs of femininity as a disguise, as a masquerade or as a form of mimicry, under which to mock "the deepest possible norms."

To conclude this incursion in the comic abilities of one of the great performers of all times, I will take a critical look at the lines that she improvises during the famous mad scene. Critics such as Vickery-Bareford have noted that, despite the nonsensical nature of her dialogue in this scene, the syntax remains "coherent" (45) and her choice of phrases is also reflective of her great erudition. That the ease with which she manipulates an abundance of foreign names or names of famous authors, such as Aristotle, or the names of mythological figures, may be a proof of her erudition, is not worth arguing, particularly since it was a well-known fact, richly proven in her own writings, that she had acquired a high standard of erudition. But that she purposely inserted famous and foreign names in order to show off her erudition is arguable and ultimately misses the point. What is worth arguing, is that her nonsensical sentences are superb examples of linguistic humor which veers into the absurd in ways that prefigure, centuries before their publication, Lewis Carol's dialogues from *Alice in Wonderland* or *Alice Through the Looking Glass*, Eugene

Ionesco's disruption of coherent language and logic in his metaphysical farces, or, better yet, the irreverent and unleashed comedy of modern feminist performance artists and stand-up comedians. Also worth mentioning is that hidden beneath the layer of nonsense and the illogic of her lines lies the mockery of the stability of language as well as of an entire male tradition of thinking and creating. Louise Clubb aptly notes that Isabella's improvisations in this scene are a combination of

> parodied bits of the imagery of love, food, war, obscenity, and classical learning plucked from the lexicons of the stock characters of comedy; and psychedelic conjunctions of visual metaphors, aural memories, and punning word associations, jumbling together Aristotle, harpsichords, butts of muscatel [265].

Let us take a closer look at Isabella's phrases and movements during this scene, as recorded in Flaminio Scala's scenario. At first, just when she appears "dressed as a madwoman," she says:

> I remember the year I could not remember that a harpsichord sat beside a Spanish Pavane dancing with a gagliarda of Santin of Parma, after which the lasagna, the macaroni, and the polenta dressed in brown, but they could not stand one another because the stolen cat was the friend of the beautiful girl from Algeria. Even so, it pleased the Calyph of Egypt to decide that the following morning both were to be put in the stocks [289].

Upon her next entrance, she tells the Captain "that she saw him among the forty eight celestial figures when the dog star danced with the moon dressed in green," after which, "with her stick she beats the Captain and Arlechino, who run away with Isabella chasing after them" (290). Then she whispers to Pantalone and Graziano to "remain quiet and not to make any noise because Jove is going to sneeze, and Saturn is going to let go of a powerful fart." And finally, when her beloved Oratio arrives, she says: "The second life of Aristotle is the spirit which was released from a bottle of muscatel in a mountain flask, and for that reason, a whaling ship was seen doing a service for the island of English where the people could not piss" (290).

There is a method to Isabella's madness. What strikes the reader/spectator most in her speech are the unexpected associations between inanimate objects and famous people or mythological figures, with the simultaneous personifications of the inanimate objects corresponding to a derisive or obscene mockery of these famous figures. Indeed, as Barreca notes in discussing women's linguistic humor, Isabella "explodes the structures of the system from within," in a process which is "in itself duplicitous in that it destroys and creates simultaneously" (17). What she destroys are the solid walls of mimetic representation and commonsensical thought, the dusty dignity of such revered masters of philosophical thought and guides of aesthetic coherence as the great Aristotle, the formidable masculinity of such personages as Jove and Saturn, the impressive power of such political greats as the Calyph of Egypt and the pretentious self-importance of the English royalty and aristocracy. Louise Clubb notes that the reference to the English may be "a hint at the marriage, politically menacing to Protestant England, of Henri IV with the Austro-Spanish powers represented by Maria de' Medici, whose symbolic association with the rainbow began during her wedding festivities in 1600 and continued for decades" (265). She also notes that Isabella puns, by using the word *isola*, on the derivations of the name Elizabeth, which is also a derivation of her own name, Isabella.

Isabella's speech illustrates the Bergsonian theory of linguistic humor to some extent. For instance, Bergson notes that "a comic meaning is invariably obtained when an absurd idea is fitted into a well-established phrase-form" (133), which is exactly what she does in making foods and musical instruments act and talk in the company of human characters, all within the structure of an impeccable syntax. Bergson also delineates "transposition" as a fairly common way of producing linguistic humor, which again is present in Isabella's speech. One form of transposition is to shift "the solemn into the familiar" or the "trivial" or even better said, "causing something to appear mean that was formerly dignified" (141). The opposite of that is placing "moral value" or turning something trivial into something solemn or dignified. Isabella performs both forms of linguistic humor. Harpsichords, macaroni, polenta and lasagna dress "in brown," dance and sit beside important figures. Inversely, the spirit of Aristotle ends up in a bottle of wine, the English cannot piss, and the all-powerful Jove and Saturn produce sneezing, farting sounds instead of the proverbial lightning bolts. A variety of nationalities are mentioned throughout these absurdist tours de force, from the Spanish to the Egyptian, to the Algerian, to the English, and all are derided and demythologized. Isabella's linguistic improvisations are coupled with slapstick humor of the kind usually exhibited in the commedia by Arlecchino, that of beating and chasing after a character. It is she who beats and chases after two of the male characters, Arlecchino, master of the comic, and the Captain, a caricature of masculine self-importance.

Most conspicuously of course, Isabella's discourse of madness illustrates Bakhtin's theory of the banquet and of "grotesque realism." According to Bakhtin, the carnavelesque laughter of the Middle Ages and the Renaissance is a laughter which brings everything down to earth and to the realm of the material. It does so by transferring that which is "elevated, spiritual, ideal and abstract on the material and corporal plane" namely to the level of "drinking, eating, digestion and sexual life" (29). This is precisely the movement of her discourse. The levels of philosophy, astronomy, politics, and aesthetics, are pulled down into the realm of food, drink, scatology, sexuality. Isabella performs the role of the buffoon in this scene, with the added dimension that she also incorporates and parodies the male buffoons themselves. She qualifies thus as a female clown or buffoon, who breaks the law and steals language and who takes the carnival to its next logical step: that of the breakdown of gender hierarchies.

Irigaray's idea of "mimesis-imposed" (*Speculum*) and of the female hysteria as a response to the imposition of mimesis is the last theoretical lens through which I will analyze Isabella's mad scene. Mimesis, according to Irigaray, demonstrates the "truth" of the centrality of man, in a mirroring system in which the female, "unable to symbolize her fantasies and desires in a male symbolic," reflects back to the male, "his Self-Same."[63] She adds, "Hysteria, on the other hand, is a female miming "that has no recognizable referent."[64] In her speech and behavior, Isabella does disrupt any recognizable referents as well as Aristotle's own rules for mimetic art in drama, even as she is taking the name of Aristotle "in vain," so to speak, and mixes his "spirit" with wine, bottles it up, as the ultimate mockery of a solid, unchangeable reality.

Mixing it all up: politics and history, philosophy and theory of aesthetics, the material world of everyday living with the elevated world of ideas, politics, languages, the low with the high, objects with ideas, allusions to famous marriages and political figures, scatology, mythology — Isabella indeed destroys and creates at the same time. She turns the very Aristotelian idea of mimesis on its head and gives the most noble audience on their most celebrated day a glimpse into an overturned world, in which hierarchies are dismantled and the recognized structures of authority, including language, or language above all, are reduced to absurdity. As in the jokes and stories of the Shakespearean clowns, she confronts her awed audience with the spectacle of their own folly and ridiculousness. In this scene, Isabella's scatological humor and demythologizing improvisations acquire Rabelaisian dimensions, namely comedy "that is broad, physical and butch," in the words of Frances Gray. Her comedy is carnivalesque, as it suspends all hierarchies, and, in Bakhtin's words, "the utopian ideal and the realistic merged" allow for a liberation "from norms of etiquette and decency imposed at other times" (9). But what is most revolutionary is that it is *her*, Isabella Andreini, best known for her stage "dignity," for being an "ornament of the stage" (Garzoni), for her feminine allure, who delivers such irreverent comedy in the presence of a most dignified audience.

Isabella's madness, akin to the present-day's feminist view of hysteria, most likely and from all accounts awed her audience. We do not know for sure if her audience laughed or found her performance funny. Pavoni's description does note in some detail the various moves of her performance, but does not really say that it was a funny performance. In one instance only, the word *dispropositi*, suggesting a certain kind of absurdity, might we have a slight notion that she may have been perceived as comical. The words that do stand out are again *valore*, *virtu*, and, once Isabella returns to her *primo essere*, her essential self, that of the sane inamorata, Pavone notes her elegant style.

But after all does it matter whether or not her audiences roared with laughter at her performances or whether they gasped with awe or whether their eyes were full of tears? Maybe it does matter a little. But ultimately what does matter is whether, from what we can fathom from her performance, we perceive her as funny today. It is a known fact that with each period, audiences have found some things funny that others haven't, and vice versa. Such is the changing nature of theater and, to some extent, of comedy.

I believe Isabella's performance would be hilarious today. Try to picture Meryl Streep going through a "revue style" performance in which she impersonates Jack Nicholson, Robert Redford, Brad Pitt, Clint Eastwood, all the *zannis*, Pantalones and inamorati in her trade, with their specific verbal tics, gestures and body movements, all while she is chasing after and kicking Arnold Schwarzenegger in the butt, then throwing in an Italian accent as she makes fun of Marcello Mastroianni. Then she goes on to ramble about how Tony Blair and his nation of Brits "cannot piss," how George Bush is going to produce a "powerful fart" and how the spirit of Edward Said has been closed up in a bottle of California Zinfandel, while the apple pie started dancing with the Mexican sombrero. At the end of it she swoons in Clint Eastwood's arms, shortly after she comes out of her delirium and starts talking like Meryl again. And all of this would be presented as one of the entertainments celebrating the wedding of one of George W. Bush's daughters with one of Sophia Loren's sons. I believe that would be funny.

As long as the world was placed back within its recognizable frame, and the virtuous Isabella again became composed, elegant, sweet and "eloquent," in that logical Aristotelian kind of eloquence, with recognizable referents, the temporary inversion was acceptable as a worthy bit of entertainment. At the end of her scene, she is brought back to her senses and she gets to marry the man of her choice. Isabella takes the de-centering of the world and of acceptable identities a notch higher, and it is maybe today, better than ever, that we can hear her at her true pitch of more than four centuries ago.

In her carnivalesque moment, Isabella has overturned and broken all hierarchies: social, gender, linguistic, as well as the distinctions between her real and her invented persona. And even if she returns to her known eloquence and to recognizable referents, the possibility of the overturn and the potential for a destabilizing of identities have been shown. After all, were she to remain in the state of insanity, the comedy would have turned to tragedy and her character into something of a pathetic Renaissance Augustine, always revolving within the parameters of her hysteria become spectacle, as the nineteenth century doctor Charcot would often impose on his female patients.[65] It is in fact the closure of her madness with regained sanity that accounts for her performance being comedic, and being a performance within a performance. Had the performance of her madness been executed in the first degree, Isabella would have been a tragic figure à la Ophelia.[66]

The fact that Isabella's creation of humor, and of a subversive kind of humor at that, has been neglected, overlooked or avoided is part of the general and century-old trend to minimize if not deny altogether women's ability to be funny and produce laughter other than as objects of male humor. Most feminist studies on humor and gender point out and often have as a departing point of opposition and contention the much-used phrase "women have no sense of humor."[67] Anne Beatts suggests that ultimately men feel threatened by women's humor because "they unconsciously are afraid that the ultimate joke will be the size of their sexual apparatus."[68] Indeed, Isabella's comedy is disruptive, threatening and does have, as the ultimate joke, at least in symbolic manner, the size of the (male) sexual apparatus. One conspicuous and curious detail of the painting of the Gelosi in the Carnavalet Museum is that of all the characters or actors depicted in the painting, it is only the woman thought to be Isabella who looks straight at the audience, as she is standing right in front of Pantalone, who wears, as mentioned earlier, red tights which reveal with very precise contours a formidable phallus, matched by the large sword hanging at his left thigh. Isabella's eyes, looking straight at the audience and ignoring the impressive display of masculinity to her left, seem to have something of an ironic glitter. Try to imagine this image next to the many others of Isabella dressed in the male attire that her own husband is wearing or that Pantalone is wearing as he self-assuredly stands in front of her. Try to imagine Isabella in a kaleidoscope of disguises, and the glitter in her eyes may just be turning into the *riso* of Chiabrera's poem, though not an innocent *riso* but a *riso* which indeed does mock the self-assuredness of phallic order.

As Frances Gray has noted,

> the field of comic discourse is perhaps the most fiercely guarded of all, against female clowns and female critics. It is the female clown who perhaps best embodies Hélène Cixous' punning image of woman as "une voleuse de langue," that is, one who steals the language, and one who also flies with the language [13].

As she impersonates the speech, specific dialects and vocal characteristics of Pantalone, Gratiano, Zanni, Pedrolino, Burratino, Captain Cardone, all male characters famous for their comic and clownish dimension, Isabella is truly a thief of language, who, by clowning the clowns, performs, four hundred years before any feminist performance theory was even conceived, the mimicry of mimesis in the second degree. Like some kind of Renaissance Meryl Streep and Marilyn Monroe combined, Isabella Andreini flies with language, breaks the rules, moves in and out of the real and the created, changes clothes, faces, roles, and accents, turns the world upside down, all before the eyes of one of the most powerful, traditional, patriarchal families in centuries, the great Medicis. Even if at the end of her performance, she is brought back "to her sense," to her *primo essere*, the potential for an upside-down world has been suggested. One can only wonder what effect the performance could have had on the French bride who so rejoiced at the sound of her native language on the lips of the Italian performer.

Did She Do It on Purpose?

Was Isabella at all aware of her subversion? Andrea Perrucci's seventeenth century version of performance theory points out that the improvisation of the commedia actors was indeed premeditated and laboriously prepared. The commedia scenarios and plot schemes, which remained and were reinvented throughout Europe in the classical comedies of the seventeenth and eighteenth centuries, have as the main target of their mockery and humor old men with pretentions of power and lusty for young women (the Pantalone types) and arrogant men who are overly confident about their phallic power (the Capitan Spaventa types). Actors and actresses alike were cross-dressing and thus destabilizing the accepted norms of gender and sexuality. Therefore, as already pointed out, Isabella was already performing within a revolutionary theatrical context.

But the most important arguments supporting Isabella Andreini's conscious subversion of gender roles and of her own idealized image are her own writings, and particularly her pastoral play *The Mirtilla*. There, Andreini reverses the traditional gender parts established by the classical pastoral and establishes her own. Thus, as Julie Campbell has remarked, "Andreini's inclusion of a heroine who is frank, intellectually astute, and free from many of the obtusely 'virtuous' characteristics seen in her foil Ardelia constitutes a critical moment in the development of the pastoral tragicomedy and in Renaissance literary characterizations in general" (xvii). If her play, written quite at the beginning of her career, and before the performance of the *Pazzia d'Isabella*, is so revolutionary in terms of the subversion of the accepted notions of female "virtue" and gender distinctions, it makes perfect sense that her so much acclaimed performance for the Medicis, as well as the majority of her performances, contain a deliberate set of reversals and subversions.

Isabella's female characters Filli and Ardelia provide, according to Campbell, "a singularly humorous glimpse of what the traditionally silent, chaste, and obedient Renaissance beloved might be like, if she were provided a voice and the agency to interact with her admirers" (xviii). Filli in particular, demonstrates the level of intelligence and independence that is not found in female characters written by male playwrights and poets of the time, such as the great Tasso. In the creation of her role, Andreini departs significantly from tradition, precisely in that area where the voice, independence and creativity of the female subject is concerned. Some of the funniest moments in *The Mirtilla* are those in which Filli frees herself by her own resourcefulness and cunning from the libidinous advances and violent entrapment by the character of Satiro. Indeed, as Campbell has noted, Andreini displays superb comic timing in creating this scene. First, as she is being tied up by the lecherous Satiro, Filli keeps her cool and reverses her discourse of woe to a feigned discourse of love, which becomes progressively funnier, as its exaggerated romantic tone contrasts with the reality of Satiro's character and with Filli's repulsion for him: "What nymph could ever see you/and not burn for you? I believe you are such that she who sees you and then doesn't love you/must be made of Caucasian stone!" (lines 1339–1342). After brilliantly tricking Satiro into releasing her and letting himself be tied to the tree on a pretense that Filli wishes to caress him more freely, the heroine savors her victory for a while longer, by teaching her trapped aggressor a lesson and teasing him to her delight and to his great desperation.

The comedy that Isabella creates in these lines is one which would give satisfaction and be appreciated by many a woman who have suffered aggression or been violated. Isabella's sarcasm in the lines in which she mocks Satiro and tricks him into believing she will satisfy his lust is no lesser than, say, the ironic tirades exchanged in Shakespeare's *A Midsummer Night's Dream*. She teases him with overly poetic and sensuous language which, by contrast with Satiro's appearance and with Filli's real feelings for him, emerges also as a form of linguistic carnival: "Certainly, I can make you wait no longer,/nor do I want to wait to embrace you and sweetly/kiss your delicate lips,/which, if I understand aright/ surpass the sweetness of Hyblean honey!" (1410–1414). To the linguistic comedy, Andreini adds abundant situational comedy which all together would make for a comic performance worthy of the most famous comic playwrights. In pretending she wants to kiss and caress him, Filli pulls Satiro's beard, twists his neck, pinches his breasts, pulls him by his horns and declares: "Alas, I can't resist/caressing you" (1444–1446).

Many of the commedia devices of physical humor (for example, the stock gestures of kicking, pulling, and pinching) are being used cleverly by Filli-Isabella, with all the elements of the grotesque derived from the combination of Filli's mock tenderness and Satiro's beast-like appearance. Filli-Isabella, the inamorata, reverses both the language and the gestures of love and romance typical of her role into burlesque comedy in which the female character emerges as a cunning trickster who has the last word and the last laugh. Furthermore, besides its comical dimensions, this scene has an ethical side to it as well, as it enacts a woman's liberation from an entrapment and the well-deserved punishment of the entrapper. This scene, together with the scene in which the singing rivalry between Filli and Ardelia transforms into female friendship and collaboration, places Andreini's performance at the innovative level of women's subversive comedy in which commedia devices, poetic discourse and conventional roles are recreated from the perspective of a female intelligent subject who does not need the help of a male savior type in order to prevail over difficult situations and who finds comfort and different forms of love in the company of other women. Breaking out of classic theatergrams and conventional gender roles is quite revolutionary for the late sixteenth century.

And is not Filli the character whom Isabella herself played and the name by which her own husband calls her postmortem, in his sentimental epitaph? Only in his epitaph he refers to her in the same language as her contemporaries had: "beautiful face, glorious name and chaste conjugal love."[69] As Campbell demonstrates, Andreini subverts the traditional theatergram of the "damsel in distress," "turns the tables on tradition," and creates in Filli "a nimble thinker and a fast talker who rescues herself with the finesse of an accomplished con artist — or perhaps, a courtesan" (xxi). And is not Isabella of Scala's scenarios quite often also a "con artist — courtesan" who, like the Filli of the pastoral, rescues herself, by her own wit and cunning, by the power of her own "fiction," or *favola*, from unwanted situations imposed upon her by authoritarian fathers, jealous lovers, and unfaithful fiancés? Having already subverted the structure of a dramatic genre as established and old as the pastoral, does it not follow naturally that she would be subversive in her own roles and improvisations onstage?

Isabella's letters are also to be considered with regard to her deliberate subversion of gender roles. As we have seen in the letter to the duke of Savoia, she presents herself as having always been consumed by a passion for learning and achieving fame as a writer, an "uncommon" desire for women of her time, she says, and one which has been throughout history the admitted ambition of male creators, writers, artists. Furthermore, in several of her letters she elaborates on what she considers to be feminine qualities, such as constancy (*Della constanza delle donne*), volubility (*Della volubilita delle donne*), thus exploding the stereotypes of the kind "frailty thy name is woman," or the generally accepted mockery of women being uselessly talkative. What she calls "women's volubility," is it not also the very essence of the women's oral traditions which account for a part of her own artistry and eloquence as a performer? Isabella in fact contrasts women's constancy with the lack of it found in many men. In *La Pazzia d'Isabella*, is it not Oratio, her lover, who pushes her to madness, precisely because of his inconstancy and because he is about to break his marriage promise to her, due to a sudden infatuation with Flaminia? Isabella also writes in praise of famous women, suggesting that women's accomplishments have been much neglected over the centuries and they merit as much praise as those of men (*Delle lodi feminili*). Conscious of her own valor as well, proud yet careful in crafting a praiseworthy image of herself for all posterity, Isabella was evidently aware of and deliberately turning the tables on accepted norms of femininity in her own performances and improvisations.

As I try to picture Isabella on that glorious Saturday of May 13, 1589, amidst a most festive and extravagant setting as described by Giuseppe Pavoni, surrounded by fountains, fruits and flowers of all kinds, watched by a large assembly of dukes, marquises and princes, exploding into a most awe-inspiring performance of madness through which, paradoxically, she demonstrates "her sane and cultivated intellect,"[70] I cannot help smiling and believing that Isabella, like Filli of her pastoral, gave the famous French bride and the other women in the audience some kind of aesthetic vindication and moral satisfaction as she relieved them, even if temporarily, for the duration of the play, from the "golden" shackles of that so much praised feminine "virtue." Like Filli, who walks away proudly, leaving the tricked Satyre tied to a tree, with readers and spectators gasping in wonderment at her astuteness, Isabella walks away, leaving behind her such "murmurs and wonder,"[71] maybe even winking at the French bride and symbolically tricking all those would-be satyrs in the audience, so eager and so fast to lust for the body of this intelligent actress.

Pavoni closes his awed eyewitness commentary of Isabella's performance with the inflamed words, "As long as the world shall last, her beautiful eloquence and value will always be praised."[72] He has a point after all. For it is maybe today more than ever that we can bring to life the true Isabella, hidden, secretly embedded in her own discourse of "madness," as the *isola*, the island of humor and subversion, akin to that other great subverter of patriarchy, Queen Elizabeth, and see her the way her own contemporaries failed to, and as our own continue to fail to see her: a subversive female clown, an ingenious creator of humor, a thief of language.

Two

Caterina Biancolelli
Seventeenth Century Trickster and Parisian Coquette

Colombina, the diminutive of the Italian *colomba*, meaning dove, is the name taken by the female servant-trickster in the commedia dell'arte of the second half of the seventeenth century. Analogous earlier female roles were Franceschina, Olivetta, Ricciolina, and Diamantina, some of whom appear as early as the Gelosi company, next to the role of Isabella Andreini. The role of Colombina appears during the period of 1653–84, as one of the main female roles of the troupe called Fiorelli-Locatelli, which later became the Ancienne Troupe de la Comédie Italienne.[1] The part of Colombine is played by Catherine Biancolelli (1665–1716), the daughter of Dominique Biancolelli (1636–88), one of the most famous Arlecchinos of all times, and of Orsola Cortesi (1637–1718), playing the role of the inamorata. Catherine was the second Colombine in the repertoire of the *commedia*, the first being her own grandmother Isabella Biancolelli Franchini.[2] Catherine's older sister, Françoise, played the role of Isabella, the one created a century earlier by Isabella Andreini.

Although Catherine Biancolelli is mentioned in most studies on the *commedia dell'arte* of this period as the one largely responsible for the creation of the role of Colombine, no full studies on her life or her character have been written. This chapter is devoted entirely to the actress Catherine Biancolelli, and in particular to the creation of her character Colombina as a superb illustration of transgressive humor and subversive performance. I argue that Caterina's Colombina takes the improvisational comedy of her Italian predecessors in the genre of the commedia dell'arte to a new level of emancipation in which the female protagonist negotiates gender, stage presence, and disguise in order to achieve personal fulfillment despite the obstacles of patriarchal structures and traditional gender roles of seventeenth-century France. As the chapter will attempt to demonstrate, Caterina's Colombina resourcefully weaves her Italian heritage of entertainment with the performative subtleties of the French coquette, and the result is a new woman who defies the place that society has traditionally reserved for her and her kind.

In his *Histoire de l'ancien théâtre italien depuis son origine en France*, François Parfaict[3] gives the following explanation of the name taken by Catherine Biancolelli onstage:

> In a little house that Dominique had bought in the village of Bière, near Paris, he had placed a portrait of his mother, painted in city clothes, carrying a basket which contained two doves, by allusion to the name of Colombina, which she carried in the theater; it is for this reason that Dominique had his daughter take this name [105].

Isabella Franchini, the first Colombina, was therefore Dominique's mother, and thus the tradition of the male-female clown was handed down to Catherine from her father's side, and that of the ingénue, or inamorata, on the side of her mother, Orsola Cortesi. According to Luigi Rasi, all the famous Colombines belonged to the Biancolelli family (430). The period between 1680 and 1697 was the swan song of the commedia dell'arte in France. The Fiorelli-Locatelli troupe, led by the actress Orsola Cortesi and her husband Dominique Biancolelli, and including many of their children, was largely responsible for the transition from Italian to French comedy.

Unlike many of the previous companies, most of the actors, particularly the younger ones, are now perfectly bilingual in Italian and French and are starting to make conscious efforts to appeal more and more to the French audiences, by mixing in their performances French and Italian (for example, *Le Divorce, Les Chinois, Les Momies d'Egypte, Colombine avocat pour et contre*),[4] and by actually asking French writers to write scenes in French.[5]

Catherine Biancolelli was a gifted actress, singer, and dancer who drew the attention of the king and of the theater reviewers of the time, such as Donneau de Visé, who wrote the theater columns in the *Mercure Galant*. In the October 1683 issue of the *Mercure Galant*, Donneau de Visé raves about the Italian troupe and the two Biancolelli sisters:

> Never has the Italian Comedy been so successful and appreciated in France, as it is presently. Never have the Italian comedians captured so skillfully our manners, as they have been doing it for some time. They unite the useful with the pleasurable and there is a lot to gain from all their plays, especially from their last one, where one learns, by the many procedures of *Arlequin Avocat*, how dangerous it is to plead.... If Arlequin is inimitable in the many parts he is seen playing in this play, his two daughters are no less so. The different characters that they play, are so well accomplished, that they have attracted the tireless admiration of the

entire city of Paris. Never have we seen so much intelligence for the Comedy, with such impressive youth. There is no character that they cannot play, and as soon as they appear in such or such scene, they seem uniquely made for the character they represent [translation mine].

While the role of Isabella, the ingénue or inamorata, was evolving into the whimsical, brazen young woman disdainful of marriage, the sassy Colombine was bringing a new dimension of female wit and humor onto the French stage and the commedia repertoire in general. Although the great Isabella Andreini was a rather hard act to follow and she had no equal in the century following her death, her role was being however transformed by Catherine's sister, Françoise Biancolelli, into a character prefiguring the Sylvies of Marivaux's theater: a more practical inamorata, with dreams of romantic love but with apprehension of marriage and of men in general, cunning and witty. Simultaneously, though, the role of Colombina is gaining in comedic intricacy, overshadowing that of her mistress and even, as Bruce Griffiths notes, converging at times with that of the inamorata or now, the *amoureuse*. The *tipi fissi* (fixed types) are not so fixed any more and Caterina/Colombina plays an impressive range of parts, from the sassy maid, to the "freelance intrigante," to the "fausse ingenue"[6] to a long-winded author, to doctor, lawyer, peddler, knight, captain, the God of marriage, judge. As Winifred Smith has noted, "Where Isabella Andreini chose one disguise and found it enough throughout one play, Gherardi's Colombine must needs keep the audience awake by tormenting Arlequin in a constantly changing personality."[7]

Though not of the erudite and literary formation which marked the personality of Isabella Andreini, Catherine Biancolelli's comic and performative creativity has probably been equally influential. Critics unanimously point to Catherine Biancolelli as the one who created and brought the role of the *zanna* to an unprecedented level of wit and complexity. Virginia Scott points out that "Colombine is actually on the way to becoming a sort of French Female First Zanni, a trickster who is, however, always successful and never gets caught. The character has no antecedent in the earlier repertory" (301). According to Duchartre, there has been through the history of commedia an entire "dynasty" of Colombines, but he too notes that it was the daughter of Domenico Biancolelli who brought the role to its most accomplished level of comedy and who, despite the claims of traditionalism and fixed types of the *commedia*, brought a modern dimension to this role, in particular that of "coquetterie" (267). Charles Mazouer notes that Catherine Biancolelli, who marked her debut as Colombine in 1683, created the most "representative" part of the French comedy destined to the Italian theater. He notes her cynical wisdom, her taste for disguise, her verve and wit, next to which even the character of Arlequin pales at times.[8] In the *Enciclopedia dello spettacolo*, Catherine is also noted to be the most famous and developed Colombina, celebrated for her pleasant voice and gestures, and the "incommensurable finesse and inimitable verve" of her performance ("dimisurata finezza e inimitabile brio"). She is also known to have appeared in many disguises, from knight to doctor to lawyer. In the Campardon dictionary of actors, Catherine Biancolelli is again presented as the creator of the role of Colombina, to which she gave energy, verve, wit and extraordinary variety. Parfaict notes that Colombina "became in little time, the most perfect comedienne of her genre, who had ever appeared in the Italian theater" (106). And Luigi Rassi, while unequivocally considering Caterina as the most famous Colombine, has noted that it was her Colombina who "created a comic universe, changing into a thousand characters" (438), and that she "achieved gigantic proportions, the character around whom all the others turn" (442). As if to exhibit to the world the grandeur of her role as female trickster according to George Sand, Catherine appeared in the magnificent costume of Arlecchina in the 1695 one-act play from Gherardi's collection entitled *Le Retour de la Foire de Bezons*, which later became popular in feasts and carnivals. This is later represented in an engraving from 1685, which later inspired Watteau in his painting *Les acteurs italiens*.[9] After the closing of the Italian Theater in 1697, Catherine was invited to join the French theater, which she proudly refused, taking her leave from the stage forever.

Materials regarding Catherine's mode of performance are even scarcer than those about Isabella Andreini's performances a hundred years earlier. Since Catherine did not leave a written body of works, and, ironically, since by the time she was acting, scenarios, or *canevas*, were being replaced by actual written scenes and plays, we have less documentation of her actual stage presence, though significantly more documentation of her actual character, Colombina in terms of dialogue. Flaminio Scala's collection of scenarios, nonliterary and succinct as they were, did in fact note all the important movements, gestures, actions, objects and costumes of the characters, which makes it relatively easy to reconstruct the general dynamics of the performances and even imagine some of the dialogues. Inversely, most of the scenes and plays in which Catherine developed her character as Colombina are gathered in the famous 1700 collection of Evaristo Gherardi, entitled *Le Théâtre Italien de Ghérardi, ou le Recueil Général de toutes les Comédies et Scénes Francaises jouées par les Comédiens italiens du Roy, pendant tout le temps qu'ils ont été en service.* Therefore, while we do have a more precise and varied image of the character of Colombina, of her actual lines and speeches, we possess less with regard to her actual performance, improvisatory work and input into the character.

The commedia dell'arte in which Isabella had so shined a century before, had become under Louis XIV, the *comédie italienne* and had lost some of its spontaneous dimension of improvisation; the *comédie italienne* was delineated and controlled by French writers hired especially to help reconcile the differences between the early commedia dell'arte and the classical requirements of seventeenth century French theater, as well as to respond to the expectations of the French audiences and of the court. A certain "Monsieur D***" who later was identified as Anne Mauduit de Fatouville, and a certain Jean-François Regnard, friend of Fatouville, are some of the better-known authors of the scenes gathered in Evaristo Gherardi's collection. Since there was obviously less room for improvisation, it is in fact harder to know how much of the roles were still the creation of the actors and how much the creation of the authors who wrote for the company. Several critics have also noted the influence of Molière on the characters of the *comédie italienne*, in particular Colombina's character.[10]

Despite this rather disconcerting convergence of the Italian actors' art of improvisation and the written works of second-rate writers who tried to contain the verve of the commedia dell'arte within recognizable and classical French patterns, or to emulate their great contemporary Molière, there is sufficient reason to believe that the role created by Catherine Biancolelli was largely of her own creation and, furthermore, it followed in the line of previous female performers, including Isabella Andreini and Catherine's own matrilineal line of performers. Furthermore, the actress immediately preceding Caterina in the role of the *soubrette*, Patricia Adami, was also a spirited, talented actress, whose stage name was Diamantine. According to Parfaict, she "shined a lot" ("elle brilla beaucoup") and was of "great vivacity in the execution of her roles" (57–58). And before Patricia Adami's Diamantine, the role of the maid was performed by a certain actress, Beatrix, who also, according to Parfaict, "brilla beaucoup" (36). By the time Catherine took over the role of the maid under the poetic name of Colombine, there was already a line of actresses who had chiseled the part of the *zanna* and prepared it for its grand end-of-the-century apotheosis.

The role of Colombine is, like its male analogue, Arlecchino, the female comic role par excellence. But, unlike the male comic parts, and similar to the role created by Isabella Andreini, or like the other female roles of the *commedia*, Colombina is to a significant degree the creation of the actress herself. Most critics seem to be unanimous on this point: Duchartre notes that, given the late appearance of women onstage, the female characters are not created by an ancient tradition, and that the "history of Isabella, Colombina, Zerbinetta, is rather, that of the comedienne herself" (248). Griffiths points out the virtuosity of the actresses playing Isabella and Colombina, who, according to him, were largely responsible for the richness of their parts.

However, the view that a role such as Colombina's appears ad nihilo and tells almost exclusively the story of the actress herself, again denies women the possibility of fiction, of the imaginary, as well as the possibility of a female comic tradition. Is Colombina just playing herself, as Lesley Ferris cynically and rather erroneously noted about Isabella Andreini, and if not, is she just the creation of some lesser seventeenth century author, a Molière emulator? My belief is that she is largely the author of her own role as Colombina, but in a way which incorporates both her own story and personality and the lesser known but nevertheless existent tradition of female comedy and performance. Much like Isabella Andreini, Catherine Biancolelli drew from what was by now an already rich tradition of female humor and, by means of the professional training specific to the trade of commedia dell'arte performers, to which was added her own improvisational genius, she brought the character of the female trickster to a level of comic richness and to a subversive dimension which, if anything, influenced the female characters of Marivaux or Beaumarchais, and certainly rivaled if not exceeded those of Molière. Certainly, all this does not exclude nor is it in contradiction with the fact that to a significant extent, the character of Colombina does emerge from the personality and life experiences of the actress herself. But, as is the case with any artist, the personal and the autobiographical are entangled with exterior influences, with a certain inherited tradition, and woven into a new form of expression. The problem with women performers is that it is harder to trace a solid and canonical, or recognizable, tradition, but that does not mean that one did not exist.

An entire century of female roles and comedy separates Caterina from Isabella. During this century the commedia troupes knew continued success, and actresses continued to attract the admiration of Italian and French audiences. As was the case with the male performers, who transmitted their *arte* much like family secrets from father to son,[11] so it was most likely the case with the female performers. In Caterina's family, we have seen that her grandmother had been a Colombina and her own daughter also turned out to be a Colombina. Furthermore, Caterina's mother was the famous actress Orsola Cortesi, who played the role of the inamorata for her entire acting career.

Besides the family ties that united the commedia performers, actresses were also the inheritors of a rich oral women's tradition, as seen in the previous chapter. As Kathleen McGill has remarked, oral traditions in Italian popular culture were quite prevalent throughout much of the Renaissance, and women's culture, being primarily one of oral expression, is largely responsible for the improvisatory competencies of the commedia dell'arte.

Italy could also pride itself on quite a rich tradition of convent drama and performance which, as Elisa Weaver has richly demonstrated, flourished in Tuscany during the sixteenth century.[12] Since many women of that time were educated in the convents, both those who became nuns and the girls who returned to secular life, it follows that the convent education and experiences had repercussions outside the walls of the convent, into the life of women in society. The convent dramas were usually commedia *sacra,* and included a variety of comic scenes, plots and subplots, as well as *beffas,* or practical jokes. Most interestingly, the nuns all played both female and male parts, cross-dressed and disguised themselves. The comic scenes and the comic subplots usually involved peasants and servants.[13]

On the other side of the spectrum of women's performative culture were the Renaissance Italian courtesans who, particularly in sixteenth century Venice, became important social and cultural figures in the life of the city and who impressed with "their talents as highly sophisticated conversationalists and cunning rhetoricians, and for their dexterity at navigating their way through a loosely organized maze of social structures and class hierarchies."[14]

This is to show that throughout Renaissance Italy, women did have, under various circumstances, from the tight walls of convents to the swarming commercial life of the city-states, a culture of performance and comedy and that even a relatively modern character like Colombina does not appear in a vacuum. There is no reason to believe that the later actresses, even when they were born and educated in France, as were the Biancolelli sisters, had lost that rich oral heritage of *contrasti,* ballads, dramatic songs, improvisatory skills, *beffas* and the taste for disguise and cross-dressing.

Despite the presence of French scenes written and inserted in their shows, the Biancolelli troupe still maintained Italian scenes in their performances. Most of the plays in the Gherardi edition have gaps in their dialogues, which are filled with what the authors have indicated as "Italian scenes," with *lazzis* and improvised dialogues to fill these gaps and, often, with the authors' comments that they are unable to reproduce in writing the Italian scenes. Caterina was particularly admired for her great versatility in all areas of performance — acting, singing, dancing, and playing instruments — and she often breaks into singing or dancing in the middle of a scene, as for instance in the play *La Coquette.* Besides, like her sister, she was perfectly bilingual and performed with ease in both French and Italian. In the play *Colombine avocat pour et contre,* Catherine performs almost equally in Italian as in French, and she acts an entire scene in Spanish, in disguise, with Arlequin. The abundant use of Italian supports the fact that, at least in the 1680s, in the first part of her career, improvisation together with traditional *commedia* material were abundantly used. Her use of other languages, such as Spanish and, later in the same play, of French dialects, bears striking resemblance with Isabella Andreini's abundant disguises combined with a linguistic roller coaster.

In general, the Biancolelli actors were known, as Duchartre has noted, for the ease with which they converted their Italian improvised dialogues into French (142). The fact that Caterina's father was one of the most famous Arlecchinos of all times is certainly not without significance, particularly since Caterina became famous for the role of Colombina, who was generally known as the lover or wife of Arlecchino, and since in her majestic appearance of 1695, she inscribed forever the image of Arlecchina in the history of theater. Even more significant is the fact that at the funeral of her father, Caterina is portrayed exactly in the center, holding her father's famous mask and handing it to the Arlecchino who followed. In this engraving by Bonnart, Caterina is again portrayed in her grand Arlecchina costume. It seems that Caterina/Colombina inherited the *arte* and the comic skills from both sides of her family, but that in fact she continued equally in her father's tradition of the comic role, as in the line of her mother, who held the roles of the inamorata and which Caterina combines at times with that of the *zanna*.

Critics are as vague with regard to the authorship of Caterina's comic part as they are certain with regard to the fact that it was she who gave this role its greatest verve and comic energy. The two positions are in obvious contradiction with each other. Even Virginia Scott, who comments quite a bit on the comic creativity of Caterina, notes ambiguously when speaking of her role in the play *Arlequin empéreur*: "Whether the invention of Monsieur D*** or of the young actress herself, Colombine is clearly not an Italian *serva* but a Parisian who has learned how to survive in a society where ideals and fine words butter no baguettes" (294). Why then, if it is not known for sure whether this character is of the actress's own creation or the product of the writers who were working for the company, is she invariably referred to as the one who created and brought the part of Colombina to an unprecedented level of comedy and complexity? On what are all these critics basing their assumptions of Colombina's creative input into this role?

It is a puzzle worth solving. First, according to documents of the time, Caterina and her sister Françoise were both playing the parts for which they later achieved fame, even before their official debut in 1683, which also coincided with the date on which they received shares in the company. [15] The official entrance of the two sisters in the company rejuvenated and brought renewed interest to their performances. Catherine was seventeen years old at her official debut, in 1683, and had been playing her role of Colombine for awhile. Isabella Andreini, a century before her, was acting and was given shares in the Gelosi company at fifteen, soon after her marriage to the actor Francesco Andreini. It was common for actresses to start acting and creating their roles for a company quite young. With a mother as inamorata and a grandmother as Colombina, it makes all the sense in the world, that the two sisters had already created their roles and were improvising dialogues and scenes, well before the mysterious Monsieur D*** and Monsieur Regnard started writing for the company.

In support of the argument that Colombine is largely the creation of the actress herself are also Scott's comments that, in ascertaining how much of the repertory of the Comédie Italienne consisted of French scenes and plays, and how much of Italian scenes, there has been too much reliance on Gherardi's collections. She suggests that, while some French plays were introduced in the repertoire of the company, "the traditional repertory continued to be played, sometimes with new French scenes added, or perhaps with traditional scenes translated into French" (275). In addition, she also points out the likelihood that some of the plays in the Gherardi edition, "especially those attributed to Monsieur D***, were originally improvised in Italian, with French ornaments," and notes that throughout the mid–1680s, "their performances were almost totally improvised" (277). The element of improvisation is crucial in ascertaining the actors and actresses' original contribution to the creation of their roles, for as we have seen in the previous chapter, in the traditional commedia companies, each performer was responsible for the creation of her/his own role, further developed onstage through the collaboration demanded by the art of the improvisation itself.

A close look at the scenes and plays in the Gherardi edition will also provide significant clues to the nature of the performances of this company's actors and, in particular, Colombina's role. In a significant number of plays, she has by far the most input in the movement of the plot and in the many comic layers of the plays. At the end of the play *Les Chinois*, from the Gherardi collection, it is Colombine who speaks in defense of the Italian actors, versus Arlequin, who defends the French actors. The scene has an unusually metatheatrical dimension, and sounds almost like an ars poetica of the commedia dell'arte, versus a caricatural version of an ars poetica of the French classical theater. Gherardi wrote:

> In fact, in order to give the universe an Italian actor, nature has to make extraordinary efforts. A good Arlequin is *natura laborantis opus*, she bestows upon him all her treasures, and she hardly has enough spirit to animate her work. But as for the French comedians, nature makes them while sleeping; she makes them of the same dough as she makes parrots, who only repeat what they have learned by

heart; instead, an Italian draws everything from his own depths, and does not borrow from anyone in order to speak, similar to these eloquent nightingales who vary their song according to their various whims [1:253, translation mine].

In this scene, Colombine is followed by all the comic actors, while Arlequin is followed by all the heroic actors. Furthermore, the scene follows one of the "Italian scenes"— that is, an improvised scene, in which the skills of the Italian actors are measured against those of the French ones. Colombine is the voice of Italian comedy itself. Her very speech at the end of the play subverts the play as a solid dramatic structure to be learned by heart and extols the virtues of Italian improvisation art, of which she appears to be the last and most notable spokesperson. In one of her very last speeches in the *Les Chinois*, Colombine states proudly that "the Italian theater is the center of freedom, the source of joy, the shelter from all domestic troubles" (255). Caterina/Colombina's speech about the particular skills of the Italian actors is almost identical to those of Evariste Gherardi, when discussing the same issue, the difference between the Italian and the French actors, in the preface to his *Théâtre Italien*. Firstly, he warns his readers that they "should not expect to find in this collection whole comedies, since it is impossible to print Italian plays. The reason is that Italian actors learn nothing by heart, and that all they have to do to perform a play is to have seen the plot for a short while before going onstage." [16] Gherardi's introduction destabilizes the texts he is about to present in his collection and favors the argument that what we see in this collection is a rudimentary image of what took place onstage and therefore of the collaborative creation and improvisations of the actors themselves. Also, Luigi Riccoboni's comments about the virtues of improvised comedy echo those of Colombina. He notes that the Italian actors are more dynamic and natural in their acting, for "one feels and consequently says better that which is created than that which is borrowed from others with the help of memory" (61–62). So resourceful were the Italian actors in their art of improvisation that even by adapting their repertory, adding scenes to their *canevas,* and shifting almost entirely to French in their performances they were perceived as serious rivals to the Comédie Française and the opera.

In trying to ascertain the originality of Colombine's role, another event seems of particular importance. In 1694, which is the date of the first edition of Gherardi's collection, *Théâtre Italien ...*, the Biancolelli troupe angrily petitioned to the king against Gherardi, maintaining that the publication was effectuated without their permission and against their will, that it contained the scenes and plays of the troupe for the past thirty years (meaning since the mid–1660s), and that it was highly damaging to the success of the troupe, for it destroyed the element of spontaneity and freshness of plays which are unpublished and are presented each time as if for the first time.[17] Isabelle and Catherine, together with their mother, Orsola Cortesi, were among the petitioners.

Obviously, the Italian actors were seeing their mythic and hard-learned art of improvisation threatened by the publication of actual scenes and dialogues, and the magic of their success, disclosed and dissipated by the proliferation of the printed word. As Peter Burke has noted, "the book was a dangerous competitor and a treacherous ally" (255) to performance, improvisation and oral culture ever since the first pressing in the fifteenth century. "The book was a treacherous ally," he points out, "because the fixing of texts in print affected the nature of the performance, encouraging the repetition, as opposed to the re-creation, of a song or a story. It has been suggested that literacy stunts the capacity to improvise, just as it removes some of the incentive" (255). The petition of the actors of the Italian troupe against Gherardi's publication of their scenes and plays expresses practically the identical fear of the transformation of the creative process of improvisation and pure performance, into the monotonous act of repetition of given texts. It is also the gist of Colombine's speech from the play *Les Chinois*, when she compares the French actors to "parrots" involved in the act of repetition versus the Italian actors, who are presented as "nightingales," therefore always involved in renewing, creating and re-creating their stage actions and dialogues. In fact so resourceful were the Italian actors in their art of improvisation, that even by adapting their repertory, adding scenes to their *canevas* and shifting almost entirely to French in their performances, they were perceived as serious rivals to the Comédie Française and the Opéra.[18]

The fact that it is Colombine who in *Les Chinois* acts as the spokesperson of the *arte* of the Italian troupes is even more significant. For if we consider the thesis that women had a crucial role in the development of the art of improvisation in the *commedia*, it was also women who therefore had even more at stake in losing that creative freedom. Having fewer opportunities to be well educated, significantly less access to books and fewer possibilities to become writers in their own right[19] women were to be the main losers in the battle between commedia dell'arte and French classical theater. All that was left to them in the transformation of Italian comedy to French comedy was to act in plays written and directed by male authors — precisely the role of female performers for some two and a half centuries after the closing of the Italian theater in 1697.

Not to be overlooked is the fact that Colombine's argument with Arlecchino is doubly an argument between the two forms of theater and between two marriage opportunities for Isabelle, Colombina's mistress. Her choices are between an Italian actor and a French actor. The final judgment is in the hands of the parterre, that is, the public in the lower seats, the cheaper places, that is the common people. As Colombina argues for the superiority of the Italian *arte,* she is simultaneously arguing for the right of Isabelle to marry the man of her choice, an Italian actor, Octave. "An Italian actor will always gain over a French one. He spends less in clothes, his share is larger, and sometimes, all an Italian troupe needs is a mediocre play in order to keep an Italian actor working the whole year" (*Les Chinois,* 254; translation mine). She is making the argument in the name of Octave, for she believes that "in a dispute, a woman is always worth more than a man" (249). Colombine's argument has yet another substratum, which is autobiographical in nature. She is vicariously arguing against her own poor choice to have married a French actor, Pierre Lenoir de la Thorillère, the son of an actor from Molière's troupe, who, according to some documents, was bringing her to financial ruination by his extravagant ways, and would spend "in a day or two what his wife saves in a month."[20] Not to be discarded is also the fact that her sister Françoise, who was playing the role of Isabella, had a most unfortunate marriage experience with a French man whose parents des-inherited him and annulled the marriage upon finding out that he had married an actress.[21]

The multilayered nature of Caterina's discourse is simultaneously a proof of the massive creative input she has into her own part, as well as of her extraordinary wit, which should have put the seventeenth century British writer Congreve to utter shame for his claim that women are entirely devoid of wit. She mixes the fictional with the real, the aesthetic with the personal, in ways which reflect both the commedia tradition of performance and improvisation, and her own original voice. Caterina/Colombina illustrates the blurring of the distinctions between the real and the fictional persona of the commedia actors noted by Taviani and Schino, Molinari and Duchartre, as well as the particular contribution brought by women performers to this form of theater. To use Diane Shemek's comment about the emancipated female figures in her book *Ladies Errant,* in Colombina also, as in Isabella Andreini, a century earlier, the "blurring of the given ... with the created" demonstrates the "inextricability of associations between "women real and imagined" (2).

Colombina's claim that women are better at arguing than men confirms the idea of a women's culture which, being largely an oral culture, has developed subtle and unmatched ways of improvising. Andrea Perucci, in his *Arte Rappresentativa,* gives ample examples of *contrasti,* and arguments (*rimprovero*) of the female *zanni* character, also called *fantesca.* He notes that, the *fantesca* must be vivacious, spirited, energetic and young. The *rimproveri* of the Italian *fantesca*, the ancestor of Colombina, are fiery and full of reproaches, usually against Arlecchino, who invariably proves unfaithful in love, as he does, for instance, in the play *Colombine avocat pour et contre*, in which Colombina haunts him with an incantatory, repetitive set of menacing lines.

As Burke has noted, women's oral culture of early Europe was separate and quite different from that of men, and was to popular culture "what popular culture is to culture as a whole" (49). As a performer in an Italian troupe, Caterina defends the interests and the art of the commedia; as a woman, she has a doubly vested interest in the survival of the Italian theater and she speaks therefore both in the name of actresses, and in the name of women in general. Her voice is combative as it is elusive, and has a different tone from that of the other performers. It is certainly different from that of the male performers, possibly reflecting the separation in popular culture between women's and men's voices. As she notes in the play *La Fille de bon sens*, she is on a mission "to vindicate all women," for "it shall not be said that Colombine stays her arms akimbo" when an insult is brought upon the female sex (v. IV, 155). It is no wonder that so many critics have expressed admiration of her verve and energy and have attributed the creation of the role of Colombina to this particular actress. Too many elements, from her personal history, the history of the commedia dell'arte and the history of women and of women performers in general meld in the creation of this character to make it entirely the creation of some lesser-known French writers.

Although quite a bit transformed in comparison with their Renaissance ancestors, the seventeenth century commedia troupes such as the Fiorelli-Locatelli were still very much functioning and working within the same system of collaboration, equality and impromptu creation which had made the early troupes the big sensation of Europe. And as seen in the earlier chapter, one conspicuous aspect of the early troupes was precisely the fact that women had equal rights with the men within the company, that their creative input was highly encouraged and cherished. By arguing for the right of her mistress to marry the man of her choice and simultaneously for the superiority of the Italian performers versus the French ones, and by weaving her own and her sister's personal stories of disappointing marriages to French men/actors into all that, Caterina is in the larger sense arguing for the rights of women to participate equally in the artistic life of society as well as to run their own lives, and is simultaneously illustrating onstage the creation of her own character, as a symbol of a creative freedom which was, sadly, soon to be lost. The Italians become, ironically, in the play *The Chinese*, the very symbol of artistic and gender equality, versus the French, who, represented by no other than Arlequin, become the symbol of the "parrot"-like theatrical art of performing a written, memorized text of bad husbands and gender inequality.

If the Italians were the first to allow women on their stages to act and create comedy, to shine with their improvisational genius, it is the French who, having appropriated the actress mostly as object of the male gaze, have largely put an end to her creative freedom. Granted, once women started playing the female roles, there were numerous French actresses who acquired extraordinary degrees of celebrity. Among them were Molière's wife in his troupe, famous actresses interpreting Marivaux's female roles, and on into the vaudeville acts of the nineteenth century and to Sarah Bernhardt. But none who like Caterina/Colombina so uncompromisingly and freely spoke in the name of a creative freedom which gave both men and women equal opportunities in the creation of their roles and in the choice of their spouses. It is not insignificant that Colombina mixes up Italian theater and Italian marriage versus French theater and French marriage. The Italian theater was based on true partnerships between the spouses, as the history of most of the commedia dell'arte troupes largely illustrates. The couple Isabella and Francesco Andreini was a superb example of true partnership in the theater, and Catherine's own parents, Dominique and Orsola, were famous for their collaborative work in the company and for how harmoniously and creatively they channeled their marital relationship into theatrical creativity. For instance, although Dominique played the role of a *zanni*, and Orsola of the *amoureuse*, and although traditionally, it was not common for the two to be amorously involved with each other onstage, they often rearranged the plots "to give the two the opportunity to play together as much as possible."[22] Later on, Catherine herself blurred the distinctions between the *zanna* and the inamorata by being at times, onstage, the lover of the master or of the inamorato and not of Arlequin. This attests to the high level of creative collaboration which was at work in the Italian troupes.

Starting with Molière's troupe, and continuing with the Comédie Française, the French troupes are led by a male performer, writer, director, the way Molière was, with the lover or wife playing the female roles created and directed by him. Later, in the twentieth century, the authority of the writer is either doubled or replaced by that of the director. In her pro–Italian theater tirades, Caterina/Colombina sets up an intentional blurring of distinctions between theater and life, with theater being not only a metaphor for life but setting an example for it. In their boldness and harsh irony, her speeches seem to foreshadow the twentieth century feminist notion that in fact the very emancipation of women is significantly connected with their access to and contributions to public performance and with their courage to make a "spectacle" of themselves.[23] And her ironic use of personal details is not too far from the comedy of the modern female stand-up comedian "willing to make a spectacle of her own problems in order to poke fun at the state of modern gender relations."[24]

In conclusion to this section, I believe the roles in Gherardi's collection are still very much the creation of the Italian actors themselves and that, in particular, the new Colombina, or *zannetta*, is a new female trickster who is very much the creation of Cathcrine Biancolelli herself. It seems likely that the plays and scenes we have in Gherardi's collection are similar to photographed versions of certain performances, and that the role of the French writers was rather to fix on paper the dialogues and plots improvised by the Italian actors onstage. This also explains the phrase inscribed on the front page in the Gherardi collection, following the title of each the play: *mise au théâtre*, "set to the theater" by Monsieur D*** or by monsieur Regnard or both. The expression suggests a form of transcription of the performances rather than an actual full-fledged creation of dramatic texts. It also explains the numerous mentions, in between lines, of *lazzis* and of scenes *à l'italienne*. Just like the previous commedia troupes, this one had its own repertoire and therefore its own set of scenarios, or *canevas*, which, instead of being collected in their scenario form like the one in Flaminio Scala's collection, are now more elaborately collected by Gherardi with their dialogues as well. But, as Ricoboni noted in his *Histoire du théâtre italien*, because of their notorious improvisatory competence, the Italian actors may present the same play several times and yet it will seem every time like a new play.

The great irony of the modernity of Caterina's character is that in the play *Les Chinois*, it is Colombina, the newest character of the commedia dell'arte who illustrates the spirit of the Italian theater, as started almost a century and a half earlier, while Arlecchino, the oldest and most representative character of the traditional commedia dell'arte is the spokesperson of the French theater. The would-be modern French theater represents, in fact, with regard to the role of women, a form of backlash against their acquired freedoms, while the Italian traditional theater, paradoxically, represents an artistic forum for the emancipation of women.

The progressive loss of creative freedom for actresses was paralleled in French society and culture by a progressive deepening of the subjection of women to patriarchal rule. Natalie Zemon Davis has pointed out that between the sixteenth and the eighteenth centuries, French women were losing even the few liberties they had acquired. They were progressively forced "to withdraw from productive labor," and "married women ... had largely lost what independent legal personality they had formerly had, and they had less legal right to make decisions on their own about their dowries and possessions than at an earlier period" (126).

There is a tragic irony. In *Les Chinois*, Colombina is triumphant and the parterre, the character representing the voice of the people, gives its verdict that Isabella marry her Italian actor, in actuality the French theater was soon to take over, the Italian theater to be closed and actresses to lose much of their creative freedom as a result of that. The role of Colombina is something like a torch of modernity before its actual time, like a cry signaling the loss of freedom looming in the near distance and simultaneously like a celebration of the freedom before the backlash. Colombina-colomba poised for flight, so elusive in her irony!

Colombina — Critic of Men

In the analyses that follow, I hope to show that, in the seventeenth century, Caterina's Colombina demonstrated "the performativity of gender" and challenged the idea that gender roles have an essential or immutable basis in so-called masculine and feminine natures. Through her performance, she destabilizes and reconstructs the feminine gender in fluid and revolutionary ways that, if exemplified in society, would give women more power and freedom. As Judith Butler argued in her 1999 preface to *Gender Trouble*, the notion "that gender is performative ... sought to show that what we take to be an internal essence of gender, is manufactured through a sustained set of acts, posited through the gendered stylization of the body" (7). However, when applying modern theories to a seventeenth century artist, one has to be consistently mindful of the socio-historical context of the artist's time and neither get too carried away with nor too disappointed in what we may perceive today as either feminist or nonfeminist attitudes. Some of Colombina's lines and actions seemed radical even to my feminist undergraduate students, while some of her other lines and actions, particularly her unabashed preaching of the use of artifice and coquettish behavior so as to have her way, are frowned upon by many modern feminists and regarded as other forms of women reinforcing "traditional" feminine ways. My position allies itself as well with that of Pamela Allen Brown who, in her book *Better a Shrew Than a Sheep*, challenges the notion that "women were tragic victims, passive ciphers, or cultural sponges" and explores jest and humor that reflects "female resistance and productive fantasy" (7–9).

Caterina Biancolelli's seventeenth century France was a place in which the emancipation of women was celebrated on many levels of social and cultural life, but it also experienced a backlash against women, their rights, and their contributions. James Collins notes, "The period 1550 to 1700 was one of critical change for women. Early modern women engaged in activities ranging from food retailing to running ferry boats, but their public position took a dramatic turn for the worse after 1550." While many women headed households and contributed in significant ways to the overall economy, they were also significantly more prone to poverty than men and were subjected to draconian laws restricting their rights to own property and to make choices regarding the regulation of their personal lives (436–40).

On the other hand, on the literary level, seventeenth century France offered the unique concept of salons — literary circles or gatherings hosted and created almost entirely by aristocratic women — where France's most revered authors exchanged ideas and first made names for themselves. Many of the celebrated women hosting the salons, such as Madame de la Fayette, Madame de Rambouillet, and Madame de Sablé, were also the initiators of the seventeenth century movement called *préciosité*, which consisted of women talking freely about issues of love, passion, and marital relations. In the book *Staging Subversions: The Performance-Within-a-Play in French Classical Theatre*, Kimberly Cashman notes, "The précieuses are constructing a social role for women in which they progress toward legal and social equality with men" (67).

Colombina is generally, but not always, the lover, fiancée, or wife of Arlecchino, and critics have at times compared her to a female *zanni*.[25] We have also seen that Caterina Biancolelli portrayed herself as Arlecchina at the Bezons Fair in 1695. However, her character is not entirely a female version of the character of Arlecchino, even though it does illustrate at times similar comic features, in particular the propensity for trickery. While Arlecchino's comedy derives largely from a mixture of stupidity, vulgarity, physical elasticity and basic cunning vis-à-vis his masters,[26] Colombina produces a subtler kind of humor through her sharp wit, cunning and spirit of revolt (in particular against older, tyrannical men), as well as through her often whimsical, coquettish behavior. Both Arlecchino and Colombina, though, are the characters who act in disguise, more than any of the other types in the Italian comedy, and who cross-dress more than any of the other characters. They are also the ones always ready and eager to trick their masters or each other, and, as Scott has noted, Colombina is always "successful and never gets caught" (301).

Although Colombina is a newer character than Arlecchino, whose origins have been traced all the way to the Greek buffoons, the servants of Atelan farces and the devils of Medieval mysteries,[27] she does also emerge from a tradition of female humor and performance that is at least as ancient as the Middle Ages. The courtesans, with their rich tradition of performance and entertainment,[28] the female jugglers and mimes,[29] the performing nuns of the Renaissance, the women entertainers at weddings,[30] the Gypsies' street entertainments,[31] the soldier prostitutes[32] of the Middle Ages and early Renaissance, as well as the actresses of the commedia dell'arte before her, can all be considered as Colombina's heritage of comedy and humor. To that, of course, it is necessary to add the professional training she received as member of a commedia family and troupe of actors, the influence and inspiration that her father, Domenico Biancolelli, must have exerted on her, and the theatrical knowledge handed down to her by her mother, Orsola Cortesi, and her grandmother Isabella Franchini.

Colombina is described as small, brunette, of pleasant voice and demeanor.[33] In a 1686 engraving by Leroux, she is portrayed in stylized, humorous attire suggestive of the maid's costume because of the apron and a cloth she is holding in her right hand, but also with a touch of elegance, with a lacy, corseted dress holding her minuscule waist and flowing to the ground with a train. Colombina is portrayed larger than life, and on each side of her, two dwarf-like figures are represented: a Pantalone, or *vecchio*, and an Arlecchino, or *zanni* type. She has an ironic smile which seems to correspond to the poem written at the bottom of the drawing: "Colombine dans ses Amours/trompe ses Amans tous les jours,/Comme un singe elle a de l'adresse,/Et plus qu'un renard de Finesse."[34] Duchartre is right in pointing out that Colombina is no servile maid character, that she expresses herself with extraordinary ease vis-à-vis her masters, even with insolence. Furthermore she is cunning, at times even harsh and has no scruples in tricking old husbands and foolish old lovers, to the advantage of the love interests of her mistress, much in the tradition of the *fantesca* described by Andreucci.

Caterina's Colombina is not only a confidante working cunningly for the love interests of her mistress, but she is also a passionate lover who when deceived can play out her vengeance like no other character and who often speaks and acts in the name of women in general. As Scott has noted, Catherine Biancolelli "developed the modern, cynical, immoral, and successful young French woman, linked to the Dorines and Toinettes of Molière, but younger, smoother, and more devoted to the feminine cause in the eternal war of the sexes" (307).

Scott is right to simply suggest a possible relation between Molière's maids and Colombine, and not a direct influence of the French writer's female characters upon the character created by Caterina, as others have done.[35] Molière himself, having acted for the Italian troupe in his youth, drew a significant amount of inspiration for his plays from the commedia plots and characters, and some of his very early plays are not much more than recreations of commedia scenarios.[36] Molière's female servants are more in line with the characters of Franceschina or Olivetta: spunky confidantes, not always very young, like Dorine, sarcastic toward their masters, and resourceful in helping their mistresses gain the spouse of their choice.

But while rebellious against tyrannical masters like Tartuffe, and supporting the causes of their mistresses, Molière's maids do not express the kind of general rebellion against *man*kind, do not actually subvert or question patriarchal structures, and are not as "devoted to the feminine cause in the eternal war of the sexes," as Colombina is. It is noteworthy that not a single one of Molière's maids, or female characters for that matter, ever cross-dress, as Colombina does innumerable times. As the poem inscribed under the portrait of Colombina proclaims, she is cunning as a fox and has an exciting sexual life herself. In fact, in Gherardi's collection, Colombina shows quite a bit of sexual knowledge and experience, in comparison with her innocent mistress, Isabella. Rather than being akin to Molière's maids, Colombina seems to have inherited some of the traits of the courtesans, or of the *cortigiane oneste*, both in character and in modes of performance: she exhibits a certain sexual freedom, is more sexually experienced than the inamorata or ingénue character, often dances and sings onstage, and exhibits an impressive amount of knowledge in various areas from law to literature to philosophy, which she uses particularly in trickery. As she says to Isabella in the play *Le Divorce*, right before creating a complicated legal stratagem in order to free Isabella from her old, tyrannical husband Sotinet, she has *une peste de tête* (a plague of a head, 164). She is educated, and an entertainer in the full sense of the word, as were often the Italian courtesans, "whose combination of sexual freedom, learning and cultural sophistication made them indispensable participants in the courtly social life of the Italian Renaissance."[37] I believe that, rather than being influenced in the creation of her character by French writers and the culture of seventeenth century French women, she is bringing into French culture her own Italian heritage of oral history, performance and attitudes. It may be exactly why she so vehemently argues in the name of Italian theater and Italian husbands.

One of Colombina's most conspicuous character traits and humorous penchants is that of sharp irony toward men. In discussing this aspect of Caterina's comic creativity, one has to resort to the discussion of the text, of lines and dialogues from the plays in Gherardi's collection. In the absence of stage directions and of abundant comments with regard to Colombina's stage movements and actions, the text remains the main source of analysis of the character and of the performance of the actress.

One type of scenario in which Caterina/Colombina's sarcastic and cynical view of men and of marriage comes out with unprecedented panache is represented by the scenes between Isabella and Colombina, acted by the two sisters Françoise and Catherine. Scott has noted that "the women's scenes are like nothing to be found in the Italian commedia dell'arte" (301). A principal reason for the novelty of this type of scene may be that it is also the first time in the history of the commedia that two sisters played together and created their characters side by side. As noted earlier, the Biancolelli sisters were already playing these parts before their official entry into the Fiorelli-Locatelli troupe in 1683. Most likely, they were developing their characters together, playing against each other from the very beginning of their acting careers. Just like the other female performers before them, they created new characters which became an intrinsic part of the commedia repertoire, so the two sisters created, not only their characters, but the types of scenes in which these two characters interacted with each other.

It was also common to the general scene dynamics of the commedia dell'arte itself that two types of characters develop a certain type of scene: in the sixteenth century, for instance, when the inamorati characters were created, which coincided with the entrance of women in the commedia troupes, a certain type of scene between the inamorati was created. The various kinds of formulae and possible dialogues for these scenes are to be found in Andrea Perucci's *Dell'Arte Rappresentativa*. Scott is not entirely correct in ascertaining that women's scenes are not to be found in the commedia repertoire. In Flaminio Scala's scenarios, there are several scenes between Isabella and Flaminia, the second inamorata, and between Isabella, played by Isabella Andreini, and the maid, Franceschina, or Ricciolina, played by Silvia Roncagli and, respectively, Maria Antonazzoni.[38] A certain complicity between these female characters is to be noted in Scala's scenarios, which may well foreshadow the scenes between Colombina and Isabella or between Colombina and Angelique in Gherardi's collection.

The general gist of the Colombina-Isabella scenes is that Isabella is generally disdainful, or fearful of, or rejects altogether the possibility of marriage and of the men who pursue her, while Colombina tries to persuade her that men, "perfidious" as they may be, are a necessary "evil," and that one must live with them as one lives "with the Turks: only for the necessity of the commerce" (*Les Souhaits*, 31). These types of scenes, to be found in plays such as *Les Souhaits*, *La Coquette*, and *Les Chinois*, remind one of Marivaux's beginning scene from *Le Jeu de l'Amour et du Hasard*, between Sylvie, who deplores the very idea of marriage, and her confidante Lisette, who tries to persuade her of the benefits one may draw from this institution. However, Colombina's level of sarcasm and cynicism in the Gherardi collection is downright shocking and by far exceeds anything encountered in Marivaux's plays.

The scenes between the two women display indeed the level of openness, of unabashed irony toward men and an element of complicity specific of sisterly exchanges or of exchanges between women friends: while Isabella has no qualms in voicing her revolt against the condition of women in society and their absence from social and political life, in lines worthy of a modern feminist,[39] Colombina has no qualms in trying to persuade her that, for all the evils of society, women need to learn how to turn their unequal position to their advantage. Maybe more than the humor of any other female character of the *commedia*, Colombina's humor displays the signs of angry humor discussed by Regina Barreca. Her lessons are harsh, her revenge unforgiving, her language cutting, her laugh merciless. Her humor is dangerous, as Barecca notes in general about women's humor, and her laughter, as Cixous has noted about women's laughter, "breaks up, breaks out, splashes over."[40]

Arguably, no male author of comedy has created female characters who so unapologetically profess the art of making the most of a precarious situation and turning one's inferior condition into an advantageous one, as Colombina does. And no comic female characters created by a male author in all of the classical period has expressed such uncompromising mockery of men, as Colombina does. In *La Fille de bon sens*, Colombina claims to be the teacher of the most famous coquettes from all the corners of Paris, and at the end of her lesson to Isabella, she cynically suggests that, just as hunters display on their doors various parts of the bodies of their conquered prey, so women should display on their doors, "the claws of the man of justice," "the talons of the banker," the "linnet of the abbot."[41] In *La Coquette* she proudly states that "man is an animal who likes to be deceived." The imagery taken from the animal realm inscribes Colombina's language within a female version of superiority humor and seems to serve those critics like Blyth, who, several centuries later, compared women to creatures from the animal realm, a bit of their own medicine.

Speaking of medicine, in *La Fille de bons sens*, she compares men and marriage to a bitter but necessary medicine: "All the important remedies have a bad taste, but one is never weary of finding them" (108). Cynical with regard to any kind of a possible match for her mistress Angelique, and particularly cynical of matches made for love, Colombina's advice is always on the side of practicality: "From whatever side may the money come, it always smells good" (108). Love matches do not impress her, for the younger, attractive men of the kind Angelique likes, are nothing more to Colombine, but fools "who imagine that all the women are in love with them" (108) and who are in love with only themselves, like Octave, the one for whom her mistress sighs (139). And at the end of the scene with Isabella in *Les Souhaits*, a scene entitled unapologetically "Contre les hommes," Colombina utters the crude line worthy of some of today's feminist performance artists such as Karen Finley: "I'm running to wash out my mouth, for I have spoken long enough about men" (vol. V, 35).

Colombina's humor is much more difficult to inscribe within any other theory of humor than that of Isabella Andreini. Unlike Isabella, who played principally a serious part and whose comic moments onstage appeared as diversions or deviations from her main lyrical mode, Caterina Biancolelli's is a comic role through and through, and it moves from the subtlest nuances of linguistic irony, to gross sarcasm, to the burlesque comedy of chases and kicks, to the most variegated disguises, to delirious combinations of all of the above, as in one of the most famous plays in Gherardi's collection, *Colombine avocat pour et contre*. Much like Isabella a century earlier, Colombina moves the plot and plays the tricks, but unlike Isabella she jumps from plot to plot, from trick to trick, from disguise to disguise, adding layer upon layer on a trickster persona unprecedented for a female character. I will therefore refrain from containing Colombina's comic diversity within any single comic theory, and, following the lead of the character herself, will discuss some of her most strik- ing and diverse comic moments through the lens of those comic theories which seem most appropriate to each particular kind of humor. In addition, I will not shy away from developing new theories of humor where necessary.

I noted earlier that the kind of humor Colombina employs in the scenes with Isabella can be relegated to superiority or disparagement humor of the kind theorized by Aristotle, Hobbs or Freud. For good reasons, feminists have a real problem with this kind of humor and with the theorizing of laughter as derived from "our perception of ourselves as superior,"[42] for invariably, women end up most often as the butt of jokes and of men's laughter.[43] Invari- ably, humor theoreticians are there to validate this kind of humor as one of the most conspicuous signs of humanity and therefore as a worthy and "supe- rior" form of expression.[44] According to Aristotle, women are more fit as com- edy characters, precisely due to their "inferiority," which brings them closer to slaves, the other type of persons fit for a comedy.[45] If Colombina's comedy contains elements of disparagement or superiority humor only in reverse, what then is its value in terms of the history of women's humor and in terms of the development of a particularly female form of comedy which could be seen as a form of feminist humor *avant la lettre*, as we have attempted to see Isabella's comedy? Critics who are not sympathetic to feminism would in no time argue that the kind of disparaging comedy and the crude mockery of men by women in exchanges like the ones cited above are nothing more than reverse sexism, or angry, vengeful humor which in no way sets an example of a specific kind of female humor, but simply repeats the humor of the oppressor. And by seeing Colombina's laughter as a female form of superiority laughter, would we not then validate and reinforce precisely that which we are criticizing male authors and critics for? Not really. The answer to these questions is a complex one.

First we could start by looking at the kind of crudely ironic language so often used by Colombina, from a different perspective than that used in this study so far, namely from the vantage point of the distinction between what Gloria Kaufman has called "survival humor" versus "feminist humor." From there we can try to interpret Colombina's laughter and irony in light of the theory of liminality developed by critics like Little or Barreca, who have in their turn taken their cues from Cixous's notions of the marginalized but not marginal laughter of Medusa. Kaufman distinguishes between two forms of women's humor: "mainstream women's humor," which in her view is often "survival humor," and "feminist humor," which "inspires changes" and "is obviously concerned with the transfer of power from those who have it overwhelmingly to those who have too little" (viii).[46] Colombina's humor in the scenes with her mistress, contains good doses of both. Survival humor, specific not only to women but to other marginalized groups, is the comic relief people get from joking about their inferior position or status in a given society, time or under particularly oppressive conditions. This humor, as Kaufman notes, is not a humor geared primarily toward social change, but one which helps disadvantaged groups get through the hard times. As Gray has noted, such laughter may even "make it easier to re-enter the system after the permitted break" (33). It is the same criticism that has been brought to carnival theory as well, where carnival, being considered in its time to be a "safety valve," is said to have also made it easier to reenter and accept the hierarchies it has broken in the form of spectacle.[47]

Colombina's irony and biting sarcasm at the ways and character of men derives from the necessity to make the most of a precarious situation and to provide for her mistress, or for herself, the tools and weapons necessary to survive as best as one can, in a man's world. Her character may not always challenge patriarchal structures in obvious ways, particularly since, more often than not, the plots end up in marriage, Isabella's, her own or both. Colombina teaches Isabella or Angelique the ways of the "coquette," who is very much a French creation of the seventeenth century. "The world may not be the most just place for women, but we have to make do with what we have, the best that we can and on our own terms." This is Colombina's philosophy and the gist of most of her lessons. Moreover, "We have to beat men at their own game, serve them their own medicine," her tricks and plots seem to always say. Therefore Colombina's survival humor emerges from the position of those who do hold an inferior position in society, and however disparaging her humor may be, it is the humor produced from the side of the marginalized, or of what Little has called from the side of women's "liminality." This makes women's survival-superiority humor quite different from men's: while women's survival-superiority humor derives from an inferior position of power and is meant to take the edge off that sharp inequality of power, men's superiority humor relies more often than not on the use of power by someone who already has it over someone who does not, and has therefore a bullying, victimizing dimension to it.

The seeds of a feminist humor are already planted within survival humor, as it also strives, deep down, toward some form of equality, but only within the confines of the system, and not by drastic changes of the system. Colombina knows all the tricks of the trade of courtesans: She is eloquent. She strives toward financial independence and urges her mistress to do the same. She continuously negotiates sex relations and/or marriage to her own or her mistress's advantage. And she has a sharp taste for performance, play, and entertainment. In a man's world, she sees role-playing as the only viable option for women, as she cunningly and unabashedly urges Isabella to do in *La Coquette* or in *Les Souhaits*. And were not courtesans after all, throughout the Renaissance, the only women whose freedom of movement and financial independence were the envy of all the other women, including noblewomen? In learning how to make it in a man's world, are not courtesans/coquettes also creating alternatives, getting around patriarchal structures, even if they are not actually changing them? At least it's a start. Margaret Rosenthal has noted, in speaking about the famous Venetian Renaissance courtesan poet, Veronica Franco, that her biography reveals the extent to which her "strategies of survival as an honest courtesan in a society dominated by men are analogous to the textual maneuvers she employs in her published works" (4). Surviving oppression is, after all, the beginning of resisting it.

Similarly, Colombina, a century later, is in possession of a set of "strategies of survival" by which she lives and which she teaches to her mistress Isabella in the empowering language of irony and sarcasm. The character of Colombine draws some of her strategies of survival from the actress playing it: always mindful of financial security, Colombina/Caterina has in the background her own experience of having to survive as best as she can, as the wife of an extravagant French actor who, according to the reports of the time, spent in a day what his wife had saved in a month. Analogously, her mistress-sister Isabella-Françoise had quite an unhappy personal life, which, ironically, seems to have confirmed and/or reflected the apprehensions and the grim view of marriage that she expresses in many of the plays in the Gherardi collection. The man she married, Constantin de Turgis, against the wishes of his parents, was later disinherited and the marriage was revoked, with a court judgment being placed on the couple against seeing each other. Although later on they entered a second marriage, and their two children were legitimized, Turgis was blatantly unfaithful to his wife and dragged her into debt and financial disaster.[48] In 1695, Françoise renounced her career in the theater. The plays in the Gherardi collection which exhibit the most acute criticism of marriage and of the conduct of men, in which Colombine is most fervently at war with the opposite sex and in which her lessons of survival to Isabella or Angelique are most cynical, were performed between 1691 and 1694, which is precisely the period during which Françoise Biancolelli was experiencing her own personal ordeal and disappointment with marriage.

The most striking example of the criticism of marriage is to be found in the play *Les Souhaits*. Isabella's unrestrained criticism of the society and rules imposed by men upon women is doubled each time by Colombina's lessons of survival. To Isabella's complaint that men are "traitors" who have deprived women of a place in society and have prevented them from participating in the life of finances, government, and all other work, Colombina answers that, although it is not from lack of military aptitude that women do not head armies, they can lead their own wars by means of deception, role playing, and using the jobs that men have deprived women of, as a means of vengeance: "If men have wronged us by appropriating all positions, these same positions can serve us every day as a place of vengeance" (32). If women have been deprived of freedom and if every move toward emancipation has been regarded as a crime, as Isabella notes (33), then women need to learn how to feign prudishness and innocence and how to turn each situation, by means of role playing, to their advantage. The following tirade of Colombine is equally a lesson in behavior as it is a performance lesson for women:

> For example, if one shows us a scandalous cigarette box, we place our hand over our eyes, but it is only in order to make a pair of binoculars with our fingers; if one sings to us a vaudeville a little risqué, we pretend to avert our eyes, but it is in order to better receive it with our ears. We are caught in the middle of an outrageous reading, well we only have to blush a little which will only enhance our beauty. This is how women have the pleasure without ever experiencing the shame; while for men, pleasure is always followed by shame [33].

The two women concur on the many indiscretions and injustices performed by men in society, from the way in which they harass all pretty women in the street to the ways in which they arbitrarily change the faces of states and countries (34–35). Colombine concludes that men have to be regarded like doctors: one must know their foibles and benefit from whatever cure they may offer. The scene concludes with Colombine's crudely sarcastic remark: "Oh, I run to wash my mouth, for I've been talking long enough about men" (35).

Colombine's irony and humor of superiority reflects the strategies of a trickster who knows how to use each situation to her advantage, whose main survival strategy is that of the disguise, and whose anger at the abuses of power in a patriarchal society is channeled into cunning ways of negotiating that power. While maybe not the humor which "breaks all possible norms" discussed by Little and not the revolutionary humor which "breaks the law" advocated by Cixous, Colombina's linguistic and survival comedy breaks some laws and is nevertheless subversive of patriarchy to the extent to which it offers to herself and her more innocent mistress a set of rules by which the two of them in particular, and women in general, can turn the disadvantages of their inferior social position to a relatively more advantageous condition in society. Colombina's humor and lessons also point in the direction of breaking to some extent the sharp boundaries between the domestic and the public spheres for women. As has been stated about courtesans and about an actress such as Isabella Andreini, Colombina's set of rules for the "coquette" illustrate the possibility for a certain participation of women in the public sphere, a certain freedom of movement and vicarious appropriation of the work and jobs of men, by means of performance and role playing. As she unapologetically teaches Isabella, women need to turn their lack of power to their own advantage and use the jobs and work of men as a means for their own happiness, precarious as that may be.

It was also in seventeenth-century France that the term *coquette* was coined, denoting "a woman who gains power over others by manipulative verbal and body language, a skill referred to as her 'art.'" Paradoxically, as Natasha Sajé points out, the word is derived from "cock," thus suggesting an aggressive maleness, which is in ironic contrast to the understanding of a coquette as someone who exaggerates the traditionally "female" fault of artifice. Colombina's cynicism toward both a highly romantic view of marriage and the prospect of staying unmarried reflects the practical sense of tricksters whose principal goal is usually to undermine the authority of his/her masters or, in the case of women, the authority of the men who run the world, while obtaining the most profit for themselves, both in terms of financial gain and personal pleasure. As coquette, Colombina is something of a female man or a manly woman. The hidden subtext of many of Colombina's teachings about marrying rich men even if they are not young or handsome is that, once one is financially secure, romance can also be obtained outside of marriage. Colombina reflects the comic strategy advocated by Norma Gravely, to "write our own jokes ... and fight back."[49] Furthermore, this is also very much the strategy of courtesans, for whom performance was not only part of their profession but also a way of life, as they had to negotiate between their private and public persona, between erotic involvement and financial stability, and among their various benefactors.

The acting techniques, behaviors and attitudes that Colombina teaches Isabella in order to make the most of her position of inferiority vis-à-vis men also reflect the playing of gender that Judith Butler discusses in her theory of gender as performance. Colombina teaches precisely the playing of the feminine to its most refined, to its most extreme and to where most advantage can be gained. At the same time, she teaches women to hold their own and stand up to the men who insult, hurt, or demean them. In *La femme vengée*, she says: "Je veux que toutes les femmes apprennent de moi aujourd'hui la manière de ranger un mari qui se donne des airs de maîtrise dans sa maison" ("I want that all women learn from me today, the way in which to put in his place a husband who gives himself airs of authority in the house," vol. II, 315). Just as submission, frailty, passivity are traits which women have learned and which have become marks of their gender, Colombina seems to say, so can they be unlearned, and so can women learn precisely the opposite: resistance, strength, action. But the trick of it is to be able to play both, according to the occasion and to what necessity requires.

Isabella always has her nose in a book (reminding us of that other Isabella who did both: performed her gender and acquired an impressive erudition) and speaks as eloquently as a modern feminist about the injustices against women. Colombina, on the other hand, guided by her good knowledge of how the world works, and by an acute practical sense, knows that, while they may not be able to change the world during their own lifetime, women can at least try to make the most of it. From this point of view, Colombina's humor can be said to be largely survival humor, and her cynicism that of a skilled con-artist or courtesan. The way she always walks triumphant from every situation by means of tricks, deceit and disguise, the way she always furthers her own interests and is mindful of financial gain, as in *La Foire de Saint-Germain* (in which she changes one disguise after another), or in the *Momies d'Egypte* (in which, together with her lover, Arlequin, she swindles gullible customers), the precision of the theatrical gestures she teaches Isabelle in order to get along in the world in (*Les Souhaits*), all call to mind what Susan Griffin has called "the considerable magic of human ingenuity," when speaking of nineteenth century courtesans who, in their turn, were inheritors of a tradition that had started in sixteenth century Venice and Rome (11). Let us also call to mind that, when discussing Isabella's character from the *Mirtilla*, Fillide, Julie Campbell calls her a "conartist courtesan," because of the ingenuity with which she manages to prevail over the most difficult and dangerous situations and walk away with a victorious smile. Colombina's survival skills are developed into an art of performance, and the virtues she preaches to Isabella are not the usual virtues expected of women but rather the virtues employed, in Griffin's words, "to defy circumstance" (11). Ultimately, the irony of her smile goes beyond that of the contentment of survival, and is a smile of triumph.

Given the lucid appropriation of gender playing that Colombine advocates, and her acute awareness of the hypocrisy of many patriarchal structures, it is also fair to say that her survival humor carries the germ of a feminist humor and that she is to a significant extent the "Flyer/Thief" described by Cixous. Like a worthy follower of Machiavelli, Colombina points out that "the reputation of honor" is often more important than "honor itself" and therefore, as long as women are equipped with "certain fundamental grimaces" and keep their eyes wide open to detect hypocrisy when they see it, their honor is safe (*Les Souhaits*, 34). Furthermore, she adds, "we would embarrass men, were we to strictly follow their own rules," for that would offer them too clear a mirror for their own behavior. Colombina's trickster acts, her "Machiavellian" philosophy, her "cynicism and insolence, vigorously expressed in racy language,"[50] partake to some extent of Barreca's notion that women's comedy is "dangerous" because it refuses to accept the givens," and with Little's comment that feminist comedy says "truly dangerous things obliquely."[51] Colombina denounces the injustices of patriarchal society while taking hold of and using all the weapons at her disposal to win in "oblique" ways, by theatrical means, and by means of what she calls the "fundamental grimaces."

It is also in view of Colombina's strategy of collapsing sexual relations and performance that we can now better understand her double argument at the end of the play *Les Chinois* about the superiority of Italian theater and marriages vis-à-vis the French ones. The Italian theater had offered women artistic and financial freedom, and Italian actors, both men and women, had generous shares in the company, while enjoying much more financial freedom and security than the French actors.[52] Despite the talk of the Italians' debauched manner and loose sexual behavior, the Italian actresses kept in fact very strict rules of comportment and marital fidelity, or at least they strove to keep the appearance of it; furthermore, no Italian actresses wanted to travel or establish themselves in France without their husbands, precisely in order to maintain their reputation and the integrity of their professional life.[53] Seeing herself at the end of that era, in a country of adoption with different customs than her own country, having the experience of her own and her sisters' disappointing and difficult marital situations with French actors, Caterina/Colombina preaches role playing and gender playing as the last resort left for women in that changing and to some extent foreign society, in which women were mostly appreciated as ornaments of the court. Colombina's cynicism prefigures in fact the tragic disappearance of the actress's artistic, financial and social freedom and integrity from the stages of Europe, and her teachings can be seen as desperate attempts to survive in a world that is changing but not for the benefit of women.

Colombina's morality prefigures also the nineteenth century courtesan-actress who, as often portrayed in Balzac or Zola's novels, keeps playing the feminine both onstage and in real life, to a point of obliteration of her actual creative resources and freedom, and to the point where she is transformed exclusively into the object of the male gaze and desire.[54] Interestingly, Colombina's philosophy does not resemble that much the philosophy of the early commedia female characters, whose tricks, disguises and overall comedy was meant to always lead to a marriage of love. Neither does it resemble the philosophy of Molière or Marivaux's maids, who generally try to guide their mistresses away from marrying old rich men. The only resemblance is with the lifestyle of both Renaissance and nineteenth century courtesans, whose financial stability was generally ensured by a rich benefactor, usually older, and under whose protection they enjoyed both a certain sexual and financial freedom and had access to the public life from which most other women were excluded.[55]

Ultimately Colombina's comedy is more subversive of marriage than either the early commedia or the plays of the classical and eighteenth century writers, as it mocks and undermines the very seriousness of the institution of marriage and looks at it primarily as a means to an end, as a necessary "medicine." Whenever needed, Colombina is as much an advocate of marriage, as she is of the breaking marriage, as she proves herself in the play *Le Divorce*, where she invents the comic stratagem of a trial presided by no other than "le dieu Hymen" (the God of Marriage) who is in town "to de-marry all the persons who are weary of marriage" (vol. 2, 164). More than anything, Colombina supports that which is in a woman's best interest, in a world which does not hold the interests of women as a priority, to say the least. Financial stability and a certain freedom of movement are what Colombina values most and that which she invariably urges her mistress to look after. In this she is very much like the courtesans of sixteenth century Venice who were often envied both for their relative freedom in comparison to the life-styles of other women, and for their economic comfort.[56] Colombina combines the strategies of the coquette and of the courtesan whose laughter turns often into a grin, whose supplementary skills also include those of the matchmaker and match-breaker. But there is more to Colombina's laughter.

Colombina's "Mise-en-Scène"

Columbina performs a most unusual kind of trick in the play entitled *La Coquette ou l'Académie des femmes*, "set to the theater" by Regnard, and performed in 1691. The comedy of disguise which ensues in the play at the initiative of Colombina is not this time one in which she herself appears in disguise, as she does in *La Fille de bons sens*, *La Foire Saint-Germain*, or *Colombine avocat pour et contre*. Rather, she is responsible for the disguise of a male character, Arlequin, suitor to her hand and bailiff of Maine. The purpose of the disguise and the direction in which she moves the plot are not, as in most plays of the *commedia* and from the Gherardi collection, her own or her mis-

tress's marriage, but on the contrary the avoidance of marriage. The comedy, unlike most comedies and contrary to the general pattern of classical comedy, does not end in marriage and joyful reconciliation, but simply with Colombina proudly getting rid of her suitor.

In order to avoid marrying the man who her father forces her to marry, a certain bailiff of Maine, played by Arlequin, she has him dress up as a woman and appear in front of her father to ask for her hand. Scandalized by such eccentricity, the father, Traffiquet, bluntly refuses the proposal and the play ends with the suitor angrily cursing at the father and daughter alike. Colombina has her last word, in which she expresses her disdain for such a suitor. Ear-

Caterina Biancolelli in the role of Colombina (engraving by Leroux, 1686).

lier in a discussion with her cousin Isabella, Colombina notes that a woman cannot get along in society with only beauty, and, touching her forehead, notes that she needs "this," meaning intelligence (119). Later she admonishes Isabella for not having remembered that Colombina "loves everybody without loving anybody." Finally, she has a lover, Octave, who, in other plays, such as *Les Chinois*, was Isabella's suitor. Colombina's tricks and comedy call to mind the women's comedy which Barreca isolates from the classical, male-created comedy, due to its lack of resolution and closure, and to the absence of the "integrative function" of marriage in the end. Indeed, the comedy that Catherine Biancolelli creates through her Colombina and which is meant to be a model of behavior for other women, as well as a lesson to arrogant, presumptuous men, is also one which "refuses to accept the givens" and which explodes in the end into what Cixous and Clement have called a woman's "anarchic point of view," from where she finds "pleasure in breaking apart."[57] In tune with this view, Barreca remarks that "the pleasure of being the girl the boy 'got' so that he can then found a nice little society around himself is not *her* happy ending" (16).

The lack of a traditional happy ending in itself furthers the argument that Colombina is the creation of a female artist, namely of Caterina, much more than that of a male writer of comedies from the neoclassical French period. Every single comedy by Molière, Marivaux, Beaumarchais, and Goldoni ends in marriage if the plot involves an amorous dimension or a couple of inamorati, and it always does. On the other hand, a significant amount of comedy written by women throughout the centuries, in narrative or dramatic form, offers different alternatives to the traditional "happy ending" of "boy gets girl and they marry and live happily ever after."

One such striking example from seventeenth century Europe is that of Aphra Behn, England's first professional female author. To an extent, Catherine is doing with performance and with the creation-improvisation of her role as Colombina what Behn has done with poetry and play writing. As Catherine Gallagher has noted, Behn, whose "life and works were alike characterized by irregular sexual arrangements," is "an advocate of 'free love,' in every sense of the phrase and a heroic defender of the right of women to speak their own desires" (33).[58] Colombina's performance skills lead her in the same direction. Whether her lovers are Octave, or Arlequin, or the master in *Les Chinois*, Colombina is never in a hurry to marry. She is content with her freedom, and through her ironic voice, women's desires are often voiced, while the iniquities suffered by women are vindicated. As she proudly affirms in *La fille de bon sens*, "It will not be said that Colombina stays her arms akimbo" while women are being insulted (155).

The form of induced disguise with the goal of escaping marriage, present in *La Coquette*, is unusual in the history of comedy. While cross-dressing by both men and women was a common comic device of the *commedia*, tricking a male character into disguising himself as a woman in order to defy and escape the will of the tyrannical father is unique. While teaching Isabella, her cousin, who is eager for marriage, all the tricks for "catching the bird" in the "noose," that is, in marriage, Colombina herself moves with ease among the many admirers and lovers in the play, without attaching herself to any, and fully illustrating her philosophy of "loving everybody and nobody." Nigaudin, Pierrot, and Arlequin disguised as captain and as bailiff of Maine, and Octave, all surround Colombine with their attentions, while she does not pay much attention to any of them, or if she does, it is to prick them with her irony. Utterly unimpressed by Octave's exalted love words and claims of desperate love, Colombina interrupts and stops his act by suddenly breaking into song.

In this unusual form of trickery, Colombina again mixes theater and sexual relations, while transforming her own personal cause of escaping an unwanted marriage, into the larger cause of vindicating the indiscretions and insults brought by men against women. The discussion of marriage with Arlequin disguised as the Marquis is mixed with a discussion of the state of the comedy and invariably leads to a discussion of the Italian theater. Through her shrewd conversational style, Colombine leads Arlequin-Marquis-bailiff of Maine toward a self-denunciation of his less than honorable attitudes and behavior towards women.

At some point, an issue is discussed that was controversial in the theater between 1680 and 1710, namely spectators sitting onstage. The practice was abused a lot, particularly by people like the Marquis, who sat onstage to distract from the play and flaunt to the parterre (the people) their costumes, wigs and would-be aristocratic manners. The audience in the parterre often acted as critics of the plays, booing, approving, or censoring plays. Self-important and arrogant, the Marquis defends the practice of sitting onstage on the grounds that it is "a veritable honour for them to see people of quality. Indeed, if all they had was that pleasure, it would be enough to make up for a bad play."[59] Colombina criticizes the practice and defends the good judgments of the people, the parterre, and states that:

> The parterre does everyone good. It corrects authors and keeps actors on their toes. A fop does not parade himself on the stage seats in front of it with impunity.... Do you really think that people in the parterre pay their fifteen sols to watch you comb your wig, take snuff and wander about the stage?

At the end of this scene, the Marquis admits that he wants to keep his place onstage and that he only pays his "ecu" in order to walk around and to fly around the actresses" (190).[60] In the next scene, he courts and harasses the seamstress preparing a dress for Colombina, right in front of her, stating that he likes her almost as much as he does Colombina, and asks her to become his chambermaid. Afterwards, he proposes marriage to Colombina. It is precisely at this point that Colombina plays her trick of having the Marquis disguised.

More than even a way to escape the unwanted marriage to what appears to be a nitwit, pompous would-be marquis, Colombina's gesture is also an act of vindication, by which she places her suitor in the very position of the women he disrespects. Again, the joining of theater and erotic relations is highly significant, for in her vindication Colombina seems to take on many different voices and causes at the same time: that of the people against the fatuous aristocrats, that of the Italian theater versus the French theater, and, most importantly, that of women against sexual predators such as the Marquis. His admission of the fact that the main reason for his going to the theater is to flaunt his clothes and "swirl" around the actresses onstage marks the beginning of an era in which the actress' role deteriorates into mere prey and object of lust for the likes of the Marquis. But at least in *this* play, it will be the actress, the woman, the trickster Caterina/Colombina who will have the last word.

Colombina pretends to accept the marriage proposal of Arlequin/the Marquis on the condition that he be initiated in the Women's Academy that she is part of, on the grounds that the women in it are linked by an oath according to which they cannot get married unless their future spouse is received in the academy. Although surprised by the request, the Marquis agrees and what ensues is a burlesque scene involving onstage disguise, in which Arlequin/the Marquis is undressed and then dressed up as a woman, with false breasts and wig, with makeup and the full works of feminine "beautification." Mezzetin, whose role was created in France in the second half of the seventeenth century, and who was initially a second *zanni* to Arlequin,[61] is the one who performs the actual initiation while singing a silly song, in which he recounts almost step by step the transformation of Arlequin/the Marquis into a pretty girl who is going to "charm everybody."

Colombina is the director of the scene, and the one to benefit from its outrageous burlesque. The humor of the scene derives fundamentally from various layers of reversals of which most are gender reversals that can largely be looked at in light of Bergson's theory of disguise comedy. As noted in the chapter on Isabella Andreini, Bergson's notion of disguise as a source of humor derives from the discrepancy between the garments that we associate with the "essence" or nature of a certain person and the new cover or garments which contradict our imagined or expected image of a person. In the case of Arlequin/Marquis/pretty girl, we are dealing with a layering of disguises that are in contrast with each other and with the initial costumes that we associate with the main *zanni* of the *commedia*. The Marquis' disguise contrasts with the costume and persona of Arlequin, the "pretty girl" disguise is in contrast with both, and in the process of this layering of disguises and false identities, Arlequin is transformed into something of a grotesque mannequin of uncertain sexuality and social class. Arlequin is called in the scene "a hermaphrodite," therefore neither man nor woman.

In her study *Crossing the Stage*, Lesley Ferris notes that quite often, cross-dressing of men into women, reinforces caricatural and stereotypical images of women.[62] Kristeva, in her discussion of the androgyne, notes that it is mostly a "masquerade" of the feminine.[63] Yes, to some extent, Arlequin's transformation caricatures the feminine, as do many other instances of males in drag. But at the same time, the context and the various dramatic motivations of the cross-dressing are of crucial significance. For here, the cross-dresser becomes so not by his own trickery but as a result of a woman's trickery. What Colombina initiates is a "mimesis-mimicry" in the second degree. The feminine is masqueraded and its conventional traits thickened through Arlequin's disguise, but since the disguise has a punitive function and ends up placing Arlequin, who earlier has exhibited "boorish" and "loutish" behavior and who, as Griffiths has noted, was one of the "playboys of the day,"[64] and since plot-wise, the disguise leads to his rejection as Colombine's future husband, the "mimesis-mimicry" has a profound practical function. Colombina plays God by experimenting and playing with gender and by placing the "boorish" play-boy in the victim's position. She tricks the trickster, as Isabella, a century earlier, mimed, impersonated and mocked the clowns. She initiates performance and comedy, while at the same time creating the path to her own freedom. By withdrawing from the scene and creating for Arlequin the dramatic opportunity to make an utter fool of himself and to give the audience the full spectacle of his stupidity, Colombina has used one of the most common classical *commedia* devices, cross-dressing, to arrive at an end which is quite unconventional, that of non-marriage and of non-integration. And while she is at it, she teaches the boorish playboy who is disdainful of the parterre and of the Italian theater a hard lesson.

It is noteworthy that Colombina is creating this comedy within a comedy in front of the very people, of the very audience she is mocking, for it was precisely during the period in which the play in Gherardi's collection were being performed that the phenomenon of the "stage coxcombs"[65] was both a fashion and a source of bitter complaints on the part of the actors. Simultaneously, as she mocks the "louts" sitting onstage and exhibiting their silly outfits to the rest of the audience, Colombina is in a dialogue of complicity with the people, the parterre who, as we have seen in the *Chinois*, and as the Marquis himself indignantly points out, favor the Italian actors and Colombina in particular. Colombina laughs with a portion of the audience, the parterre, at the expense of another portion of the audience, the "stage coxcombs" just as she laughs at the character who is impersonating the latter portion of the audience. Thus she blurs the distinctions between the fictional and the real, the inside and the outside of the performance, while at the same time destabilizing the very cohesiveness of the audience. She plays for the parterre, for the people and for the women in the audience, as, possibly, Isabella Andreini may have played for the women and in particular for the French bride at the magnificent de Medici wedding.

Finally, Colombina's comedy of disguise equally destabilizes and mocks the phallic self-assurance of the likes of Arlequin/the Marquis, who shamelessly boasts about preying on actresses in the theater. By having him dress as one of the actresses he may be harassing or lusting after, she is in fact depriving him precisely of the masculinity he brags about and turns him into not only a ridiculous suitor but a nonexistent one. Dressed as a pretty woman, he becomes worthless as a male lover or husband. This comedic structure calls to mind the unforgettable scenes from *Some Like It Hot*, in which, the crossdressed Tony Curtis and Jack Lemmon pose as women band members. Thus they are able to get closer to the voluptuous Marilyn Monroe and into her bunkbed, but as long as they are dressed as women they are nonexistent as potential male lovers or husbands for Marilyn's character.

Colombina has created the masquerade to end all masquerades in a play which is supposed to offer a lesson of behavior and sexual negotiation for women. The coquette, like the courtesan, has been not only the performer but also the creator and director of her own performance, and through her voice, the voices of deceived women, objectified actresses, dissatisfied wives and oppressed daughters have found a voice as well.

Her comedy has done little in the direction of an integrative closure and has done its best at disintegrating and exploding accepted notions of what a woman's fulfillment and virtue may reside in. Though she has made attempts at helping Isabella find a spouse for herself, no marriage plans are mentioned for her at the end of the play either. Rather than the fixed script of marriage, she chooses the coquette's freedom of improvising. The greatest advocate of the improvisatory performance specific to the classic commedia, Colombine rejects the fixed endings in marriage of that same genre. At the end of the play *Le Divorce*, in which she plays the role of marriage breaker for Isabella, Colombina glibly accepts the marriage proposal from a certain Cornichon, with the line: "Ah, très volontiers, à condition qu'on nous démariera au bout de l'an" ("Oh, very willingly, provided that we will be de-married by the end of the year," vol. 2, 182). Such sarcastic attitudes toward marriage are revolutionary even within the genre of the *commedia* itself, usually marked by the happy ending of marriage.

Colombina mixes the old with the new and the classical with the modern to best suit her own sense of self and to have the last laugh. The relation between Colombina's defense of the creativity of improvisation to be found in the Italian theater and her vehement attack of the rigid reliance of the French theater on the text, is paralleled, at the sexual level, by the elusive performance tricks she seems to always have up her sleeve, as the queen of Parisian coquettes, and, ultimately, by her cunning avoidance of the fixity of marriage.

Colombina's Disguises as Weapons

Critics have noted with a certain amount of awe the variety of Caterina's many disguises within her part of Colombina,[66] and Griffiths is right to point out that the richness of the character comes from the versatility of the actress. The aspect of disguise and cross-dressing brings Colombina closer to the line of commedia female performers and in particular to the great Isabella Andreini. The two of them, a century apart, seem both to have broken the record of disguises for their respective times. If Isabella appeared in disguise or in drag in at least half of the plays she acted in, Caterina/Colombina often appears in several disguises, one after the other, within the same play. Her disguises, like those of Isabella Andreini, are mostly of the nature of cross-dressing. She appropriates, in disguise, many masculine professions. In *Les Souhaits*, Isabella complained that they belonged exclusively to men: soldier, captain, lawyer, government representative, doctor, judge.

Colombina's disguises, just like the mise-en-scène of Mezzetin's disguise as a woman, have an equally practical and moral, punitive function. She is always the one who has the last laugh, who gets her way, who arranges for her mistress to marry whomever she pleases or not to marry at all and, equally for herself, to end up with the partner of her choice, *if* she chooses to have one at all. While Isabella's disguises and comic of cross-dressing had primarily the function of enabling her to escape unwanted marriage and/or marry the man of her choice, Colombina's disguises are more punitive for men and have the value of lessons for women. But at the same time Colombina's punishments are not motivated by gratuitous vindictiveness, but, generally, by the desire to establish an equal footing between men and women in relationships, as

well as in society at large. As she states at the end of the play *La Femme vengée,*
after having indeed received the judicial vindication vis-à-vis a husband gone
mad with "airs de maîtrise" (airs of authority), "One never derives any honor
from insulting one's husband, it is enough to bring him to reason," ("On n'a
jamais d'honneur d'insulter son mari, c'est assez de le mettre à raison," vol.
2, p. 323).

At the end of the play *La Fille de bon sens,* in which she wears three different disguises: that of lieutenant, captain ("capitaine de dragons") and government representative, Arlecchino addresses the parterre with an invitation:
"You, if you have daughters to marry, send them to our school" ("Vous, si
vous avez des filles à marier, envoyez-les à notre école," 198). The "school"
he ironically refers to on behalf of Colombina is, more than anything, a "performance" school. Just as Colombina has given lessons of performance about
how to best be a coquette in *Les Souhaits,* and how to "play the feminine" in
order to achieve at least some vicarious forms of participation in the social
life from which women have been excluded, in *La Fille de bon sens* she gives
a performance lesson to women about how to find justice in a world where
justice is construed, governed and distributed exclusively by men. As Isabella
notes in *Le Divorce,* "those young beards of judges" do nothing but "laugh in
the faces" of women like her, who, dissatisfied in their marriages, would dare
complain about a husband.

Cross-dressing gives Colombina a chance to take justice in her own hands
and to reverse the object of laughter: in the end she is the one who laughs at
all the men who have tried to deceive her and her mistress, and at all the
"young beards of judges." Indeed, laughter is almost literally for Colombina,
as Barreca puts it, "a weapon." Colombina's tricks have the value of weapons
by which women can find justice, punish men for the insults and iniquities
they have brought upon them, and achieve a level of personal satisfaction if
not even happiness, whenever possible. Colombina's irony boldly denounces
the great hypocrisy and corruption of the judicial system. As she mockingly
plays the part of the government representative, the *commissaire,* in charge of
the imparting of justice, she simultaneously assumes his power as she subverts
it, by exposing the great abuses of that same power. As she sits down to start
the judicial procedure, she comments: "Orfus, mister captain, let us well
observe the judicial order and, provided that no one offers us money in order
to stop the course of justice, let us begin our procedure" (191). At the end of
the mock trial of the two "rascals" who wish to marry her, Mezzetin and
Pasquariel, she triumphantly announces:

> Oh, you rascals, I am Colombine and here is Arlequin. You have played heads
> and tails to see who will marry me, I made you play the king of hearts to see

who will be hanged and I'm marrying Arlequin. Cintho and Octave were mocking my mistress, she mocked them.[67]

Colombina teaches women to make a "spectacle" of themselves. When she cross-dresses, either to punish unfaithful lovers, as in *Colombine avocat pour et contre*, or to get rid of unwanted husbands/suitors and/or obtain for herself and/or her mistress the husband of their choice, Colombine teaches women to assume the power that comes with the attire. Her cross-dressing reflects the "critique of maleness"[68] and is used with the same goal as much of the female-to-male cross-dressing is used in modern theater: "to protest the injustices caused by the sex-gender system."[69] It is no wonder that more and more news and rumors about the insolence of the Italian players were reaching the king around the middle 1690s.[70] It is not the obscenities or the vulgarity of their language that probably most offended the king, but the unrestrained manner in which the Italian actors were poking fun at the entire system of justice and the arbitrary organization of power under the monarchy. And more than any of the other characters, it is Colombina who pulls the ropes of trickery, invents ingenious *mise-en scène*, and changes from one disguise to another, all with the double goal of punishing those who in real life hardly ever get punished for the insults or iniquities they may bring against women, and to bring justice to herself and her mistress. Rasi is right to note that Colombine's "gigantesque" comic dimension is also seen in that all the other characters ultimately revolve around her, each for a different reason: some for help, others for jealousy, others for despair, love, "per ... tutto" ("for ... everything." 442).

The passion and vehemence with which Colombina consistently defends or vindicates her mistress may well echo the sisterly indignation hidden behind her act, for it is precisely during the times of these plays that her sister Françoise was going through the humiliating legal ordeal of the dissolution of her marriage. Colombina so blurs the distinctions between onstage and offstage performance; her speeches, like her actions onstage, are so inflammatory; her relation to her audiences so direct; and her mockery of patriarchal institutions so bold, that it is a wonder the Italian players were not chased from France even earlier than 1697.

The comedy that Catherine Biancolelli has created through her character has nothing of the "gentle, subtle, reconciling" humor that theoreticians like J. B. Priestley[71] have claimed feminine humor to be. Instead, it has all the elements of the "very challenging, angry and subversive comedy" explored by Barreca in modern women writers. Colombina's biting irony, trickster personality, lessons of performance and her many disguises are not the "safety valves" of carnival; neither do they always lead to integration and happy reconciliations. Rather, they often have the value of an "inflammatory device, seeking ultimately not to purge desire and frustration, but to transform it into action."[72] Caterina/Colombina's gesture of refusal to join the French company after the brusque dismissal of the Italian one is significant: as part of the French troupe she would have lost half of her freedom of expression, and she would have had to modify her comic verve from that of a critic of the status quo to a supporter of it.

Catherine Biancolelli's Improvisation

A strong proof in support of the thesis that the character of Colombina is largely the creation of the actress Biancolelli is the discovery, in her speech and performance, of cues, formulae and techniques that illustrate the dynamics and the art of improvisation of the *commedia* actors. One of Colombina's funniest, most dynamic and most provocative plays in the Gherardi collection is *Colombine avocat pour et contre*, in which she takes her revenge on Arlequin's unfaithful behavior, by going through a continuous change of identities and languages. She changes identities no less than six times within the space of a single play. Upon the moment of revealing her true identity, she repeats each time these formulaic words: "Perfido, traditore, m'avrai negli occhi se non m'hai nel core" ("perfidious, traitor, you will have me in your eyes if not in your heart," 1:372).

I will attempt to demonstrate that this play illustrates to a large extent the improvisatory dynamics of the commedia dell'arte actors, of the repertoire of the *servettas*, or, in Perrucci's language, of the *fantesca*, and of the improvisational skills of commedia women performers in general. In discussing the play, I will take into consideration both the elements noted as necessary for the success of the improvisation by Andrea Perrucci, in his *Dell'Arte Rappresentativa*, and the performance cues analyzed by Kier Elam as necessary for improvisation.[73] Kathleen McGill's article on improvisatory competence in commedia dell'arte performance constitutes a crucial guide in my analysis. Elam's cues are: space, grammar, props, story, discourse level and voice. As Taviani and McGill have demonstrated, and as Perrucci argued several centuries before them, the art of improvisation is largely premeditated, and the actors based a good part of their dialogues and stage actions on a set of learned texts and gestures, which they would rearrange and combine with each new play and often with each new performance. This play is a perfect example of a certain number of linguistic formulae and repetitive stage actions which the *commedia* actors possessed each for their respective character.

Space

As in the case of the earliest *commedia* scenarios and stage dialogues, or *contrasti*, the references to space are vague, suggesting that many of the scenes can be acted anywhere: a public place, Isabella's room, or they are altogether nonexistent in many of the scenes. Although there is mention that such and such a scene is for instance taking place in Paris upon both Arelquin and Colombina's return to the city, no other more specific cues with regard to space are given. Exactly as described by Perrucci under the category of *soggetto*, which corresponds to Elam's category of "story," the mention of space is general and often refers only to the city: "At the head of the subject, there needs to be noted the place where the story takes place: Rome, Napoli, Genova, Livorno."[74]

Props

Unlike the *contrasto* or the stage dialogue by Isabella Andreini on which McGill bases her theory of improvisatory competence, and coordinate with the fact that the scenes we are discussing derive from an actual performance and are not a model dialogue for a performance, there are numerous mentions of props. Much of the burlesque of the scene derives from Colombina's overwhelming number of disguises and use of objects. The objects and costumes used in the scene are similar to the "properties" listed at the beginning of each scenario in Flaminio Scala's collection: costumes for various occasions, both male and female, of which one in particular, the "mauresque" costume used here by Colombina, is reminiscent of some of Isabella's disguises as Gypsy dancer and Persian astrologer. Other props include a sword, a mirror, the frame for a painting, some of which also appear in the lists of properties in Scala's scenarios (such as the painting for the play entitled exactly *The Painting*). Like Isabella a century before her, but at a much faster pace, Colombina uses the most varied disguises, impersonating both male and female personages of various nationalities or ethnic groups and of various professions: she appears as a Spanish signora, a French servant, a Gascon woman, an Arab or Mauresque slave woman; as a doctor, she tricks Arlequin by replacing his head in a portrait and in a mirror with her own, and at the end of the play she acts an entire scene in a lawyer's disguise, this time pleading in order to save the life of Arlequin after she has brought him there in the first place.

Colombina's rapid succession of disguises and tricks follows a certain pattern of covering and uncovering. With each new disguise, except for the final one, she tricks Arlequin into taking her disguise for real and not recognizing her as such, and at the climactic point of each mini-scene, just when Arlequin has revealed a little more of his lack of loyalty to her, or of his dishonest plans, she reveals her true identity by uttering in Italian these incantatory verses: "Perfido, traditore, m'avrai negli occhi, se non m'hai nel core."

This rapid succession of disguises, tricks, and grimaces, punctuated by linguistic formulae, illustrate to a degree Perrucci's guidelines with regard to *gestualita*: the totality of gestures which produce laughter and which the actors must use in abundance. Of these many performative tricks, he enumerates disguises and use of swords, ridiculous ornaments and ridiculous gestures. Not only does Colombina use an overwhelming array of disguises, but she does make use of the sword against Arlequin when she is dressed up as a Mauresque slave, and drives Arlequin crazy by appearing and disappearing and doubling his image in the mirror and in the portrait. It is noteworthy that this gesture in particular is one of the *lazzis* used by the Italian actors and first performed in Paris in 1685.[75]

According to Mel Gordon's classification of *lazzi*, this one is part of the *lazzi* of stage properties. It was first used in 1685, when Catherine was officially employed in the Troupe Italienne. Since this *lazzi* is listed as always being performed by either Colombina or Mezzetin, it is highly probable that it was Catherine herself who invented it. In any case, *lazzi* were *not* the creation of French authors. They were part of the repertoires of the *commedia* troupes and were the exclusive improvisatory creation of the actors. Furthermore, the reaction that Arlequin exhibits upon each revelation and upon hearing Colombina's vindictive incantation is a perfect illustration of the "*lazzi* of fear," first noted in the manuscript of Basilio Locatelli in 1622.[76] It is also significant that the troupe which the Biancolellis were part of was initially the troupe Fiorelli-Locatelli; therefore these *lazzi* were part of their repertoire and of Catherine's repertoire as well. Arlequin's exclamations of fear, just like Colombina's incantation, are in Italian: "Misericorde, aiuto, spiriti, diavoli, demoni, fantasme"; "Hoime! Ainto! Spiriti! Demoni! Larve!" or "Ah, poveretto mi!" ("Pity, help, the devil, demons, holy spirit"; "Oi me! Aiee! The spirit! The Devil!" 1:372)

Discourse and Voice

At the linguistic and rhythmic level of voice, Colombina's incantatory formula and Arlequino's exclamations of fear clearly illustrate the system of improvisation by which the actors would be in the possession of a set of memorized texts, dialogues and lines in verse or in prose, or both, and use them according to the various needs of the plot and in perfect collaboration with each other. The fact that Colombina's lines are in verse and that, moreover, there is a rhythmic cadence suggestive of verse and even rhymes in some of the dialogues between Colombine and Arlequin, further strengthens the argument of the improvisational and oral quality of the scenes. As McGill and other experts of oral literature have noted[77] most improvisation is in verse, for very obvious mnemonic reasons. A large part of what Molinari has called the "moving blocks" of improvisation often derives from lyric poetry.

The rhetoric figures of gradation, antithesis and accumulation, specific to oral poetry and improvisation,[78] are used in the Italian as well as in some of the French lines exchanged between Arlequin and Colombina in this play. Colombina builds up her line by starting with a set of double invectives: "perfido, traditore," then creating an antithetic syntactical structure: "m'avrai ... se non m'hai ..." Arlequino answers by an accumulation of exclamations which pick up the aural cues of both assonance and consonance in Colombina's line (the repetition of the vowels "i" and "o" and of the liquid consonants "r" and "l"). There are roughly five rhythmic beats in each of their lines: "perfido/ traditore/ m'avrai negli occhi/ se non m'hai/ nel cuore" and "hoime/ainto/spiriti/demoni/larve." Each one of Arlequin's words forms a rhythmic beat or cadence, which corresponds to each rhythmic beat in Colombina's line. Arlequin's "oime" picks up the three main vowels in Colombine's "per<u>fido</u>," only in reverse order: "o," "i," "e." The exclamation "a<i>into</i>" picks up the same vowels in Colombine's "tra<i>d</i>i<i>tore</i>" in the exact same order: "a," "i," "o." The third rhythmic units, "m'av<i>rai</i> negl<i>i</i> occh<i>i</i>" and "spiriti" contain in both lines the vowel "i" three times in conjunction with the liquid "r." The fourth rhythmic unit contains in both lines the labial consonants "m" and "n" in reverse order, and the three vowels "e," "o," "i," in the same order: "<u>se</u> <u>non</u> m'h<u>ai</u>" and "<u>demoni</u>." Finally, the fifth unit, "nel cuore"—"larve," contains the repetition of both liquids, "l" and "r," in the same order, and both lines end in the same vowel, "e."

The set of aural cues, and rhetorical figures set to a well-balanced rhythm, illustrates a "basic rhythmic structure of parallelism."[79] The melodic quality of the exchange, enhanced by both assonance and consonance, reflects equally the cueing specific to collaborative improvisation. Even more than parallelism, one can detect in this short exchange a subtle system of cueing by which Arlequin picks up, in his first word, the main sounds in Colombine's last words: the last rhythmic block of Colombina's line is "m'hai nel cuore," in which the vocalic cluster "hai," the vowel "o" and the consonants "m" and "r" are predominant. Arlequin picks up exactly on the same vowel sounds, and the "m" in the onomatopeic expression: "hoime" which combines the three vowels in Colombina's previous cue, almost as if it were a musical phrase. This system of cueing illustrates exactly the one noted by McGill in her study on the improvisational technique of the commedia dell'arte: "What is of special interest to the cueing of performance is the way in which these assonant/consonant markers function at the beginning and end of alternating lines of dialogue, so that the responding speaker picks up the sound of the final words of the other, and uses it to construct his or her reply" (120).

Grammar

The structure of parallel rhythms and, in McGill's terms, of "melodic variations" (119), is also present in the French dialogue: "Arlequin: De tout ce qu'il y a de marquis en France, sans vanité, je suis un des plus donnans." Colombine: "Folle qui s'y fie. Depuis l'histoire arrivé à une nommée Colombine, il pleuvrait des hommes que je ne voudrais pas en avoir ramassé un" ("Arlequin: Of all the marquis in France, without being vain, I am one of the most giving." Colombine: "Crazy is she who would trust that. Ever since what happened to a certain Colombine, it can rain with men that I wouldn't want to pick out any"). Firstly, the two lines rhyme with each other: "donnans"—"un." Secondly, the synthetic structures of the two lines are very similar: they each start with the subordinate and not the main clause, and with similar sounding prepositions: "de" and "depuis." Thirdly, for each segment of Arlequin's phrase, there is a segment which corresponds and is parallel to Colombina's sentence: the segment "De tout ce qu'il y a de marquis en France," referring to a general characterization or state of things, corresponds to Colombine's "Depuis l'histoire arrive à une nommée Colombine," which places Colombina at a distance from herself, and turns her into something of an example of injustices done to women. To Arlequin's "sans vanité, "without vanity," Colombina responds with "il pleuvrait des hommes," "it could rain with men;" his false modesty is counteracted by Colombine's hyperbolic reference to men in general, suggesting that, contrary to Arlequin's claim, all men are vain, or that he is no better than most. Finally, Arlequin's self-praise, "Je suis un des plus donnans" ("I am one of the most giving"), is counteracted by Colombine's rejection of men altogether: "Je n'en voudrais pas un" ("I wouldn't want any"). The parallelism is to be noted also in the fact that both phrases start with the first person personal pronoun "je." Grammar-wise, both sentences rely upon the use of first person personal pronouns, relatively simple verb forms (all present indicative in Arlequin's speech and two present conditionals in Colombine's) and a relatively simple vocabulary. From the point of view of discourse, the style is not the elevated, lyric style of the inamorati, but the lower, comic style specific to the *zannis*, involving invectives, exclamations, truncated lines, threats, and negations. The combination of all the elements of grammar, spatial reference, melodic and rhythmic structure, discourse and props correspond to the techniques of oral expression characteristic of the improvisatory competence of the *commedia* actors. The versatile combinations of aural, semantic and syntactic units reflect Molinari's theory of the textual "moving blocks" which the commedia actors, according to him, manipulate and combine like the jazz soloists, who, while in possession of a certain set of learned musical segments, are able to use and constantly re-create these segments, while cueing each other and creating the overall effect and "melody."

As for the subject matter of the exchanges, although the dialogues take place between two *zannis*, since they are also in a position of being in love with each other, and since Colombina is often also an "amoureuse," the gist of their lines is similar to that of the *contrasti amorosi*, the lover's quarrels of the traditional commedia. The dynamic of these dialogues is centered, like the exchange between Colombina and Arlequin, on a game of seduction and contains generally an initial refusal or rejection of love from the part of the female character. The very dialogue McGill uses for her analysis is called "Amorous dialogue in disapproval of love." Most love dialogues or *contrasti amorosi* in Isabella Andreini's *Fragmenti* are lovers' quarrels, with a pattern of disagreement, contradicting, and final reconciliation.

Finally, Colombina's incantation and the exchanges between her and Arlequin are reminiscent of the "greetings," or *saluti*, and the *rimproveri* (reproaches, scoldings) that Perrucci includes in his study, to be used by the character of the female servant, or *fantesca*. They are also reminiscent, respectively, of certain parts of the dialogues that he proposed for the roles of the inamorati. The greeting of the Tuscan servant and the *rimprovero* to the servant are particularly relevant, the first one due to its accumulation of insults and the alliterative nature of the pejorative words used by the servant, and the second one due to the vindictive tone and language which makes it sound practically like a curse. The servant's greeting is addressed to the *zanni* who is her lover and who is represented as a traitor or unfaithful; the lines in the traditional greeting alternate between praises and the expression of her love, and insults and expressions of her rage. The last line of the Tuscan servant's greeting is particularly relevant to our discussion: she calls her lover: "bove, becco, caval, porco et somaro" ("bovine, cuckold, horse, swine, ass"). It is similar to the gist of Colombina's verses and actions. They exhibit rage and vindictiveness; in her revenge she suggests cuckolding Arlequin (as when she goes away with Pasquariel), and stylistically the insults are alliterative or asso-nant and/or rhymed, or arranged according to an incantatory rhythm. The *rimprovero* as well ends in a violent curse in which the *serva* wishes the *servo* a painful death by hanging. And to put the last touch on this analysis of the improvisational nature of the play, it is to be noted as well that in the mini scene of the portrait, another one of the zannis, Pasquariel, is disguised as a painter, one of the disguises that Perrucci suggests as most ridiculous.

In addition to the specific scenes and exchanges analyzed so far, it is also noteworthy that the scene in which Colombina recounts to Pasquariel her misery with Arlequin, as well as the scene toward the end of the play in which Colombina, now worried that Arlequin might end up being hanged, confesses her love for him and her desire to save his life, are acted mostly in Italian. This supports Scott's comment that many of the plays in the collection, particularly the earlier ones, are versions of old commedia plays translated into French. Or in this case, the translations are only partial. This play was first acted in 1685 and contains more Italian dialogues than the other plays in the Gherardi collection. Also Pasquariel, in the dialogues with Arlequin, often answers Arlequin's French lines in Italian. Furthermore, there are more scene summaries of the kind of the original commedia scenarios in this play than in the rest of the collection (such as AIII, s. 4,5). Often, there is no dialogue at all, just a summary of stage actions and some snippets of lines, such as "le diable, le diable" (AIII, s. 4). As Gherardi himself notes in his preface to the collection, "the Italians learn nothing by heart," therefore it follows that particularly the scenes acted in Italian and that the scenes which are only recounted, not rendered with full dialogue, are improvised according to the traditional commedia style.

In demonstrating the input and improvisational competence of Catherine it is important as well to show, as I have tried to in this section, that the other actors working with her in the scene are equally well timed and are basing their own performance on improvisational skills. Such is the example of Arlequin and his use of language, rhythm, and timing. As McGill has noted, "the best improvisation is profoundly social," due to its "reliance on the other in responding to the performative demands of the moment." In proving that the entire play is largely the result of the improvisational skills of the commedia actors themselves, strengthens the argument that Catherine made significant input into her own character. Her performance was brilliant, as her contemporaries and later critics noted, but her creativity exemplifies at best the collaborative work style of the Italian actors and actresses, and the rich tradition of female improvisational virtuosity.

Colombina Meets Isabella

Other than the high level of improvisational competence and orality reflected in this play, Colombina's use of many disguises and, in particular, many languages, dialects, accents and discursive styles, brings to mind another spectacular performance of multilingual versatility and of comedic virtuosity:

the scene of Isabella's madness of 1589. N.M. Bernardin remarks that the play *Colombine avocat pour et contre* transports us to "Babylon" with its delirium of languages, impersonations and disguises.[1] And, as noted earlier, Winifred Smith has already compared Isabella and Catherine in terms of the increased number of disguises that Colombina uses to torment Arlequin. Some have argued that Isabella's use of languages had the underlying motivation of showing off her erudition. Rather, I would say that both Isabella and Colombina illustrate their extraordinary improvisational skills and erudition in their multilingual theatrical expression. Catherine is no less talented than Isabella on that account. In fact, it may even be argued that she exceeds her, as she carries an entire scene in fluent Spanish, then another in a mock combination of French and Italian, and another in Gascon dialect. In the Italian scene with Pasquariel, Colombine tells him that she can speak "francese, spagnolo, provenzale, franco" (vol. 1, 303), which she later proves in abundance.

Colombina's Spanish scene in particular is impressive and the humor she creates by speaking in a language Arlequin does not understand is largely of the nature of superiority humor: she goes on to mock Arlequin and to recount his acts of betrayal in fluid Spanish. The satisfaction is hers and the laughter was probably shared only with those in the audience who knew Spanish. The general humor of the scene illustrates to some extent the kind of humor noted by Pavis, of the action which fails its projected goal,[81] for there is no actual communication in the exchange, just an overlap of unrelated lines. Catherine's linguistic versatility has a precedent in Isabella, and is most likely the expression of the actress's competence and talent, and less the creation of a French author.

The motivation of the disguises and impersonations in *La Pazzia d'Isabella* and *Colombine avocat pour et contre* is similar as well: both Isabella and Colombina use disguise, impersonation, and multilingual expression in order to defy, punish, and frighten disloyal lovers and would-be husbands. There is also a hint of madness in Colombina's behavior and speech, in the precipitated change of appearance, personality, accent, and language. As in Isabella's scene, this gives a sense of breakdown and rupture of logic and is reminiscent of the figure of the hysteric, the one dismantling and collapsing linguistic as well as social order, "the paradigmatic rebel against reality-testing."[82] Again, Colombina illustrates that "comedy is dangerous."[83] The incantatory line she keeps throwing in Arlequin's face with each new disguise has a menacing and painful edge to it. The "hysteric often laughs even as she howls," notes Barreca (16). Columbine produces this strident, repetitive verse at the culminant moment of each mini-scene of disguise, at the point when Arlequin is revealing his dishonest intentions of marrying Isabella. Colombina's outcry spells revolt, rage, indignation, triumph and vindictiveness all in one, just as Isabella's madness spelled all of that in what Scala notes in his scenario as "rantings" and "ravings."

But Colombina has an added note of malice. Colombina's carousel of languages and impersonations is like a carnival gone sour. The haunting character of both her stage actions and the repetitive nature of her speech is reflective not only of the "woman on top" motif, but of the Medusa type of vindication. Her lines and actions are directed at Arlequin's sight; they are meant to freeze, immobilize, and incapacitate him with fear. As she reveals herself from each disguise, she obtains indeed the projected effect, as Arlequin is half dead with fear, particularly when she appears in the portrait and in the mirror. Indeed, Colombina's comedy is joined here with what Catharine Clement has pointed out to be the "monstrous" element of laughter.[84] The mirror and the portrait, such essential symbols in the history of the objectification of women and their transformation into objects of men's gaze, are transformed into means of vindication. The object of the gaze talks back, the image becomes an element of torture: wherever he turns, Arlequin sees Colombine, and the sight of her freezes him with fear. A combination of a comic Erinie and a Medusa, Colombina's comedy is poised on that fine line defined by Cixous and Clement as the "the cultural demarcation beyond which she (the woman) will find herself excluded" (33). Arlequin, wanting to marry Isabella for her wealth and thus take Colombina out of his heart, will have to face, at each step of the way toward his goal, Colombina's refusal to be excluded and the insistence of her ever-present image.

Not only is it not far-fetched to compare Colombina with Medusa or an Erinie, it is in fact quite in line with her repertory and theater experience. In 1684, a year after her official entry into the Italian troupe and a year before the premiere of *Colombine avocat pour et contre*, Catherine played Colombine/Medea in the play *Arlequin Jason*, a burlesque parody of the Medea story. Colombina's familiarity with the "monster" females of history and mythology is significant. In this play Colombine/Medea takes revenge on Arlequin/Jason, who, as in *Colombine avocat pour et contre*, wants to marry Ipsiphilia/Isabella. The comic elements of the character Colombine/Medea/Medusa derive largely from her use of sorcery and the vindictive transformations of humans that she performs: she transforms Jason into Arlequin, who is supposed to be ugly and stupid, so that Ipsiphilia/Isabella will stop loving him; and she turns a handful of men who have insulted her into statues. Among them are a doctor and two actors, a French and an Italian one. The French actor is punished for having bored her and the Italian actor is punished for having made her laugh so hard she became sick. The figures of Medusa and Medea collapse within the character of Colombine: she both freezes men to stone and has the power of sorcery. In the end, everything turns out in her favor, as she not only marries Arlequin/Jason but makes him promise he will stop being jealous "like an Italian," be faithful and stop going to the tavern.

Colombina is largely responsible for the creation of a truly burlesque dimension in this play: everything elevated, of mythological, tragic and serious nature, is demystified and transformed into object of laughter. The mechanical is literally imposed on the human to the very extreme, to use Bergson's terms,[85] as Colombina/Medea/Medusa turns humans into statues one moment and then turns them back into humans the next. The carnivalesque reversal of the high and the low takes unprecedented proportions, as not only does Colombina dismantle any dignity that was left of the character of Jason from ancient mythology and tragedy, but she teaches a lesson to all the would-be heroes of her time — doctors, bankers, actors — on behalf of all women, in her enchanted garden of petrified men. The combination of the Medusa and Medea figures into one female trickster rounds up Colombina's character to the full range of comedic possibilities she explored throughout her many performances and illustrates at best the aggressive, transgressive and subversive humor of women artists.

What Isabella Andreini started in the late 1500s, Catherine Biancolelli brought to fruition in the late 1600s: a comedy which is ostentatiously created from the vantage point of the liminal, like the comedy discussed by Little, a humor which brings the margins to the center, as recommended by Cixous, a laughter which is "allied with the monstrous," as advocated by Clement.

Isabella's madness is taken several steps further in Colombina's controlled hysteria; Isabella's disguises proliferate at a dizzying pace in Colombina's plots; Isabella's carnival of gender role reversals and her use of language(s) to explode patriarchal linguistic self-assurance acquires the slightly bitter, slightly frightful dimension of the laughter described by Cixous, a laughter which "breaks up, breaks out, splashes over" (33). While Isabella's comic performance is embedded within the serious part of the inamorata, Colombina's comic role of the *zanna* encompasses both the clown and the deceived but angry female lover and unapologetically acquires the dimension of a social manifesto on behalf of women. Each according to the social context of their own time, though, shakes things up with her laughter, and each unabashedly "makes a spectacle of herself." And if Isabella was the first to explode mimesis and mock it in the linguistic delirium of her famous mad scene, Colombina goes a step further and turns mimesis on its head, while using it as a means of revenge. To Arlequin's self-assured expectation of seeing his own image in the mirror and in the portrait of himself, Colombina responds by an erasure of mimesis altogether: for all he sees is her image, and all he hears is the sound of her promise to forever haunt him. Colombina's performance trick is to fixate the gaze — Arlequin's eyes — onto its object — Colombina's face — forever and ever, to the point where the gaze ends up being its own punishment. And Medusa laughs on, and "She is beautiful"![86]

Finally, both the *Pazzia d'Isabella* and *Colombine avocat pour et contre* end with the marriage of the female protagonists to the man of their choice. In Colombina's case, she does so only after she has impressed Arlequin with her "lawyer's" talents and after she has saved him from hanging. Arlequin, so avid throughout the play to marry Isabella, for her money, is now eager to marry a woman who would be the feminine version of his lawyer. This time, Colombine's uncovering occurs with a positive rather than a vindictive note, as she turns out to be just that woman. Although this play does end with the classic resolution of classic commedia, the reconciliatory act of marriage, it does so entirely on Colombine's terms as she makes herself wanted in marriage due to and for her intelligence and "professionalism" as a lawyer, which turns out to be more expert than that of the expert male lawyers themselves. Again, Colombina manipulates and negotiates the power status of male characters, and proves, via performance, that women can be at least as good at the jobs that men hold exclusively, but from which women have been banned. Her performance within performance, her cross-dressing and playing the male gender and professions, not only subvert gender roles and societal conventions but actually create a virtual reality of role reversals and offer a glimpse into a possible, though not yet for that time existent, world: a world in which women would actually find themselves in those positions of power, as lawyers, judges, government representatives.

Let us now ask the same question we asked when discussing Isabella: beyond all comic theory, would Colombina be funny today? And as an answer, let us imagine her, as we have done with Isabella, as a modern-day actress, Catherine Zeta Jones, for example. Catherine Zeta Jones is deceived by her lover, played by the actor George Clooney, who had sworn eternal love to her; in the meantime, she finds out he has been leading a double life and plans to marry Gwyneth Paltrow. To take revenge on her deceitful lover, Jones keeps appearing in the rear view mirror when he is driving to work, in his bathroom mirror when he is shaving, seated in front of him at a restaurant just when he is about to order his meal, disguised as his doctor when he is having his physical examination, in the guise of the gas attendant filling up his car, and in the place of his secretary when he goes to his office in the morning. Every time, she repeats the following line, first with a Spanish accent, then with a Louisiana accent, then with a French accent, then with a New York accent: "Traitor, cheater, since you won't have me in your head, you'll have me in your eyes instead." That would most likely be funny. Similarly, you could take out the gore, the knives, and the steaming sex scenes from *Fatal Attraction* and have Glenn Close, appear repeatedly in Michael Douglas' way, each time uttering "I won't be ignored." That *could* be hilarious.

Rasi is right to consider that the Gherardian Colombina has acquired "gigantesque dimensions" and that she has created an entire "world of comedy." Quick, ingenious in trickery, vengeful when betrayed yet always sure of herself, versatile and unpredictable, Caterina's Colombina is something of a seventeenth century Claudette Colbert/Catherine Zeta Jones/Julia Roberts combination: a female trickster who always has the last word, whom no man can fool and who, on top of it all, is largely responsible for her own script — which doesn't even always end with "They lived happily ever after," but with "She lived happily whichever way she chose." Jill Dolan's suggestion that today's theater critic, teacher, or spectator should in fact pay attention to "who's there (or who appears to be there), using and surpassing metaphors of performativity" seems well suited to the analysis of Caterina's Colombina ("Geographies of Learning," 440). Ultimately, Colombina and her "tricks" seem to urge us to view her in the full flamboyance of her female power and in the richness of her humanity, beyond gender lines and past all her disguises.

THREE

Franca Rame
Militant Isabella, Feminist Colombina
in Twentieth Century Italy

Franca Rame: Feminist Performer
in the Commedia dell'Arte *Tradition*

In the Prologue to the collection of one-act plays entitled *Female Parts*,[1] Franca Rame notes that, at the premiere of her play *Abbiamo tutte la stesa storia* (*We All Have the Same Story*), at Palazina Liberty in 1977,[2] she failed to understand why she could only hear women's laughs and no men's laughs. Furthermore, she would sometimes hear women saying things like: "Do you recognize yourself, cretin?" (22). Later, she says, she started to also hear men's laughs, but they were poorly timed, and seemed to say "I'm not one of those" (22). No wonder the men in the audience did not laugh and no wonder that the play would often, as Rame notes, start quarrels among spouses, lovers, or fiancés. This bitter comedy, like that of most of Rame's plays, is harsh, unforgiving, and unapologetic. The protagonist, a married working woman, like many of Rame's characters, use abundant sarcasm veering toward the fantastic and the surreal to voice women's feelings regarding sexuality, contraception, conception, pregnancy, birth, and motherhood. The play begins with the protagonist miming the sexual act and interrupting it in order to voice her discontent or apprehensions: "That's it, yes, I like to make love, but I would like to make it with a little feeling." It ends with the image of the girl grown into a woman, sitting under a tree with other girls turned women and sharing the fact that they all once had a little doll who used to utter obscenities. Rame ends her act with a song about the child she has produced and whom she is breastfeeding

119

with rage and fright, whom she will bathe in blasphemy and obscene songs in order to send her all armed against the *padrone*, the owner, the Master.

Franca Rame is a unique twentieth century Italian performer, playwright, director, and comedian who draws all the strings of the women's comic tradition we have discussed into a new, explosive and unapologetically feminist comic performance. By feminist performance I mean a performance which "pays attention to women," which addresses numerous issues regarding women's status in society, from sexuality, to motherhood, to relations with men, to violence against women, by means of performative and discursive techniques which differ radically from conventional mimetic realist theater, and which subvert conventional drama by means as varied as breaking in and out of character, speaking directly to the audience, and especially by always placing the woman's voice and presence center stage, as subject and not as object of the male gaze.

Rame exemplifies at best the category of female comic creativity whose portrait I have been trying to delineate in this book, but which comes into fruition only through her performance: unpredictable and avoiding definitions of the feminine, transgressive of traditional forms of expression to the point of entirely breaking with the conventions of classical theater, speaking from the vantage point of women and their marginalized positions, carnivalesque in its shocking reversals and highly sexual discourse, angry at times, bitter at other times, with deep overtones of the Baubo open laughter and strident notes of the Arachne sarcasm at patriarchal values; always honest in its direct approach to and inclusion of the audience.

Franca Rame emerges from and continues to a significant extent the Italian tradition of commedia dell'arte, which she explores in terms of performative and comic techniques, while redirecting it toward the creation of a militant and fiery feminist theater. She was born into a family of puppeteers who turned to regular comic acting, which they called *teatro di persona*[3] in direct derivation and continuation of the commedia dell'arte in terms of characters, plots and burlesque comedy. The family can trace its roots to seventeenth century itinerant troupes.[4] So important were the contributions of her family in the history of Italian comedy that some of their theatrical belongings are on display in the Scala museum of theater.

Rame started acting at eight days old in her mother's arms and has continued to do so until today. In the words of Ron Jenkins, "Franca Rame is one of the few living performers in the Western theatrical tradition whose theatrical knowledge has been passed down by experience through the generations of a single family."[5] Antonio Scuderi also points out that Rame "literally grew up in the theater," very much like the actors of the commedia troupes, and that she is "truly a *figlia d'arte.*"[6] Throughout her childhood and adolescence she acted in variety shows that "were viewed as a form of 'lesser' theater, a direct descendant of commedia dell'arte, retaining many of the characteristics of popular performance."[7] She grew up learning directly, onstage and at home, the trade of acting and the art of improvisation, for which she showed particular talent, from early childhood on. In 1951 she joined the theater of the Italian playwright and performer Dario Fo, whom she married three years later. Together, they wrote, directed and performed an abundance of comedies, which, throughout the years, and following Italy's tumultuous political journey, acquired a progressively sharper political edge. In 1977, Fo received the Nobel Prize for literature. In his acceptance speech, he stated that it belonged to both him and Franca, yet it was him only who stood on that podium to receive the prize. Little consolation that was to Franca, who indeed was responsible for much of his success.

With the important exception of their divorce, this couple who write, direct, perform comedies together and tour the world with their performances bear striking resemblance to Isabella and Francesco Andreini. The collaborative method of script writing and directing which Rame and Fo started to use once they created their own company and broke off from conventional theater is very much in the style of the commedia troupes. Very much like the work style of the commedia troupes, this consisted of "all the members of the company musing collectively over an idea brought forth by one of them and developed through additions and changes until it is 'rehearsed' several times as a piece."[8] Antonio Scuderi notes, "It may even be argued that their collaboration has no equal historically in all of European theater, for even the great Andreini family of the sixteenth century, with the stellar presence of Isabella, lacked a collaboration that produced an equivalently vast corpus."[9] Of course the supposed "lack" of identical collaboration of the Andreini's that Scuderi notes is arguable, and is contradicted by important evidence, such as Francesco Andreini's epitaph letter to Isabella, the very scenarios they played, reports of contemporaries, and Francesco's very gesture of giving up the stage upon Isabella's death and devoting his remaining days to the posthumous publication of her works. If differences in the degrees of the collaboration between each of the two couples do exist, they must be looked at in terms of the respective historical and societal conditions. In the sixteenth century just about any real artistic and professional collaboration between a husband and wife was something of a revolution. One has to wonder why it is that in the modern era collaboration like that of Rame and Fo is such a unique occurrence. Moreover, why have Franca's contributions for so long been overshadowed by those of her husband?[10] In any case, Scuderi's comment is helpful in that it presents the two theater couples side by side and their theatrical collaboration as comparable.

Writing, directing and performing together, touring all over the world with their company, creating a set of recognizable roles and characters, establishing themselves both on and off stage as charismatic personalities, it all follows in the line of the commedia dell'arte troupes. The one significant apparent difference is constituted by the blatantly revolutionary and anti-establishment dimension that Rame and Fo's theater acquired in the seventies. Even when creating characters, scenes and a type of humor which mocked the status quo of patriarchal figures or of certain social classes, the commedia troupes did so within acceptable forms, in the context of the carnivalesque representations, and generally refrained from directly attacking their sponsors, without whose protection and financial sponsorship they would not have been able to continue acting, except in the streets. For when the Italian troupes *did* start attacking and making fun of the establishment, as in the case of the Italian troupe playing for Louis the XIV, they were summarily expelled from France. Similarly, "Because of their militancy and provocative disruptiveness, both Fo and Rame have been denied regular public subsidies or performing spaces."[11] Fo has some revelatory things to say about the role, history and importance of clowns throughout the history of theater and in his and Franca's theater in particular: "Today's clown," he says, "has lost both his ancient capacity to shock and his political moral commitment. In other times, the clown used satire as a vehicle against violence, cruelty, hypocrisy and injustice."[12]

There are several striking similarities between Franca Rame and Isabella Andreini. In a study entitled *Commedia dell'arte*, coauthored with Fo, Rame talks with great admiration about Isabella Andreini and about women's comedy and sexual humor throughout the centuries. She praises Isabella for her acting, particularly in the famous mad scene, and presents her as an example of high performative professionalism to modern actresses, who, in Rame's opinion, tend at times to overact and overdo their stage acts.[13] The most conspicuous similarity between Franca and Isabella is the simultaneous creation of both powerful stage and real-life personae which, while at first responding to the needs of their respective societies for a certain feminine construct, becomes with time and in performance layered into several other transgressive, often carnivalesque or buffoonish personae. Walter Valeri notes, "Like no other performer today, Franca has created a stage persona that artfully combines powerful acting with formidable presence of personality" (4). Franca Rame also resembles Isabella Andreini in terms of her extraordinary artistic and intellectual range of expression. What is being said today about Franca is similar to the descriptions of Isabella by some of her contemporaries: "Franca

Rame is not only an exceptional actress, but a theatrical personality of unmatched talent on the contemporary Italian stage and endowed with extraordinary intellectual and professional resources."[14]

Both Isabella and Franca blurred the distinctions between their stage and public image and, like Marilyn Monroe, they became symbols of an ideal of femininity for their respective historical periods: Isabella fit the image of the beautiful, innocent, virtuous Renaissance woman, and Franca that of the "50's svampita airhead, a role that was a combination of the dumb-blonde type of the Hollywood cinema and the chattering housewife of popular theater."[15] In her film roles, she also projected the Monroesque image of the "eye-catching blonde sex-bomb."[16] However, Isabella did not project the image of a "dumb blonde"; but on the contrary, she was praised and admired for her erudition, intelligence and eloquence, in addition to her beauty and virtue. Franca, much like Marilyn, fit into the feminine mold of the 1950s which in fact represents quite a regression vis-à-vis the Renaissance ideal of femininity, as women are both desired for and encouraged to uphold that all too "lofty" feminine ideal of the "dumb blonde." On these terms one is hard pressed to argue for progress or evolution with regard to the status and representations of women in the twentieth century. However, as feminist critics have noted, the screen and stage physical image that Franca promoted throughout her acting career was also something of a mockery of the same image she incarnated, precisely because of its thick, exaggerated lines. Elin Diamond notes, "Rame exploits, more dubiously, her dyed blonde hair and heavy make up to mimic the gender signs of heterosexual femininity."[17]

One crucial element which makes Franca Rame the twentieth century sister of Isabella Andreini and Catherine Biancolelli is the extraordinary level of her improvisational skills. When Franca was asked, during a tour in Scandinavia, how she prepared for her roles, she scandalized her audience when she said simply: "I read it through and go onstage."[18] To a trained author in the conventional modern theater, such a comment may seem glib, boastful, altogether not serious. But nothing could be more authentic, in fact, when one recalls that the most famous troupes of the commedia dell'arte had precisely this same approach to theater: they read or saw the plots, then went onstage and acted them out. She exemplifies beautifully that miraculous skill about which Evaristo Gherardi speaks in the preface to his collection of plays, granted with an arguable level of exaggeration: that the Italian actors "only need, in order to play a comedy, to have read the subject a moment before going onstage."[19]

Franca's family was known for its extraordinary ease in the art of improvisation. Just as the early commedia troupes did, the members of Franca's family "had consigned to memory a range of dialogues and exchanges relating to situations which might arise in several different plays. "On other occasions, when spending a lot of time in one town on their tours, Domenico, the father, would explain to the family a certain plot, they would inquire about local legends, customs and stories, he would devise parts for the outline of the plot "was pinned up in the wings, and the family would take their cue from it between entries and exits.... The adaptation unfolded spontaneously onstage."[20] This production dynamic is almost identical to that of the early commedia troupes. Perhaps the only exception is that the women of the early troupes, according to reports by Tomasso Garzoni and others were truly the stars of the art of improvisation, and were often the leaders of their troupes. Antonio Scuderi argues that in fact Rame and Fo's improvisational style follows directly in the tradition of *recitare a sogetto* of the commedia dell'arte and that the acting and production style of Franca's family is practically identical to the commedia production style as described by Allardyce Nicoll.[21] Furthermore, he even likens the scenarios and plots in the repertoire of Rame's family to scenarios from Flaminio Scala's collection (178).

If the general system of production, improvisation and performance in Rame's heritage follows directly in the tradition of the ancient commedia troupes, it seems that in terms of gender relations, things have not only stagnated but possibly even regressed. Franca Rame's accounts of the gender relations and roles in her family's troupe reflect something of a deterioration of the equal status between the men and women. She recounts that the women were in charge of the costumes, the box office and the household chores, and never "appeared up front to speak directly with the audience," and only her father, the actor-manager of the company "knew how to address the audience directly, to entertain them, to crack jokes or to provoke them in the prologues."[22] On the contrary, four and five centuries earlier, the women of the commedia troupes were usually center stage. They awed with their improvisational art, were often in charge of their companies, and, as we have seen in Catherine Biancolelli's Colombine, made it almost their duty to address, provoke and dialogue with their audiences. Kings and princes referred to "Isabella's troupe," and all accounts of Catherine Biancolelli concur that she was the center of vitality of the troupe and of the plays they performed.

Franca's legendary improvisational skills reinforce McGill's argument about the essential role that the women of the early commedia played in the development of the genre, precisely because of their remarkable ease at improvising onstage. Many wonderful anecdotes, told by both Franca and Dario, attest to her talent and professionalism in this area. The best-known is the one when Franca entirely lost her lines onstage, acting next to Dario, in the play *He Had Two Pistols with White and Black Eyes*. Despite the great panic in Dario's eyes, and the even greater panic of the stagehands who were signaling to pull down the curtain, she saved the show by starting to improvise as if nothing had happened, until she remembered her lines. Farrell notes plainly that "Dario learned improvisation from her" (30). In the one-woman shows that she has been doing since the 70s, Franca consistently breaks in and out of character to speak to the audience and listen to them, to entirely include them in the show. The relationship to the audience is of great importance to Franca and she cannot conceive of performing without including, talking to and even listening to her audience. "Many times," Rame muses, "actors and directors are in danger of making the audience irrelevant to their art form."[23] Walter Valeri remarks, "It is Rame's singular ability to combine, and sometimes confound, the roles of performer and listener that has, more than any other aspect, distinguished her theater" (3).

As I noted in the introduction and reiterated throughout this study, it is of great importance to both women's history and to feminist art and expression to discover, establish and ascertain the continuity of a women's tradition of comedy and comic performance throughout the centuries. Rame herself touches upon this notion and comments that ever since the Middle Ages, although unrecognized, women did contribute and did create a comic tradition, be it in the form of comic acrobatic performances by female jugglers in taverns, or in the form of storytelling in stables and rural settings, of convent drama, or of joke telling after the children are put to bed.[24] Her own plays at times draw directly from the tradition of certain commedia forms, such as the famous *contrasto*. She calls one of her plays *Contrasto ad una sola voce*, and in the prologue to *Récits de femmes*, she calls this play a "contrasto con canzonatura" (dispute with joking) whose origins she traces back to popular traditions of Italy, from Venice to Sicily. One of the first roles she played upon her return to the theater in 1958 was the commedia dell'arte female role of "a peasant woman, rich in popular wisdom,"[25] in a play which Fo had converted from one of the scenarios, or *canovacci*, of Rame's family. From then on, the couple relied more and more in their comedies on the use of commedia performance tricks, such as the famous *lazzi* as well as song and music.[26] Cottino-Jones notes that Fo and Rame's theater

> avails itself of a very vast repertoire and of performing techniques characteristic of the most valid European traditions, combining the improvisation technique and use of masks and dialect typical of commedia dell'arte, with the rigorous facial gimmicks of mimes, or the contortions and physical exhibitions of acrobats, or the comic farces of clowns.[27]

Drawing from an almost five-century-old tradition of comedy, Franca Rame illustrates at once the humor of the commedia, the improvisatory competence of the commedia women performers, and the many layers of feminist humor theorized and analyzed by feminist performance and humor theorists that I have often referred to or used thus far. At the time when she was creating one-woman shows all over Italy, experimenting with theatrical forms, and bringing women's issues to the center of her performances, feminist performance theory was only in its incipient stages. She is at times taken as a point of reference by feminist theoreticians, though, in my opinion, not often enough.[28] Franca Rame's is the practice which generates the theory which leads to more practice. A feminist performance theorist has noted that this cycle is specific to the tension between feminist performance and theory.[29] Cottino-Jones is right to point out that "Rame's role as performer fits perfectly" Lizbeth Goodman's notion of the female and feminist performer. In the words of Elin Diamond, Rame "plays gender with a vengeance,"[30] while continuously deconstructing and subverting society's conventional gender images. However, when discussing Franca's performance in terms of feminist performance techniques and discourse, one has to avoid pinning her down to any specific form of discourse or to apply too rigidly any particular performance or comic theory. As Farrell has rightly noted, in response to critical remarks brought against Rame by a feminist critic,

> Authentic liberation, in Franca's eyes, was to be found embedded in the experiences of the women featured, not trumpeted in an abstract discourse on patriarchy. Her theater was an arena of voices, all speaking of their distress, but expressing, however awkwardly, a brave optimism that conditions could be changed [203].

It is indeed Franca's polyphony of voices and the carousel of her many faces which constitute the strength of her theater and the freshness of her humor. Rame's theater and her varied female voices and characters illustrate artistically Theresa de Lauretis' broad definition of *women* as "real historical beings" and as "historical subjects," as opposed to *woman*, "a fictional construct," a product of "hegemonic discourse."[31] It is within this historical immediacy and this variety of female voices joined by a common desire to be "respected at home, in the street, at work, without the paternalism with which we are so often gratified" that Rame creates her humor and deliberately converts a tragic reality into a source of laughter and a point of lucid questioning. "The show is comical and even grotesque," she says as a preface to her performance. "We have done it purposefully, for we have been crying for two thousand years, us women. Well! This time we are going to laugh, and even laugh at ourselves."[32] At the same time, she warns her audience that, as Molière once remarked, when one laughs the brain also opens up, and with that the "nails of reason" are planted in it. It is Franca's wish that our brains be planted with the nails of reason produced by laughter.

Franca's Carnival

"As a superb comic performer," notes Cottino-Jones, "Rame has overcome the institutional taboo that sets the comic muse out of the reach of women, and has established herself as an internationally recognized comic interpreter and writer."[33] She further points out that Rame has devoted her professional life to making her and Fo's theater the essential comic space for a satire aimed first at social conventions and then more and more targeted at "the unfairness of the economic and political conditions of contemporary society."[34] At the time when she was experimenting with the genre of one-woman shows and some variety of stand-up comedy and improvisation, in the Italy of the '60s and '70s, her voice and her humor were truly revolutionary and a great act of courage. It even cost her a gruesome attack: a beating and gang rape by a group of neo–Nazi youths.[35] The words that Mayakovsky once uttered about the Stalinist terror might apply to the various steps of women's revolutions as well: "If we weren't really important, they wouldn't be shooting us in public places." If the women's resisting voices and their various forms of comedy weren't as powerful as they are threatening to patriarchy, they wouldn't be repressed with such vehemence. It has been rightly noted that Franca is one of a kind and does not have much of a precedent in the history of theater: a militant feminist writer, performer, director, comedian, improviser.

While Franca's uniqueness as an artist with a larger-than-life social and stage persona is undeniable, I believe it does her a disservice to disconnect her art and comedy from a women's tradition of performance. I will therefore attempt to look at her comedy and to analyze the various layers of her transgressive humor in light of the tradition of women's performance developed in the commedia dell'arte genre, to detect links with other forms of women's performative traditions, such as storytelling and vaudeville, as well as place her special kind of humor within the context of feminist performance and comedy.

As we have seen in the discussion of the many links between Franca and the commedia dell'arte, she, like Isabella Andreini and Catherine Biancolelli, also learned from and started her performing career, in emulation of female family members: "I learned to move and speak onstage quite unselfconsciously, and picked up the parts by listening to my mother and older sisters act them out night after night."³⁶ Many of the plays that she and Fo co-wrote and performed together often had as a starting point either stories handed down in Fo's family or, as noted earlier, scenarios kept in Rame's family. Fo's mother notes, "The stable was everything for us peasants, in those times, especially for women, it was a church, because we prayed there, it was a theater, because storytellers would sing and narrate for hours."³⁷

What I believe to be particularly interesting and awe-inspiring is the way in which Franca Rame incorporates in her art and comedy some of Italy's richest performative traditions: the carnivalesque dimensions of the commedia, the improvisational art of the early commedia actresses, the tradition of subversive women's humor, and the narrative soulfulness of storytelling. She channels all of it toward the creation of a revolutionary, political, feminist theater, giving voice to women from all walks of life. Her comment that she was surprised to hear only women's laughter at the performance of *Abbiamo tutte la stessa storia* validates the theories of several feminist humor theoreticians that, while women's humor remains more often than not unrecognized as such by men, it is usually understood and appreciated by other women.

In Rame's comedy all the forms of women's humor discussed so far coexist and culminate in a performative experience, which may be as embarrassing and threatening to men as it is comforting and satisfying for women. Her performance draws from a wealth of sources — from the art of jesters and buffoons,³⁸ the carnivalesque reversals of hierarchies, the art of improvisation, the biting sarcasm of the Colombinas, the madness of Isabella, and the general bawdiness of the commedia — to create a comedy which is overtly angry. It gives voice to the liminal in society and breaks with "norms four thousand years old," exploding the law and breaking up the language, as promoted by Cixous, which itself turns the tables on the Freudian idea of woman as lack and, in Frances Gray's words, "takes the idea of lack out of language."

Franca's is the carnival to end all carnivals with the big difference that through the parts she creates, the world upside down is supposed to stay like that for a while, at least until the most vulnerable and the marginalized of society achieve some equality and the distribution of power is balanced out between those who normally have it and those who don't. Franca's performance is the best example of shifting positions of power at the level of gender roles through subversive humor and transgressive comedy.

Franca discusses the specificity of women's humor over the centuries, and points out the fact that it is precisely the comedy and the humor of women, whether jugglers, storytellers or professional actresses, whose main goal has been to combat the various anxieties related to sexuality, through bawdiness and laughter. "Obscenity has always been," she says, the most efficient weapon against the threat that authority has installed in the heads of people, by instilling the notion of error, shame and the anxiety of sin.... To combat this anxiety through laughter has always been the main task of comic actors and in particular of actresses.[39]

Entirely faithful to her principles, Rame has developed the stage persona of a *giullaressa*, or female jester, dealing in her monologues with a wide array of sexual matters, anything from the linguistic stigma placed on the vocabulary of female sexuality and body parts, to sexual violence, to female orgasm, to various aspects of sexual politics and domination, to the various aspects of sexual pleasure and enjoyment. D'Arcangeli has rightly noted that Rame has revived the tradition of the female jester who is quite different from her male counterpart, "mainly through the overt eroticism in the comic part freed both from religious guilt and the heavily erotic innunedos of modern theater but maintaining the ingenuousness and naturalness of the peasant world."[40]

Franca is the full-fledged twentieth century female clown or trickster, whose performance bears all the signs of modernity while resuscitating the theatrical professionalism of the traditional commedia troupes and returning to the buffoon or clown character the full intensity, passion, and devilishness of ancient times. In the show entitled *Toss the Lady Out,* for which Fo and Rame trained with the Colombaioni brothers, the two were called Clown Dario and Clown Franca. In his discussion of clowns, Fo recognizes the female jesters as one of the two main sources of the commedia dell'arte: "It could be said that the characters of the commedia were born of an obscene marriage between female jesters on the one hand and storytellers and clowns on the other hand, and that, after this act of incest, commedia spawned hosts of other clowns."[41] It could be said that Franca Rame is precisely the offspring of such a marriage. Her humor, her performance, and her characters contain the full register of the commedia comic parts, while dealing with the widest array of issues pertaining to the condition and status of women in today's world.

However, one aspect of Rame's comedy needs to be noted. She never acts in drag or cross-dresses and both she, as a performer, and her women characters are fully, unabashedly heterosexual and female. Franca believes in creating and rediscovering the female tradition of the buffoon, not an androgynous or primarily male version of it which women performers would copy and emulate, but one in which the female body and that which may be specific to women's personality is brought into relief and not erased. She is critical of the female mimes or clowns who try to crate a male persona by effacing the signs of their femininity in costume and act, though she does acknowledge the theatrical and comic value of acting in disguise. But, she notes, this is done only after the identity of the woman has first been established as such in front of the audience.[42] This attitude is of course at odds with a certain trend of feminist performance theory, particularly with advocates of Judith Butler's theories of the relativity of anything that might reek of a gender "essence." And Rame did in fact find herself under attack by various feminist groups (Farrell). To such actual or potential attacks, the open defense of pluralism within feminist theory and performance advocated by such critics as Annette Kolodny or Patricia Schroeder is, I believe, the most constructive position to hold. As Schroeder has eloquently articulated it,

> the variety of available theatrical forms is one of the strengths of the contemporary theater, and feminists can and should take advantage of this variety. To deny women playwrights this freedom, to insist that their plays cannot be considered feminist unless they adhere to a particular ideological stance within feminism or that they take shape in a certain prescribed dramatic form, is to create feminist literary canon which, like more traditional canons, would become self-referential and self-reinforcing, a touchstone system.[43]

Rame goes back to myth for inspiration about comic females and notes, "The first comic beings, in the first mythological discourses, were women," and that "the comic spectacle was a fundamental act in all rites of initiations." All space first had to be rendered sacred by the "comic woman." This first comic woman is the shameless Baubo, the one responsible for "the return of joy and of life in creation ... in the world of men."[44] Rame's humor is as complex as it is unapologetically female. It defies definition while inscribing itself in the line of a women's tradition of comedy. It is carnivalesque in its sexual discourse and in the subject matter, in its questioning of hierarchies based on gender differences, though celebrating difference at the same time.

The first example I would like to look at is Rame's open and comical discussion with the audience of the linguistic differences in status and between the terms designating the male and the female genital organs. Indeed, on both literal and symbolic levels, Rame's discussion does what Anne Beatts has noted to produce the number one fear in men vis-à-vis women's humor: the mockery of their sexual apparatus. Rame's technique appropriates the carnivalesque reversals between the low and the elevated levels of discourse, and is illustrative of Bergson's notion of the linguistic humor of "transposition," in which the solemn is changed into the familiar or the trivial, or vice versa, in which something trivial is turned into something solemn or dignified. In light of the history of performance, Rame inscribes herself in the line of *dell'arte* and medieval farce bawdiness, with the difference that the female organs are introduced and named as well. Appropriating the discursive form of classical tragedy, Rame creates a hymn to the Phallus, after which she uses Dante's terza rima from the *Inferno* to illustrate the stigma carried by its female counterparts in an open and ironic mode which prefigures Eve Ensler's *Vagina Monologues*, her famous exploration of female sexuality and the discriminatory dimensions inherent in the language which expresses it.

The elevated language of Euripides becomes, under Rame's magic improvisational wand, the vehicle for demythologizing the mighty Phallus:

> Here appears in all his glory, the noble Hermion;
> In front of him, all armed, raising his visor,
> The invincible Phallus and Gland, his older brother
> Splendid, rising his puffing stallion
> Scrotum, erecting high between the flags
> The heroic Penis attacking the enemy.[45]

When she attempts to perform a similar aesthetic leap by using the terms which designate female parts, Rame ironically points out the incongruent dimensions of such juxtapositions by stressing, on the contrary, the vulgarity of the terms: "When Briseis the sweet advanced slowly,/love of the Pleiades, one saw rebelling/Clitoris in furor." She stops the recitation in the middle and comments: "Clitoris, it's awful, repugnant. But vulva, vagina, ovaries, it's not any better. Who therefore nailed us with such names! Brrr ... I get goose bumps only at the thought of a poem with the word 'vulva' in it.... Maybe in a passage in Dante, in the song of Hell" [she goes on to improvise in Dantesque discourse] "A terrifying beast appeared to my eyes,/hairy, horrible and grinding its teeth,/ferocious/All trembling, I immediately recognized its traits: this beast was the vulva, and I was snapped up alive" (20).

In direct conversation with the audience, which is one of her great strengths,[46] Rame picks up on the most common stereotypes of gender and sexuality, and turns the tables on them. Rame laughs in the face of century-old beliefs, first articulated by Aristotle, which strictly glorify and validate Man and Phallic dominance as almost exclusively worthy of the tragic mode, while allocating for Woman, her experience and her sexuality, the liminal space which is neither the tragic nor the comic, but some form of the grotesque and the ridiculous. As has been noted before, Aristotle denied women "the capacity to exemplify tragic virtues"[47] on account of their inferiority which places them only a notch higher than slaves.[48] He more indulgently accepts the presence of women in comedy, particularly at the level of the grotesque and the ridiculous, precisely due to their inferiority. As Gray ironically comments, the fact that, according to Aristotle, women are inferior beings "would be no obstacle to their providing suitable butts for laughter — indeed, inferiority would give them a head start" (25).

In anatomical terms, Rame plays on the age-old beliefs which started with Hippocrates, were further developed and enforced by medieval and Renaissance treatises and cherished all the way into the twentieth century, about the female body being a grotesque or deviant version of the male body.[49] Consequently, the language which designates female body parts and sexuality must partake of that same sense of the grotesque, the ridiculous, and the abnormal as the reality it is supposed to point to. Franca has a big Baubo laugh at all this and in her Dantesque rendition, she laughs at the *vagina dentata* motif, exemplifying precisely the kind of female humor that men could easily do without, as suggested in the *Feminist Dictionary*: "There is no imputation of humourlessness if she does not find impotence, castration and vaginas with teeth humorous." As Franca goes on to play with and to explore the potential for grotesque poetry in the terminology for female body parts, she also obliquely explodes Dante's own dichotomic representations of women in his *Inferno*, where the desexualized Maria, Beatrice, and Lucia are given divine and angelic status and represent the positive side of femininity, while Medusa, the Furies, and ancient prostitutes like Thais are given the status of monsters and represent the reprehensible side of the feminine.

Parodying canonical works of art and changing high literature into burlesque comedy is not unknown to the commedia tradition. We have noted, in the discussion of Colombina, the hilarious parody of the Euripidean tragedy *Medea*, in which Catherine Biancolelli plays with the ancient myth and turns the feared character of Medea into a no-nonsense woman who not only stands up to Jason/Arlequin, but exposes him in the full glory of his fatuous arrogance. Parodies of classical plays were part of the general repertory of the commedia troupes. Rame's use of classical tragedy and Dantesque discourse to discuss male and female sexual parts contains both elements of the commedia tradition of the burlesque and that of the sexual humor of the carnival. At the same time, her use of the commedia tradition acquires an overtly feminist dimension when she breaks the taboo of women not using obscene or sexual language and when, in the words of Ron Jenkins, she deals, in her monologues, "with sexual politics."[50] Jenkins comments on Franca's extraordinary ease in talking abut sex and using richly sexual language onstage, which even made him blush several times in front of the audience. Rame breaks up the Freudian notion that all sexual humor is "smut" which inherently implies man's aggressiveness versus woman's passivity, and which invariably leads to the real or imagined presence of a woman. According to Freud, "smut" "will force a woman to imagine her own sexual organs, or herself engaged in the sexual act, and it will make it clear that the teller of the joke is also doing so."[51] Thus, through "smut" humor the woman is invariably objectified and made fun of. Rame's sexual humor is the opposite of Freudian "smut." Franca's characters resist objectification, resist their position as butts of male humor, and reveal simultaneously their own desires for sexual fulfillment together with their anguish, revolt and despair at the multiple forms of sexual domination.

The character in *Una donna sola* (*A Woman Alone*) exposes, with bitter sarcasm and winning candor, the brutality of sexual and physical abuse, the layers of hypocrisy hidden behind the word *love*, the daily indignities this woman has to suffer from her husband, brother-in-law, a perverse phone prankster, and ultimately even her young lover. The woman in *Contrasto ad una sola voce* (*Dialogue in One Voice*) tricks her lover into letting her achieve sexual climax and literally "be on top"; the woman in *Abiamo tutte la stessa storia* (*We All Have the Same Story*) reveals, like the one in *Una donna sola*, the female character's sexual dissatisfaction in the relationship with her husband, and pours her anger into the milk she is feeding her newborn baby. The woman in *Sesso? No, grazie tanto per gradire* (*Sex? No, Thanks for Asking*) teaches women a variety of "performance tricks" for faking orgasm. Rame turns "smut" upside down and then explodes it altogether. Her characters expose the authors of "smut" in the full glaring reality of their politics of sexual domination and demolish the dignity of the mythic "Invincible Phallus." Through her characters, Rame combines the ancient female jester with the sarcastic Colombina and the militant feminist all in one.

In Franca's carnival, the motif of "the woman on top" is given a literal existence onstage. In *Contrasto ad una sola voce*, she incorporates medieval and Renaissance discourse of love poetry reminiscent of the *lais* of Marie de France, of courtly love poetry, and of lovers' dialogues of the kind written by Isabella Andreini or given as example by Perrucci into a modern monologue in which the female character leads the audience, step by step, toward the discovery that she has played a trick on her lover in order to achieve sexual satisfaction. Almost the entire monologue follows the different steps of the sexual act. The woman has both the voice and the lead in guiding her lover's actions. She controls and slows down the man's desire, step by step, in a language which, in its archaic tone and poetic expression, in its fluidity and sensuousness, bears echoes of the famous discourses of love throughout history, from the lovers in the stories of Marie de France, to the epic love poem of Tristan and Isolde, to Romeo and Juliet, to the inamorati of the commedia dell'arte. And she does it all in subtle parodic form and with tinges of irony. She gently undresses her lover herself, saying "My beautiful honey, my spring, you are all in flames, do you have a fever?" As her lover, who has just climbed into her room through the window, soaked from having stood under her window in the rain all evening in courtly love style, is trying to warm up next to the fire, she warns: "Move away from the fire, you will fry your little round buttocks...." She calls him "my lotus," "my sweet sugar," "tender flower of love," "the beautiful animal that you are," "my little mouse," "my angel." She guides her lover to undress her, but slowly, not like "a brutal adored tearer." As they are both naked and foreplay is on its way, she again guides his desire and slows him down, calling him this time "barbarian invader and Turk and Sarasin, what are we already ready to hit the sack?" The woman controls the man's desire and speech all at once, "Sht, let me speak, I have enough words for both of us! ... No, stay there ... slowly, without rushing, don't go alone on the waves, swim on the sea next to me ... I don't want to stay alone, I could drown.... You know how to draw from me unknown sounds, and flowers and cries like poems. You are like the sea which swells." She thus guides both of them to the sexual climax, in gentle speech and sensuous action.

The next day, in Juliet style, realizing they have slept too late, she complains that "neither the lark, nor the rooster, nor the other birds" have woken her up. She reveals with a cunning laugh that her parents were not at home, as she had let him believe in order to subdue his noisy sexual rush, and confesses with great satisfaction that she has enjoyed the sexual reversal of the previous night: "I had to try! Always submissive I had to stay in the game of love ... the man on top and me at the bottom, like a prey, always. This time I reversed the roles! And well, I have greatly enjoyed this new situation." She ends by also reversing the well-known metaphor of the woman as a bird caught in a cage: "Oh, my beautiful love: you have come to set a trap and I caught you in the trap! Go, poor bird catcher!!" The ending love song celebrates the *jouissance* and love of both the man and the woman.

Rame's discourse and performance makes use of canonical poetic and dramatic forms, of common places of love poetry and, just as her character reverses her sexual position and the rhythm of the sexual act, Rame reverses all of these forms and re-inscribes them within a new discourse which acquires a level of intimacy, of discontinuity and openness which constitute a breakthrough in modern theater. These reversals and new dramatic discourse and theatrical action bear common points with that which many feminist theoreticians from Cixous, to Irigaray, to Gayatry Spivak, have attempted to delineate as "women's writing." As Christine Miller has remarked, "Women's writing may be like quilt making; both stem from the 'organization of material in fragments,' a process that encourages rearrangement, new form."[52] And Anaïs Nin notes that "writers know their text as a form of intimacy, of personal contact, whether conversations with the reader or with the self. Letters, journals, voices are sources for this element ... expressing the porousness and non-hierarchic stances of intimate conversations in both structure and function."[53] In theater, "the performance of a play, poem, or story by a woman, in a woman's voice, onstage or some public space, can still be a powerful thing, made more powerful by the presence of an audience," says Lizbeth Goodman.[54]

At the time when Rame started writing, producing and performing, her one-woman shows were not only "a powerful thing," but quite a revolutionary thing. As Valeri has eloquently phrased it, "In today's world of female stand-up comics and one-woman shows, it is hard to imagine the pioneering courage that was necessary 35 years ago for a woman to engage in this act of theatrical 'virility'" (3). Indeed, while creating a discourse and performance which bear the marks of women's writing and performance, Rame's reversals of canonical forms and of gender roles can be equated with "theatrical virility," in the sense of appropriating, as Colombina did many centuries before, male-created forms, poses, behaviors and re-creating them, with humor and irony, in a voice and a performative mode which subvert them as it simultaneously transform them into useful tricks for the female character-performer-voice. The character in Rame's *Contrasto* unfolds as a sensuous, poetic Colombina, as she plays her trick of role reversal for the purpose of reaching sexual satisfaction. Indeed, Colombina was the "dove" who, like Rame's woman, always caught the "bird-catcher." If Colombina always turned social relations and structures on their head by means of cunning, trickery and cross-dressing to achieve a level of personal contentment and justice, Rame's character does that at the level of intimate relations and sexuality. Though Rame never cross-dresses, the actions of her character in this play clearly illustrate the reversal of the conventional status of women as passive objects of male desire. The beautiful irony of the *contrasto* is that the heroine is simultaneously taking possession of language as she is asserting herself sexually, being literally "on top" in the sexual act and metaphorically, in the act of communication.

The positioning of the woman at the balcony and then in the intimacy of her alcove or room continues the tradition of courtly love, and to some extent that of the early commedia dell'arte. In Scala's collection of scenarios, Isabella alone or together with Flaminia quite often conducts entire scenes from a balcony. The balcony delineates the private space to which women are most often confined, as opposed to the piazza, or public square, as the space where men act, function, and interact with other men. But rather than the man being allowed access into the private space of the woman and proceeding to a seduction, it is the woman who takes all initiative and leads the game of love with words accompanied by gestures. The man's reactions or words are only implied or suggested in the heroine's monologue, as when she asks him to not be so noisy, to slow down his desire, to not raise his voice, to not get too close to the fire, to let her breathe and take it easy. As Cottino-Jones has noted, Rame's theater illustrates Lizbeth Goodman's "feminist performance art theater," which "emphasizes the role of the performer as the representer of herself— her body as text; her self as character ... her movements as symbolic of the gestures and rituals of everyday life."[55] What is remarkable is that Rame indeed creates a feminist performance which even bears some of the signs of postmodern art and performance[56] while re-creating, modernizing and giving new life to traditional theatrical forms. But since the commedia dell'arte was the first Western theatrical form which gave women a central place onstage and in the creative process, it makes a lot of sense that Rame would make use of precisely those forms.

The language and the rhythm of Rame's discourse also bears resemblance to the early *commedia* "contrasti" of the kind written by Isabella Andreini or given as example by Perrucci, with the difference that, rather than the two-voice exchange of the *commedia*, Rame's play is a one-voice monologue and the voice is always a woman's. The terms of affection derive from the discourses and *contrasti* of the inamorati, only they become comical because of their unexpected, often exaggerated tone. For instance, a lover's exchange in one of Perrucci's *contrasti* consists of a rapid succession of affectionate terms between the Uommo and Donna: "Mia speme/amor mio/mia vita/mio bene/mia luce/mio respiro/mia Dea/Idolo mio" ("My love/my life/my good/my light/my breath/my Goddess/My Idol"). Syntactically, Rame's heroine uses the similar formulaic structures of the possessive pronominal adjective preceding a noun, such as "tesoro mio," (my treasure), "amore mio," "caro mio." But besides these common ones, most of her terms of affection are rather unexpected, as for instance in the following passage: "my perdition, my saliva, my rose liquor," "my lotus," and "my flower of tender love." It is as if the woman had appropriated both the male and the female's terms of endearment from the traditional *contrasti*, thus extending the role reversals to both language and action, and blurring gender signs at the level of language and sexual initiative altogether. The usual poetic comparisons specific to Renaissance poetry between the woman and the flower are reversed and appropriated by the woman to express her own feelings of love and desire.

The humor of this piece is gentle and full of poetry, though not in the least deprived of irony. The reversals of linguistic and sexual initiative contain an implicit criticism of the conventional behavior of men: silencing the woman, objectifying her in the sexual act, giving sexual heed to their desire without consideration for the woman's experience of pleasure or lack thereof. However, the humor and poetry of the play derive, not so much from proselytizing about women's sexual liberation, but from the full and unashamed expression of the character's experience of pleasure in the newly discovered literal and metaphoric position of power. Though filled with irony toward the man's rush to consummate the sexual act, the woman's discourse and performance are neither demeaning nor do they try to dominate; they just lead, guide and, yes, trick the man into a form of sexual democracy, wherein both partners can fully experience the pleasures of sexuality. This form of humor is in line with that mythic fertility ritual laughter, in which, as Gray has subtly noted, "the emphasis was rather on the sexual power and pleasure of the goddess." It is precisely the kind of comedy that Rame creates in this piece. The sensuous and often unexpected or downright funny terms of endearment used by the woman reflect, even in their controlled, syncopated rhythm, a humbling, a bringing to human dimensions and vulnerability of the all too powerful "invincible phallus." The rhythm of her discourse, following the rhythm of her guided sexual pleasure in which the man's uncontrolled urgency is implied, would bring smiles to most women's faces: "Stop, stop, let me breathe, slowly my love. The earthquake will wake up the entire neighborhood.... Golden Sarasin, go slowly, no need for such hunger. Calmly, calmly, breathe, give me my breath, there is still a lot of time until we will hear the song of the birds" (91).

The woman's voice in *Contrasto*, as she simultaneously contains and makes ironic the man's words and gestures, in a constantly "dialogic discourse," performs what Judy Little has called "humoring" and "carnivalizing the sentence."[57] Little argues that the comic style of a large number of women writers and playwrights displays the characteristic of a juxtaposition of voices, in which the voice of authority is both contained and parodied, or deconstructed. Such a comic voice, argues Little, "may not be typical of realistic drama, but in some experimental plays by women juxtaposed styles occur occasionally within a voice, and the result is carnivalized discourse" (158). Rame performs this carnivalization throughout the piece, through the voice of her female character, not solely at the level of discourse, but at the level of gesture and action as well. One can divine the man's words and gestures from the voice of the woman, only in parodied, transformed and ironical manner. For instance, as the man climbs into the woman's room, soaked from the rain, the dialogue that must take place between the lovers is contained in the woman's speech alone, and both the man's gestures and words are transformed into an ironic discourse:

> Holy Virgin how you are soaked! ... No, one moment, stay away, you have completely soaked me! Couldn't you have shaken yourself a little before climbing up, as dogs do! Look a little bit on the floor! No, no, my sweet love and sacred ... forgive me ... I do not want to mock or scold you. Yes, you are right but I beg you, don't raise your voice, with your thick voice, they are going to hear you [89].

"The juxtaposition of the two voices may result in ridicule of one of the voices and of the ideology it brings along," says Little. Rame's monologue performs this juxtaposition with gusto. As it passes through the woman's voice, both the man's voice and actions appear in their glaring insensitivity or in their tyrannical urgency. But the most succulent humor derives from the woman's incorporating of the man's sexual unrestrained sexual appetite into her own lyrical voice:

> What is it? A tempest! Calmly! How? In order to enter into the fortress, it's useless to tear down the walls.... Oh! What a barbaric invader and a Turk and a Sarazin! What! Are we already ready to hit the sack? Stop, stop! Let me breathe, assuage your love! The earthquake will wake up the entire neighborhood! Quiet for a moment.... Let me listen [91].

Rame "carnivalizes" not only the sentence but the entire stage. Not only her voice but her very performance is dialogic and subversive of the voice and the actions of the male partner. On stage, she is both the woman and the man, and the man's authority, desire and voice are re-inscribed within a voice and a performance which assert themselves as strongly female in their search for circles of pleasure, of laughter, of play, and which ultimately subdue and redirect the performance of the man away from the established canon of linear narrative and linear sexuality, into the spiraling meanders of the woman's own sexuality and lyric voice. The woman in this text and in this performance does that which Cixous has urged women creators to do in "The Laugh of the Medusa": "Woman must write herself: must write about women and bring women to writing, from which they have been driven away as violently as from their bodies.... Woman must put herself into the text — as into the world and into history — by her own movement."[58] Cixous hopes for women to be able to proclaim: "I, too, overflow; my desires have invented new desires, my body knows unheard-of songs."[59] It is what Rame's woman proclaims as well as she laughs joyously and announces at the end of the play: "I greatly enjoyed this crazy inversion!" (93).

The use of trickery by female characters with the goal of obtaining pleasure or turning a disadvantageous situation on its head is not new to the tradition of female humor. Isabella Andreini's inamorata character uses every means at her disposal, including dressing up as a man and feigning madness in order to reach her romantic/sexual goals. The display of a certain amount of sexuality onstage is inscribed in that same tradition. As already noted, in the play *The Old Husband*, Isabella is seen coming onstage all flustered, red, and perspiring "from exertion" after an encounter, right behind her old husband's back, with her young lover. The suggestion of sexual satisfaction and pleasure is rather clear in Scala's scenario. Colombina's maneuvering of social situations which place women in positions of inferiority is mostly aimed at obtaining the most financial and/or sexual gain for herself or her mistress, much in the tradition of the politics of the courtesans, as discussed earlier. And Isabella's Filli from Andreini's play *La Mirtilla* cleverly tricks her male attacker, an aggressive satyr, into giving her her freedom; she then is also free for the union with the man of her choice. As noted in that chapter, Andreini's character is something of a "con-artist courtesan."

Rame's character in this play and others takes the tradition of female tricksters to an extreme where the woman's position of inferiority is entirely reversed, suggesting the possibility and the hope for a new era of better relations between men and women. Indeed, as Farrell has remarked, many of Franca's characters voice "a brave optimism that conditions could be changed" (203). Her laughter is not meant to destroy, demean, or degrade men, even at its angriest. It is meant to stick "the nails of reason" into our heads, it is meant to produce change, it is meant, as Colombina noted at the end of the play *La Femme vengée,* not to insult one's husband, as "it is enough to bring him to reason" (vol. 2, p. 323). Rame's humor is a good illustration of Gloria Kaufman's definition of feminist humor, whose "dominant undercurrent is the pickup, an obvious reversal of the putdown" and which "is based on a vision of change."[60] Rame's humor is also a superb example of the specificity of women's humor across the centuries, which, as noted by Mahadev Apte, does not display the level of aggressiveness of male sexist humor but rather is a humor which reflects the marginal position of women in society while subverting that very marginality. The ultimate goal of Rame's comedy is to instill the confidence, energy and will for both survival and change, for, "By joking we remake ourselves so that after each disappointment we become once again capable of living and loving."[61]

Performing Pleasure — Franca's "Improvisation-Performance" Lesson

Quite a different side of Rame's carnivalesque theater is developed in the most recent piece, coauthored, like most of her pieces, with Dario Fo, and entitled *Sex? Thanks, Don't Mind if I Do.* In discussing this piece, Cottino-Jones remarks that the main goal of the play "seems to be to give reliable information about sex while teaching especially young people to care and respect for the other in their life, and to search for love, pleasure and long-term commitments together" (41). She also notes that, not only does this theatrical piece largely illustrate Lizbeth Goodman's theory of performance art, it "moves even further into feminist performance art theater, by concentrating, in its central part, on Rame as performer representing herself ..." (42).

Since the path I am trying to follow is that of the comic in performance, I will pay particular attention to the central portion of this unusual piece, which consists of Rame's lesson to women about how to fake an orgasm. I am purposefully choosing this piece immediately after the monologue of the woman searching for and experiencing sexual pleasure because I believe these are two facets of the same coin: performing in order to either achieve or pretend the experience of sexual pleasure. Both pieces are poised on the tension between performance and sexuality and the humor in both is, by various degrees, of the kind so much feared by men: it mocks the male "sexual apparatus." As I noted earlier, although Beatts mentions only "the size of the sexual apparatus," I believe this can be extended symbolically to what Franca herself touches upon in her prologue to *Female Parts*: the great arrogance and self-assurance of what men would like to believe is "the invincible phallus," hero of tragedy and epic poetry. The humor of both pieces is comforting for women and humbling for men, and one hopes, it may implant the "nails of reason" into the heads of some lovers and husbands. It is always Franca's hope that it may initiate better sexual relations among men and women. The kind of comedy and laughter Rame produces in these pieces can only be a woman's humor. I find it worth discussing and drawing some conclusions about it.

Although again, this may cause certain feminists to react negatively and some men to respond in anger, Rame is quite open and unapologetic about what she sees as the differences between men and women. In an interview given in 1984, she says the following: "Us women we are made differently from men, even in the way of thinking. We see things in different ways than men, because of the conditions of our lives. There are things to which men could not even arrive."[62] The intensity and the humor of much of Rame's theater derives largely from the unabashed exposing of these differences, from the conflicts which often arise from them, from the power struggle involved in the relations between men and women. These two theatrical monologues dealing with women's sexuality are therefore funny in different ways for women and for men: the women's laughter is open, spontaneous, the kind of laughter which seems to say, "That's exactly how things are, I know exactly what you are talking about"; the men's laughter, as Rame herself noted in her prologue, sounds strained, guttural, almost with "inhuman" tones, as it tries to say "I'm not one of those." There is, however, one simple goal for both types of laughter: love and the achievement of some harmony or understanding in the relations between men and women.

Again, I would like to present Franca's theater in the context of the tradition of female performers of the commedia dell'arte. Negotiating with, manipulating and shaming authoritarian fathers, husbands, and fiancés through performance is a means, for women, of acquiring some level of emancipation, freedom, or, in Rame's own words, "independence from this blessed male."[63] As we have seen, the very idea of theater is linked, at the turn of the twentieth century, according to Susan Glenn, to the emancipation of women, and the very rise of feminism is associated "with the idea of women provoking controversy by making spectacles of themselves" (2). I believe the commedia dell'arte as well did offer women precisely a kind of emancipation which could be seen as a precursor of feminism itself. The female commedia performers were the first ones to appear on the European stages in a variety of comic roles and to assume, proudly, the lifestyle that came with their participation in the theatrical life, and which was in itself a form of emancipation: leaving the house for the public sphere, making themselves seen, admired, desired in public, traveling with male companions halfway across Europe, exposing their faces, voices, bodies, and talents to wide audiences, in short "making spectacles of themselves."

Furthermore, these women took performance and improvisation to its limit by weaving it into their lives, or creating a variety of stage personae which contradicted traditional images of women. It was Isabella's performance in the role of the virtuous, the perfect, the sweet, the innocent woman, the feminine ideal of the Renaissance, that gave her the key to social and professional success and the freedom to travel, to write, to appear publicly, and act in drag onstage, while still being taken seriously in her own time. In Gherardi's theater, it was the many performance lessons of the coquettish Colombine, her many disguises and carousel of performances within each performance, that allowed her and her mistress the freedom to chose their husbands or lovers, or to not chose any for that matter, as well as achieve some vicarious participation in public life. We have also seen that Colombina vehemently argues for the superiority of Italian theater versus French theater, precisely because of the freedom, the thrill, and the creativity involved in the art of improvisation. In conjunction with that, Colombina argues in favor of an Italian husband for her mistress, as opposed to the French suitor. At the time of the commedia, the marriages within the troupe were also emancipated by comparison to the rest of society, as husband and wife together collaborated, created, and improvised, with the woman often taking the lead. The Andreinis and the Biancolellis are excellent examples of these working marriages.

However, judging by Franca's monologues and by what she has to say in her interviews with regard to Italian men and husbands, things must have changed for the worse over the centuries, or at least not improved much. In her own case, her image was tied for decades with that of her husband, and her massive input into his work has often been overlooked. It is after Fo was awarded the Nobel Prize that Franca reveals, with a poignant metaphor, the role and the burden that she carried in the collaboration with Fo. She calls him a "monument" and herself the "pedestal" on which the "monument" is resting. Anderlini D'Onofrio is right to point out "the absurdity of exclusively awarding the prize to a man who claims he could not have deserved it without the contributions of his collaborator and wife of 45 years, namely actress, activist, editor, co-writer, archivist, and *fille d'art* Franca Rame."[64] Strange as it may seem, the theatrical and artistic collaboration of the Andreinis 500 years prior seems to have been more democratic, more emancipated and more to the advantage of the woman than that of Fo and Rame. Critics of various orientations, both male and female, have by now acknowledged and proven in abundance that it was Rame who taught Fo the art of improvisation and that it was only through her creative input and insight, through her feminism and activism that Fo's theater has taken its political and subversive direction. Yet it is only for the past couple of decades that Franca has started to be recognized fully as a comedian and writer in her own right. Inversely, five centuries ago, Isabella and Francesco Andreini and their troupe became world famous due to the many talents of Isabella, who was encouraged to shine and admired as a creator in her own right.

By reading comtemporary reports about Isabella and about and by Franca, one can conclude that commedia dell'arte, with its freedom of improvisation and with the appreciation it once gave female performers, offers at least a productive metaphor of the emancipation of women both privately and socially. Franca herself deplores the fact that of all places, Italy is now the country where one sees the fewest outdoor or street theater performances, while they flourish everywhere else in the world.[65]

In Franca's theater, it is the private, intimate realm of women's lives in which the element of performance and improvisation is introduced and used as means of emancipation. Franca, like the commedia performers before her, and like the famous French actress Sarah Bernhardt, and like many of the comic performers of today, has also "built a public persona by deliberately acting out of the bounds of traditional female behavior, in part by calling attention to her own self-importance."[66] She is also part of a line of performers who "became agents and metaphors of changing gender relations,"[67] asserting women's rights to equality both in society and in the bedroom. The relationship between women's emancipation, sexual relations and improvisatory performance is a fascinating one and it can give us a valuable insight into the mechanisms of negotiations that women have and can use in their relations with the other sex, in both the public and private realms.

Why is a piece like Franca's section from *Sex? No, Thanks for Asking* so outrageously funny? Precisely because improvisation, performance and sexuality are tied to each other in what becomes ultimately a huge mockery of male insensitivity in sexual relations. Somewhat in the line of the sexual mockeries and impersonations by women in various societies that Mahadev Apte analyzes in his study on the anthropology of humor, Rame's mock-didactic performance on how to fake an orgasm is as funny and comforting for women as it is shaming for men. If public performance gave women the chance to participate in the artistic life of society, the private performance of women in the bedroom frees them to some extent from the pressure of anger and discontent of their husbands. Although the very idea of "faking an orgasm," or performing pleasure rather than experiencing it, is counterintuitive and cannot replace the actual feeling or sensation, the very act of exposing women's expressions of the throes of passion as *performance* is an indirect denunciation of the inadequacy of certain men in the performance of the sexual act. Rame is giving onstage the performance of a performance of faking something, in this case, sexual pleasure. She illustrates the palimpsest of roles and performative tricks that women are often conditioned to play, like the many disguises of Colombina, at all levels of their lives. At best, says Rame with unfazed sarcasm, this multilayered performance may eventually, lead the woman to actually experience pleasure: "American sexologists have studied this problem and come to the conclusion that if a woman can successfully fake an orgasm, with a credible acting job, twice a day for at least three years, in the end, miraculously, she'll actually have one." At worst, it may lead to "frustration ... neuroses ... and instead of reacting by educating ourselves and trying to find the reason for it ... we cry and we stuff ourselves with pills."[68]

As with so much comedy by women, the core of their laughter is either angry, sad, or both. The answer to the question that Rame gives the audience to her — "Why do we fake it? — is simple as it is unnerving: "So as not to disappoint ... to gratify.... You're fantastic!"[69] She elaborates on that: "Men are so sure of their innate splendor, of their sexual potency, that they would never imagine, 'You don't enjoy it with me???!!!'"[70] For, if truth be found out, it may be that, just like "the prophets of the so-called sexual revolution of the late sixties" your partner may just find you as the perfect illustration of the well "proven" theory that "a woman's inability of having an orgasm is simply the unconscious refusal to have one, in order to get revenge on the husband."[71] Therefore the ultimate goal of miming sexual pleasure is first and foremost that of reinforcing even more the centrality, the omnipotence of the male subject. The woman, as Irigaray has theorized, "is positioned as mirror to the male, reflecting back to him — thereby demonstrating the truth of his centrality — his own image, his Self-Same."[72] Before Irigaray and the development of performance theory studies, Virginia Woolf noted the same thing: "Women have served all these centuries as looking glasses possessing the magic and delicious power of reflecting the figure of man at twice its natural size."[73] The "ohs," the "aaahhs," and in particular the "Dio, Dio, Dio" produced by a woman in the performance of faking an orgasm, have precisely the function of offering men this delicious size enhancement of their own image.

Only Rame breaks the mirror, through her mimicry of enthrallment. Turning sexuality into performance and, furthermore, into a miming kind of performance, brings us to Bergson's notion of the mechanical overlapping the human as major source of comedy, giving one "the illusion of a machine working inside the person." Furthermore, as Glenn has noted, "Imitation and mimicry brought laughter ... because 'our gestures can only be imitated in their mechanical uniformity'" (83–84). That the most natural, intimate and what can be the most physically pleasurable human activity is turned into a mechanical activity is both tragic as it is comical: it is grotesque. By performing the mechanics of sexual miming onstage, Rame exposes, deconstructs and destabilizes precisely the "truth of the centrality" of man, "his own image, his Self-Same." The woman may not experience sexual pleasure, but she will at least have a last laugh: "Ha, I fooled *you*!" Just like in the famous orgasm-faking restaurant scene performed by Meg Ryan in the film *When Sally Met Harry*, it is ultimately the man who, once the mimicry is exposed, is left to wonder, question, worry about whether his partner is or is not having an actual climax, and it is his own confidence which is shaken. Rame addresses the men in the audience with wicked satisfaction: "Men, now that I've put the flea in your ear, I'm going to give you the key for discovering whether your partner, during sex, simulates or really reaches." And she proceeds to give a set of signs which would show that the woman is actually reaching orgasm: the curling of the toes, the dilating of the pupils. The whole thing becomes so absurd that the entire mystique of sex is exploded right there in front of the audience. Imagine the husband who, in the middle of intercourse, tries to pry open his wife's eyes to see the size of her pupils, or to turn around from whatever position he may be in, to watch the status of her toes. Sex itself becomes a huge comedy in which everybody in the audience is exposed. Rame fakes regret at having spoiled it for men: "Men, I'm sorry to have ruined your next sexual encounter.... I can see you now ... there you are ... working away ... ready for the big moment ... sweating all over ... and as soon as she [moans] 'Ahhaaha' ... you'll be saying [mimes inspecting of toes and eyes]: 'Eyes-toes-eyes-toes.'" (82).

By miming the sexual act and deconstructing it into its various stages,

Rame destroys the very mystique of sexuality and pleasure in the Western world. After her last "ohhhh" has quieted, she resumes the dialogue with the audience by stating, "We in modern times are the first people in history to confront the problem of pleasure" (85). Her performance in no way sends the message that men and women should not search for pleasure, but it does send the message that something in the hunt for pleasure has gone awry and, in the process, women have suffered from various forms of objectification, which in itself is a degraded form of sexuality. For the relations between men and women to regain authenticity, freshness, and to unfold on the basis of trust and mutual pleasure, the mystique, the routines, the "performance" of sexuality must be denounced and overturned. Ultimately, Franca's performative mimicry in this scene subverts itself as it becomes an anti-performance statement. There should be instances in one's life, her underlying message seems to be, when there should be *no* roles, *no* playing, just "being" in the first degree, truthfully, with no masks, no mirrors, no performance.

The comedy of mimicry has also a rich tradition among female performers and represents a fascinating facet of the many ways that women performers throughout the history of theater, and women in society, have subverted mainstream culture and destabilized the very notions of authenticity, of high culture, and patriarchy in general. Susan Glenn offers, in her book on female spectacle, an ample and insightful analysis of the female vaudeville comedians who specialized in mimicry at the turn of the century. This form of comedy, she argues,

> did more than merely facilitate and legitimate new forms of female aggression and competitiveness, which in any case constituted only one element in the mimic's vaudeville repertoire. More significant was the way mimicry engaged both its practitioners and its audiences in a wider conversation about questions of selfhood, individuality, and creativity in the urban industrial age [80].

Most revolutionary, claims Glenn, was the challenge from "those who claimed that to mimic was not just to copy — it was also to originate" (83). In other words, mimicry is a form of art in itself, and mimicry, by the laughter it engenders and the questions it elicits, is just as good a form of art as any. The art of mimes over the centuries has already taught us that. Rame herself talks about female mimes in her interviews, and it is a well-known fact that miming was one of the most important tricks of the trade of the commedia dell'arte performers. Rame mimes women's miming of an imaginary idea of what the woman's response to sexual pleasure may be in a "ahhhhahhhhah" or "Oh Mamma," or the "religious epiphany" kind: "Dio. Dio. Dio. Dio. Oh Dio!," "Holy virgin!," and with the appropriate gestures: "lift up your hips. Feet

firmly on the ground. Shoulders back. Arms free. Undulate. Don't lose your
balance. Count to twelve" (85). She concludes, "Orgasm achieved," with the
satisfaction of acting well done. If not the physical pleasure, the woman may
at least claim to have experienced the pleasure of having fully drawn her audience, that is her sexual partner, into her performance, with no suspension of
disbelief.

Rame's miming and lesson in miming illustrate beautifully the techniques
of improvisation of the commedia actors: it contains parataxis, "formulaic
wording" as well as gestures which can be rearranged in a variety of possible
combinations; it has a repetitive dimension, is combined with a level of spontaneity, and has "a rhythmic base."[74] Rame gives her female audience a mock
lesson into the art of improvisation: learn a set of expressions and gestures
and use them, combine them, according to the situation, the context, the
partner. Like the commedia actors, you will have the same and yet a different
play every night. You have your main *topos*, the "fixed part"[75] of the wife
enraptured by her husband's charm and potency, you have a set of formulaic
expressions, your "Oh Mamma," or "Dio Dio Dio," or the various sounds
and moans which are supposed to express pleasure and thrill. For instance,
when she gives as a possible exclamation of pleasure the expression "Oh
Mamma," she warns women to be careful when and with whom to use it, for
if the man is an orphan, he may just start crying for his mother in the middle
of intercourse. In that case, she continues, they can use the "religious
epiphany" formula. For each moment in the sexual act, Rame gives women
a set of variants that they can use according to the situation. The abundant
ellipses, interruptions, and the generally fragmented nature of Rame's discourse
illustrate precisely the element of spontaneity involved in the art of improvisation. Parataxis is used throughout this scene with practically no subordinate
clauses, with all the verbs being in the present indicative or imperative, which
are the tenses of choice for commedia improvisers, as they are simplest and
most direct to invent and use onstage. Rame gives women the "stable blocks"[76]
of the show which they can use and recreate in the context of their "audience,"
their "stage," and according to their own imagination. Moreover, Rame illustrates with her own body, as the commedia actors used to do, what Tessari
has called "an efficient rhetoric of gestures,"[77] and proves that a good actor of
improvisation makes use of her/his entire person and body words and gestures
combined.[78]

What is funny in a bitter sort of way is that, while actual improvisation
onstage involves lucid collaboration between the acting partners, in this particular case, the success of the particular improvisation she is teaching is based
solely on the woman's act and the man's total ignorance of it as such. The

woman is the better actor, but at the end of the performance, her success as an improviser is achieved at the price of her lack of actual pleasure, and the lack of authenticity of the experience. Ultimately, the entire play is a failure from the start. As critics of the commedia starting in the fifteenth century have pointed out, the success of the genre depends largely on the fact that all actors involved must be on their toes to be equally versed and to collaborate with their onstage partners for the show to be successful. In the case of Rame's mock sexual improvisation, the two actors are entirely at odds, badly timed and uncoordinated in spirit and gesture. Thus the woman's "co-actor" actually becomes her audience, but an audience which has derived pleasure from the selfish act of objectifying, and using the actress to reinforce his centrality. In fact, this is ultimately an example of bad improvisation, for the best improvisation of the commedia actors was the collaborative, the interactive kind, and as critics like Molinari have noted, the unique dimensions of the *commedia* improvisation consisted in the level of camaraderie established among the actors, in the fact that, by the very nature of improvisation, no one could actually monopolize the stage and be a solo player for too long. What is also funny in a bitter sort of way is that the element of spontaneity involved in both good improvisation and good sex is destroyed and turned to a mechanical and repetitive activity which involves pre-learned expressions and gestures. Thus the imaginary scene that Rame creates onstage using her own body ends up being in fact an example of failed improvisation, and illustrating, more than the fluid and creative use of improvisatory techniques, their transformation into a Bergsonian set of mechanical actions which give "the illusion of a machine working inside the person."

Ultimately, as the woman is the one who shortchanges herself in this act of solo mechanical improvisation, the goal of Rame's outrageous and raw comedy is to instill a level of lucidity, receptivity and attentiveness in the male "performers" to their female partners, and, for the female "performers," to NOT follow her lesson in *performing* sex, but her lesson in actually *experiencing* it. The good kind of improvisation, like good sex, is the one which, although based on certain learned actions, gestures and expressions, or rather, on a certain experience and on a certain feel, is like jazz improvisation: fluid, with moments of spontaneity, collaborative, with the partners "performing 'solos' against a given rhythmic base."[79]

The good kind of sexual improvisation is beautifully illustrated by Franca's character in the lyrical piece analyzed earlier, in which the female performer is truly improvising in a creative dance with her partner, cunningly, but poetically "tricking" him into mutual pleasure. Taviani has noted that the best art of the commedia actors is not *arte del ridicolo* ("art of the ridiculous") but *arte comica* ("comic art"),[80] which has the gracefulness and fluidity of song and of ballet. With her caricature of sexuality, in the orgasm scene Rame creates in fact "an art of the ridiculous," which is in contrast with the graceful ballet of the "comic art" of the woman in *Contrasto*. Ultimately, Rame's "performance lesson" has a self-subversive dimension, as its underlying message is, on the contrary, that most of the "text" of the "sexual" performance should actually be created *in* performance, and not mechanically learned and applied. At the same time, as she explains and discusses with the audience later in the play, good sexual relations do involve a certain amount of learning about one's own and one's partner's body, as well as learning about how to achieve the harmony, the collaboration in improvisation, but should ultimately become a dance in which the steps are created together, *all'improvviso*, as they said in sixteenth century Italy: "Yes, it's a dance, like the waltz, but the steps aren't set. It's a kind of synchronized telepathy."[81]

Comedy, improvisation, mimicry and sexuality form an indestructible bond in Rame's theater, with the ultimate goal of actually achieving a certain level of authenticity in the relations between men and women, but only after all stereotypes, pretenses, arrogance and power games are exploded so that the play can begin again, and so that it can be truly a play of delight and pleasure for all the "actors" involved. The comic and the improvisational are in themselves related, as the very birth of the commedia dell'arte has shown: the emergence of comic theater in the Western world is almost synonymous with the emergence of a theater of improvisation. A non-literary form of artistic expression, this theater once quivered with beauty, delight, and humor on many stages, in the street, in public squares and palaces alike. Taviani has pointed out precisely "the very improvised character of the comic," ("il carattere improvviso pur del comico"; Taviani and Schino, 269), due to both the "fragmentary nature" of the comic and to its "elasticity" (269–70). The repertoire of the commedia troupes consisted mainly of comedies, an occasional pastoral, and sometimes parodies of canonical plays, particularly tragedies, as we have seen the example of *Medea* turned into a burlesque. Women, having had a crucial role in the development of the art of improvisation and collaborative theater production, were therefore crucial in the development of comic performance itself. Simultaneously, their creative participation in the development of Western theater coincided with their emancipation at the social level, as they crossed the boundaries between the domestic and the public sphere, between the *casa* and the *piazza*. Furthermore, as we have seen throughout the examples studied thus far, and in the examples of female clowns, tricksters, and comic mythic figures, there is a persistent tendency in the humor, the performance and the improvisation of women to be overtly erotic, sexual and, at times, downright bawdy. Yet, as Gray has noted, women's humor tends to be "sexual, without being sexist."

Franca Rame's theater takes these three elements, the comical, the sexual and the improvisatory performance, and combines them in a powerful theatrical experience which speaks both of the role of performance itself in the lives of women and of the sexual politics that they have to negotiate in today's world, be it in the public sphere or, most delicately, at the level of intimate relations. At the same time, her own example, as a woman comic performer, writer, and activist who has for years exemplified collaborative acting, scriptwriting and directing with her life partner Dario Fo, is poignant. It is particularly poignant because, although it has given birth to a rich body of works, it has also exemplified the marginalization of the contribution of women to the development of comedy in general. Her contribution, her creativity, her role as a scriptwriter and director has consistently been in the shadow of her partner of half a century. Taviani has noted about the contribution of women to the development of improvisation in the commedia dell'arte that it is the "best kept secret" of theater history. So for too long have also been ignored Rame's input, her talent, her innate knowledge and understanding of the art of improvisation which has accounted for much of Fo's success.

Rame's consistent return in her monologues to sexual relations and to women's experience of sexuality, by means of a performance art which is comic and improvisational at once, is intriguing. Her last play *Sex? Thanks, Don't Mind if I Do*, offers, I believe, a brilliant insight into the connectedness in women's lives between performance, comedy, improvisation and sexuality. As she uses her own body to advance and support the sexual emancipation of women, reinforcing the very notion that performance has been a powerful tool for that very emancipation, Rame is also subverting her own text and performance, showing the double-edged sword of risk that performance can be for women.

The improvisational performance of the early commedia actresses allowed women to appear in public and free themselves to some extent from the very shackles that medieval and Renaissance society was trying to place on them. By portraying erotically awake and independent women onstage, they managed to create the subversive image of a new kind of woman. Inversely, the demise of improvisational theater and its replacement with a text-oriented theater, in which the sole role of the actress was that of an interpreter of fixed texts and roles created by male writers, shifted dramatically the role of performance for women to a dangerous art of objectification, idealization, mystification.[82] While having the potential of a powerful tool of emancipation, freedom, and social progress, performance can also turn women into their own enemies, as it can lead them equally on the path of becoming either objects of the male gaze or mirrors of male subjectivity, to the point where they lose their own identity and self, and where the performative act becomes, like the faking of orgasm, a set of grotesque automatisms whose sole function is to mirror the "greatness" of man to the detriment of the woman.

Inversely, performance based on improvisation, in which at least part of the text is being created as it is being performed, allows the woman performer and women in general to keep creating and re-creating themselves and their roles according to place, time, and context. We have seen that, in fact, it was the female actresses who, like Isabella and Catherine, subverted and exploded the very fixity of the roles initially created by the commedia dell'arte, and that their roles are the most fluid and varied of the entire Italian repertoire. Performing too much of a fixed role from a given text has a destructive potential for women, both onstage and in real life, as women are always more susceptible than men to being perceived in real life as they are onstage and vice versa. Women in society are already trapped within a limited number of roles, a good number of stereotypes, and are expected to perform in terms of an idealized image, significantly more than men are.

From one end of history to the present, we can see the entrapment of women within roles created for them by society and patriarchal institutions. As Ulysses descends into the underworld, in Book VI of the *Odyssey*, all the women he encounters are named as someone's mother, sister, daughter or wife. Throughout the Middle Ages and the Renaissance, women were largely dichotomized within the role of the "virtuous," asexual, or virgin woman akin to Mary, and the courtesan or whore. Making a huge leap into our own time, the Guerrilla Girls gathered an impressive inventory of stereotypes of contemporary women, from the Barbie type to the "soccer mom," to the "hot tamale" Latina, and, of course, the eternal "dumb blonde." The fact that, as Franca Rame comically shows, a woman would have to even perform her orgasm, therefore be an actress even in her most intimate moments of her life, in order to please the ego of her male partner, is an example of the dangers and negative effects on women's lives of performing from a fixed text, and, ultimately, of too much time spent performing the gender models which have been imposed on them by the society, desires and rules of men.

On the other hand, improvisation gives actresses onstage and women in general the opportunity to be literally and symbolically "on top," to achieve personal, creative and sexual fulfillment, on their terms, in a collaborative dance with their acting or sexual partners. Improvisation, because of its fluid, nonlinear nature, and because of its immediate and oral dimension, is one of the most stunning examples of female creativity which over the centuries has had to bypass the rigidity of male-dominated societies, the canons of writing and the book, if it was to make itself heard at all. As they have built, throughout the centuries, a tradition of storytelling, poetry, and performance as an alternative or secondary tradition to the main patriarchal, canonical and written traditions, women have relied more on what Albert Lord terms as "composition in performance."[83] Lord's analysis of women's lyric songs in south Slavic oral poetry explodes the notion of the memorized text and reveals a system of creative improvisation, which, similar to the commedia actors, has a basis of "small blocks of lines intermediate between the formula and the theme" to which "new elements are added," thus opening up the text and the performance, to practically an indefinite number of variants and possibilities.[84]

　　The element of the comic encompasses all this, as it is through the various kinds and degrees of laughter that women can free themselves, explode their "fixed" roles, shame the men who constrain them as either objects of desire or mirrors for their egos, implant "the nails of reason" in their male partners' heads, find relief from their own frustrations and subvert the roles that men have written for them. Women tricksters of the kind created in Franca's *Contrasto* subvert gender roles as they creatively improvise the dance of sexuality and as they achieve both "the last laugh" and a fulfilling sexual experience. The trickster woman in Rame's lyrical piece *Contrasto*, laughs joyously at the end of the piece. Her laughter coincides with her *jouissance* and with the satisfaction of a good improvisation. The woman performing the mock orgasm is also a trickster, but of a different kind: the aggressive, angry kind, whose act is self-subversive and produces in women a bitter laughter of recognition, in men, the tense laughter of shame. Her trick is an example of improvisation gone sour, and therefore her laughter has an angry edge to it. But in the end, through its sharp irony, it points in the same direction as the creative improvisation of Isabella or Colombina, or of the sensuous woman of Rame's *Contrasto*: in the direction of the unpredictable, the elastic, the improvised comedy which is often sexual without being sexist, in which women can act independently, yet in collaboration with "this blessed male," and for whose very invention they are largely responsible.

　　In these overtly erotic pieces, which re-enforce Franca's role as a *giullaressa*, comedy is akin to the performance art of Baubo. As I have already pointed out, in Gray's felicitous formulation, the emphasis is "on the sexual power and pleasure of the goddess," or of the woman. Rame mentions Baubo as well in her discussion of the role of women in the creation of laughter and describes the possible act she might have performed for the grieving goddess Demeter: "Baubo, who in the rite of Eleusis is considered 'the girl of the earth,' undresses, and paints on her chest two large eyes, a nose, and above the pubis, a little mouth. Let's say that her ombilic is her third eye." Rame goes on to describe how Baubo hides her face under an enormous shock of hair and, very importantly, how "she improvises for the goddess a dance with obscene episodes and sings bawdy verses. Demeter smiles, even laughs, she is having fun." She concludes that this represents "the return of joy in life and in creation ... in the world of men.[85]

What Rame describes is similar to her own performance in her monologues: her body becomes both her text and a source of comedy and laughter. Like Baubo some four thousand years ago, Rame draws on her body, speaks with her body, performs sexuality, pleasure, the search for pleasure on her body, with her body, in ways which produce laughter and joy, among women in the world of men. The desperate, grieving, depressed women in the audience, like Demeter, smile, even laugh. If Baubo is the first example of a performance artist, Demeter is the first example of a female audience. She was sad because of awful deeds of aggression done unto her and her daughter by the male gods. Thanks to Baubo, she can smile again, like the many women in the audience whose laughs resonate in the theater spaces where Rame performs.

What is also fascinating is that we have in the example of Baubo a female comic improviser of sexual and bawdy acts and racy discourse. Rame, like Baubo, creates liberating laughter in her female audience by uniting the three elements of the comic, the sexual and the improvisational. If the nature of the comic itself is improvisational, is not the nature of happy sexuality for women also improvisational? The comedy of women, like the sexuality of women, is in its best expression improvisational in the sense of being completely freed from rigid canonical structures and texts (according to Tessari, improvisation *is* a deviation from the canon), in the sense of its unpredictable character, of its cyclical, yet often disjointed nature. And is not the very idea of feminine pleasure inscribed, then, within the guided freedom of the improvisational, which is equally the place of female joy and laughter? While remaining mindful of the risk of essentializing, I believe the notion of improvisational laughter and sexuality is an empowering notion for both women performers and for women in general, precisely because of its lack of closure, because of its opening toward a plurality of experiences, texts, discourses and performance techniques. Certain feminists, like Nancy Reinhardt, connected the linearity and the precise progression toward a climax, specific to traditional Western drama, to "the male sexual response,"[86] and the often cyclic, poetic dramatic forms, more specific to women writers and to female sexuality. The theory is attractive, though of course not without its dangers. However, what is worth retaining is the refusal of a rigid, linear established text, discourse, or performance when it comes to some of the best and the most satisfying comic experiences for women.

Rather than uniting all women under the umbrella of an essentialist view of comedy and sexuality, the improvisational is, on the contrary, an excellent strategy for achieving what Annette Kolodny has called "a playful pluralism," which, in Patricia Schroeder's words, is synonymous to "recognizing and respecting the legitimacy of differentness."[87] Franca Rame's theater, although drawing upon the commonality of women's experiences in the sense of the struggle for freedom and the suffering under various forms of oppression, offers precisely a polyphony of female voices. Most of them laugh and most of them improvise.

The link between comedy, improvisation and sexuality which Rame establishes in her theater and which is noticeable in the work of other female performers, is provocative not only because of its more obvious element of the spontaneous, the unpredictable and the freedom involved in the art of improvisation, but, paradoxically, also because of the element of preparedness, of work and deliberate creativity. As most critics of the commedia dell'arte and the critics who discuss Rame's improvisational art agree, theater improvisation is far from being a random and unleashed flux of words and gestures that the actress/actor produces onstage. Perrucci has called the art of the commedia dell'arte "arte rappresentativa *premeditata*" (emphasis mine). Tessari, Molinari, Taviani, McGill, Farrell, and Scuderi, as well as the experts on orality Perry, Lord, and Foley, all reveal the various facets of memorization, of premeditated creation, of preparation of a role, of lines, texts, as well as the training of voice and body for performance. In fact, the best improvisation is not in the least the one in which an actress or actor would go onstage and start doing and saying whatever strikes their fancy.

The best improvisation is the one in which skill, preparation, learning, experience and a certain amount of memorization are harmoniously united with the addition of new elements, with inventiveness, with interactions with the audience, and with a certain freedom of discourse and gestures. Many of the famous *lazzi* were created in performance, as were many of the texts of the performances. But for that freedom of expression to be possible, the linguistic, acrobatic and physical skills of the performers had to first be developed to the utmost level of perfection. It is why *commedia* is called *dell'arte*: of art, of skill, of professionalism. This is very important with regard to women's input, creativity and ultimately sexuality as well. It would be yet another disservice to women to consider that women are good at improvisation because of its randomness. This would again connect female creativity invariably to the emotional, the irrational alone. While the emotional and the irrational must reacquire their lost dignity, and writers like Cixous and Irigaray have done a lot in that direction, on the other hand, the cerebral, precise, rigorous work must as well be accepted as a dimension of women's artistic expression. Although Franca Rame says that going onstage and acting is for her like breathing, it is also a well-known fact that she works hard for her shows and that she is a playwright in her own right. Her texts are not randomly produced onstage but well thought out, written and directed in advance. Isabella Andreini produced a large body of stage dialogues and was well known for how she ingeniously used her knowledge, erudition and intelligence to create her roles and to better improvise.

Returning to the connection between sexuality and improvisation, Franca Rame follows her faking orgasm scene precisely with a detailed discussion about the male and the female sexual organs, a series of potential sexual problems such as premature ejaculation, impotence, and sterility, and stresses precisely the importance of knowledge, of being well informed, of research, discussion, and awareness. She goes into detail about exercises for women to strengthen their pelvic muscles, relaxation techniques, in short learning and preparing. And then she says that the sexual dance can unfold in its full beauty and the partners can improvise with full confidence: "Your body moves itself ... possessed by a mysterious rhythm ... keeping time with liquid movements and shivers that transform the inside of her sex into an amusement park of delirium."[88] This is the "new love" which Cixous passionately advocates: "The new love dares for the other, wants the other, makes dizzying, precipitous flights between knowledge and invention."[89] The flights "between knowledge and invention," in creation and in eroticism are what allow women, who have had to learn how to "fly/steal," to be birds and tricksters at once throughout the ages, and to "blow up the law, to break up the truth with laughter."[90] The complex art of improvisation is, at its best, a fruitful metaphor for life and sexual relations. Similarly, Colombina four centuries ago used the very existence of the Italian theater as a metaphor for life and marriage. Acquiring the confidence of learning, of the solidarity and connectedness with other women, and then allowing themselves the freedom to go onstage and create in performance is ultimately what also allows women to have the last laugh, and a good *jouissance* together with that laugh.

Franca's Madness

With the freedom of improvisation may also come the flight of madness, or of that which in our culture has been considered madness, particularly when it comes to women's creativity, language, and sexuality. Improvisation, as it veers away from the fixity of the text, as it deviates from the canon, is to the canonical texts as madness is to sanity. Shoshana Felman closes her article on "Women and Madness" with the provocative statement: "If, in our culture, the woman is by definition associated with madness, her problem is how to break out of this (cultural) imposition of madness without taking up the critical and therapeutic positions of reason: how to avoid speaking both as *mad* and as *not mad*."[91] Women poets, writers, and performers have often tried to do precisely that: create a discourse which both illustrates by various degrees that which modern psychology has labeled as madness or hysteria, and raise these concepts above their negative connotations to the status of a form of creativity which, although different from and subversive of the reason bound, logical patterns of phallogocentric discourse, asserts its own truthfulness of what Felman has called "feminine difference."[92] Since, as Phyllis Chesler has noted, "the ethics of mental health is masculine in our culture,"[93] the woman's revolt against masculine ethics, discourse, and against the roles assigned by that ethics to women, appears as unrecognizable, as anomalous, and is ultimately dismissed to the no-man's-land of madness, therefore of "the absence of womanhood," therefore of an annihilation of difference altogether. But it is precisely from that no-man's-land that many women artists *do* want to speak, and to validate their "madness" not as madness, but just as a *different* voice.

We have seen that, for the first actresses of the commedia dell'arte, the mad scene, or *scena della pazzia*, was seen as a stepping stone, the highest form of artistic achievement onstage. Vincenza Armani, Vitoria Piissimi, and, of course, Isabella Andreini all developed mad scenes and were praised by their contemporaries for them. And of course Isabella's highest moment of performative achievement was the famous mad scene she performed in front of the Medicis in 1589. While the fathers of the church considered those scenes just another proof of the depravation and devilish nature of the actresses, the audiences — the people and aristocrats alike — appreciated and greatly admired them.

As part of carnivalesque reversals, and precisely because it was the commedia troupes which introduced real women on the stages of Europe, the actresses' mad scenes were regarded as high entertainment and considered the highest form of artistic achievement for a female performer. Of course that comes with its set of good and bad repercussions. The good ones are that at least in its stylized forms, as a form of performance, and as long as the actress resumed "sanity" and logical discourse at the end of the comedy, the spectacle of female madness was turned into something awe-inspiring and accepted as a valid form of artistic expression onstage. It is also to be noted that it was Renaissance drama, and Shakespeare in particular, who introduced the character of the fool, the clown, as the one who, paradoxically, is the sanest of all and always tells the truth. But female madness is different from that of the Shakespearian fool and one only has to consider the character of Ophelia to see that her madness veers into the tragic, the pathetic, and is not really accepted as truth revealing. The downside of the mad scenes for actresses of the commedia was precisely that they relegated women even more to the realm of the emotional and the irrational and, while madness was seen as a good trick for female characters to play in overcoming a difficult situation, such as an unwanted marriage, for the comedy to have its happy ending, sanity had to be regained and the very act of regaining of sanity coincided, as in *La Pazzia d'Isabella*, with the woman recognizing her lover and marrying him. Nevertheless, the positive aspects of the representation of female madness onstage and the acceptance of women as possible tricksters, clowns, and buffoons are not to be discarded.

Franca Rame creates her own carnival of madness. Her discourse and performance also veer at times into the hysterical and into the realm of that which, according to masculine ethics of mental health, is considered madness. I will close this section by going back full circle to the first play I mentioned at the beginning of the chapter, *Abbiamo tutte la stessa storia* (*We All Have the Same Story*). The analysis of "madness" in this monologue may also offer a more profound explanation of the fact that it is the women who laugh most at this piece. Franca addresses her audience of women in particular with the complicity of the special laughter, which connects them. She tells the story of the woman who gives birth to a little girl who marries an engineer; she has a little mischievous doll who says obscenities and who sticks her head in the engineer's behind so that he feels like he is giving birth and so that the wife has to call the midwife, who explodes into wild laughter at the sight. At this point, Franca addresses her audience: "And like all the women ... (To the audience.) You too ... you know what happens when the wild laugh takes over us ... (Shouted.) 'Pipi! It's coming out ... I am a midwife but I am under a spell.... I'm making gallons ... help! ... I don't want to cause catastrophes ... floods.... I don't want to cause deaths! Give me a pail!" The midwife finishes peeing in the pail, "with dignity," and then asks the wife to make her husband drink it, for it is "magical," all mixed up with vermouth, marsala and raw eggs.[94] The husband drinks and drinks until he explodes, and the doll reappears, whole, unharmed, and "laughing like mad." She tells the little girl: "You see ..., bitch of my balls! You are free now, mistress of your body, of your choices, of yourself, you are freeeee! Let's go!" The little girl, who has by now grown up, holds her doll against her chest and little by little the doll disappears into her heart.[95] Next, she walks alone and reaches a big tree, under which there are lots of little girls who have grown up like she has, and who realize they all had a little doll like she did, and they all explode into more mad laughter, realizing they all have "the same story to tell."

The laughter of all the female characters in the play and of Rame herself is linked to "insanity" and "hysteria," inasmuch as it explodes gender roles, hierarchies, expected boundaries of modesty and prudishness for women. It is "insanity" and "hysteria" by male standards of discourse and behavior, but to other women, this laugh is liberating. Rame turns a discourse which is explosively unconventional into a dramatic and comedic tour de force. Using several comic devices and "theatergrams" taken from as far back as medieval farce and certainly from commedia dell'arte, such as the drinking of the urine of a woman (which was also one of the *lazzis* of the commedia) and a man who gives birth and explodes, Rame pushes all carnivalesque reversals to the extreme and makes of her discourse, performance, comedy and laughter a powerful expression of female liberation. In the end of the play, it is only women who are gathered under the big tree, laughing with each other and with the women in the audience. The women in this piece achieve their happiness, their sense of self and their laugh, precisely as a result of growing up and breaking up with the men who objectified and abused them.

In her analysis of Balzac's story entitled *Adieu*, Felman points out that for as long as Stéphanie, the female protagonist of the story, fails to recognize her lover Philippe, she is both mad and unfeminine. She becomes unrecognizable as a woman, precisely because, in her "madness," she fails to recognize him. "'Woman,' in other words, is the exact metaphorical measure of the narcissism of man," notes Felman.[96] Rame, on the other hand, creates female characters who explode this metaphorical measure, who stand up to and undermine the "narcissism of man," and it is why the men in the audience do not laugh or produce "inhuman" laughs, and why the women in the audience laugh wholeheartedly. Rame legitimizes as non-mad her female characters' "madness," thus achieving that which Felman notes to be precisely the biggest challenge of female artists: to be "both mad and not mad." The main female voice of this play defies male sexual politics, unwanted pregnancy, unwanted abortion, unwanted labor, against everything that is imposed on her by the men in her life. In a complete reversal of a sex scene, the female protagonist acts as if it were the man "under her" who risked getting pregnant. All of these theatrical moments partake of the madness of carnivalesque reversals of gender roles. The reversals, however, stop being simply reversals or images of "the woman on top," as "madness" becomes a way of being, a form

of liberation, and, in fact, a different form of sanity altogether, one that is
not defined by "the narcissistic economy of the Masculine universal equiva-
lent." It does not try to eliminate "under the label 'madness'" the "feminine
difference," but instead validates a form of sanity and of artistic expression
which breaks through the "sociosexual stereotypes"[97] that women have been
cast in, and which confidently affirms itself and its own truthfulness. By dismantling all traditional plot and character lines, as well as conventional forms
of discourse and the ending of classical comedy in marriage, Rame validates
women's experiences and women's laughter as legitimate.

Franca's monologue bears resemblance to both Isabella's mad scene and
Colombina's unforgiving sarcasm. Inscribed within the carnivalesque discourse
are Franca's mixing of elevated, spiritual and lower bodily domains. As Isabella
brought together in her "rantings" the Greek philosophers, the queen of
England, foods, and bodily functions such as urinating and farting, that which
Bakhtin has called "the lower bodily stratum," so Franca mixes the pompous
political jargon of the sixties and seventies, with the Vatican, with capitalist
multicorporations, with female sexual organs, contraception, urination, birth,
love, emancipation. As she complains about her partner's insensitivity during
the sexual act, the female protagonist notes that:

> if a girl doesn't immediately take a comfortable position, skirt up, panties down,
> open legs, then she's a bitch full of complexes, paralyzed by the sentiment of
> honor and prudishness instilled in her by the reactionary-imperialist-capitalist-
> massonic-catholic-conformist-Austro-Hungarian and repressive education! I
> know things, hein? And a woman who knows things is a bitch.[98]

Confessing that she has stopped taking her pills, she complains that they
used to make her breasts look like the "cupolas of the Vatican." The flood of
urine produced by the midwife who has come to rescue the engineer from
the mischievous doll bears resemblance to Rabelais' scene in which Pantagruel
floods Paris with his urine. To Isabella's "mad" impersonations of all the buffoons in the commedia repertoire, of their behavior and language, corresponds
Franca's reversion of sexuality and biology altogether, in the acting out of a
dream. In this dream, the woman is now on top of her partner, who has
become "a female man" with large breasts, and is talking to him/her in a mock
reassuring tone resembling both the masculine discourse of seduction and
something close to a woman's fantasy of how a man would speak to her, *if* he
were a woman:

> How beautiful you are ... lie down ... (She is lying down as if the man was under
> her) Let's go, undress yourself, I have to talk to you.... What is it? I sense you're
> nervous, tense. You are not taking the pill anymore? That's all right! I still love
> you! Calm down, I'll be careful.... That's ok if you haven't taken the pill ... if

you get pregnant, there is the law 194 which protects you.... If not, I'll have you do it clandestinely, and I'll pay for it, general anesthetic ... but if you want to have it, your baby, I'll marry you. Let's make love, let's make love, it doesn't matter if you become pregnant: a man doesn't accomplish himself unless he becomes a mother! (shouted) Mother! Moooooother![99]

The humor of such scenes derives equally from the carnivalesque reversal of gender roles and biology as well as from a kind of mimicry in the second degree. The woman is miming both the man's discourse and behavior as perceived through the eyes and experience of a woman and is simultaneously acting out her own fantasy of the caring, sensitive reactions and tone that the man would have *if* he were like a woman. The "male woman" on top expresses the urgency of her desire, while at the same time reassuring the "female man" with regard to all the possible consequences of their sexual act. Rame's carnivalesque reversal explodes that which Felman has referred to as "the logic of resemblance,"[100] wherein neither the man nor the woman resemble their conventional images or act according to the expected behavior as dictated by the various "sociosexual stereotypes" created by patriarchal society. They are both the product of a dream, and dreams are tied to "madness," and therefore are both true and untrue.

Elin Diamonds' comment that most feminist performers "perform gender with a vengeance" acquires new meaning in Franca's show, for she acts out both genders as she simultaneously subverts them. She almost literally performs "with a vengeance," as in her carnival of mimicry, mockery, and gender reversals Franca vindicates women of the burden and pain of the negative stereotypes and roles that imprison them.

Colombina's acrid humor echoes through Franca's monologue as well: "When you want, you can be so sweet ... almost human, a true partner," she says to her lover. In the midst of the pains of labor, Franca's character asks where the father of the child is, and when she is told he is outside smoking, for he is nervous, she replies: "Poor man, he is nervous, tense! He would have better been more careful before, instead of getting me pregnant."[101] Shaming the men in the audience through irony is one of Colombina's comedic fortes. Franca's "almost human" is similar, in its cutting, superior humor, to Colombina's remarks about the less than human behavior of certain men, in plays like *Les Souhaits* or *La Fille de bons sens*. The rebellion, anger, and aggression of Franca's female characters is also similar to many of Colombina's outcries against the inequities suffered by women or against the vulgarity, hypocrisy and dishonesty of certain men, as in the case of the fatuous would-be Marquis, Arlecchino's infidelities, or Octave's narcissism.

The sex reversals in the play, all the way to the delirious "labor" scene in which the engineer, with the "help" of the midwife, explodes and "gives birth" to the mischievous doll through his behind, are akin to Colombina's carousel of disguises and tricks, in which she invariably inverses the conventional power roles between men and women and always ends "on top." Franca draws into the sphere of her laughter and carnival all the women in the audience, and this corresponds to Colombina's complicity with her audience of women.[102] However, Franca's "madness," sexual reversals, openly sexual discourse and her overall comic performance push the carnivalesque to that place where it meets with feminism by giving birth to what Kathleen Rowe has called the "unruly woman" who "has cackled at the margins of Western history for centuries."[103]

Both Isabella and Colombine illustrate several characteristics of the "unruly woman," but it is in Franca's carnival of female voices, faces, and bodies that she comes most poignantly into existence. Franca and her female characters illustrate several of the characteristics of the "unruly woman:"

> she creates disorder by dominating, or trying to dominate, men. She is unable or unwilling to confine herself to her proper place; ... her speech is excessive, in quantity, content, or tone; she makes jokes or laughs herself; she may be androgynous or hermaphroditic, drawing attention to the social construction of gender; ... her sexuality is less narrowly and negatively defined than is that of the *femme fatale*. She may be pregnant.[104]

Most of Franca's characters display at least one, but usually several of these characteristics. The character in *Abbiamo tutte la stessa storia* illustrates all of them: She and her doll, as an extension of herself, break out of their submissive roles and dominate the men in the story; she utters what would easily be considered "excessive speech" for a woman; she draws attention to the social construction of gender by the blatant gender and sexual reversals; she is *not* a femme fatale; and she is pregnant.

Bakhtin's theory of the carnivalesque, though of great importance to feminist scholarship on comedy, appears limited in terms of the discussion of gender. As Rowe has noted, his "idealization of the women as the 'incarnation' of the 'lower bodily stratum' falls into one of the most enduring and misogynistic of philosophical traditions, that of relegating the feminine to matter, and the masculine to spirit" (34). However, Bakhtin's theory is open enough to lend itself to fruitful developments in the direction of feminist interpretations of comedy, which is what critics including Natalie Zemon Davis, Katheleen Rowe, and Judy Little have done, and which is what I am myself doing in this study. Franca Rame's performance and comedy in a play such as *Abbiamo tutte la stessa storia* is a superb example of a feminist and female carnival in which even the dolls, the ultimate symbol of the objectification and idealization of women,[105] become "unruly women," and which is built, to use Rowe's phrasing, "on transgression and inversion, disguise and masquerade, sexual reversals, the deflation of ideals, and the leveling of hierarchies" (9). Furthermore, madness and the carnivalesque come together in Rame's monologue, as logical, conventional discourse is exploded, as dreams and wild fantasies are acted out and, most importantly, as the female breaks the rules and taboos of "resemblance" and resists male subjectivity and narcissism. Unrestrained laughter, anger and disorder rule in this piece. As she validates them through the commonality of women's laughter, she also legitimizes female anger which, as feminist critics have noted, has been consistently denied in our culture "as an available and legitimate response to the injustices they experience" (Rowe, 7).

The doll pouring out obscenities, sticking her head into the engineer's behind, and leading him to his embarrassing demise, the midwife's flood of urine, the woman's sarcastic tone even as she is giving birth, and even the closing song in which the mother turns a lullaby into something which sounds more like a war song, all are carnivalesque images in which anger, madness and laughter become one and create that which Rowe has referred to as "strategies of danger" (5). The women's carnival is equally a women's war, just like the grotesque giants in Rabelais' world that Bakhtin takes for the subject of his study engage equally in carnivalesque activities such as banquets and everything else that has to do with "the lower bodily stratum," as well as in just wars against unjust invaders. The laughter of Rame's women "expresses anger, resistance, solidarity and joy."[106] The framing of the play with the phrase "abbiamo tutte la stessa storia," by the title on one end, and the final phrase uttered in unison by the women gathered under the tree at the other end, legitimates women's experiences and turns their liminality into a position of empowerment.

The play *Abbiamo tutte la stessa storia* bears significant marks of improvisational comedy. Franca is well aware of the commedia tradition of "*recitare a soggetto*," or "performing on a theme,"[107] and she makes abundant use of it. Underneath the rich and often surreal turns of events in *Abbiamo tutte la stessa storia*, there are several of the common themes of classical commedia and of popular fairy tales. The boy meets girl, boy gets girl theme underlies a good part of the monologue and is a recurrent one as it is simultaneously entangled with echoes of known fairy tales. For instance, as the daughter of the woman who starts the monologue grows up, she goes deep into the forest to find her mischievous doll, to save her from a mean red cat that has grabbed her. There she meets a dwarf who is excreting phosphorescent urine. He kills the cat with his flood and wants to marry the doll when he hears it utter one obscenity after another. Then the big bad wolf appears and says that he wants to marry the doll. He says he is an electrical engineer whom a wicked witch has transformed into a wolf and if the little girl kisses him on the mouth he will recover his human form. The girl does just that and the engineer, turned human, impressed by the girl's beauty, wants to marry her, which he does, and they live "happily ever after" (82). The basic fairy tale scheme of obstacles in the way of the protagonists, and the usual ending in a happy marriage are all too evident, though several fairy tales are mixed up: Little Red Riding Hood, Snow White, Beauty and the Beast. Franca breaks the tales' boundaries and turns them into an irreverent comedy filled with anachronisms and sexual and scatological language. She abandons the familiar "ever after" in favor of the impending "day after" (82). The day following the marriage starts with an inflammatory speech by the revolted doll who calls for "a general assembly" and addresses the young married couple as "my young newly weds of shit" (82). She entirely challenges the illusions of the young woman that she may be happy in this marriage.

The improvisatory nature of the play is evident in the fluid development of several basic themes and their development into several unpredictable turns of events which at times veer into the fantastic, but which are nevertheless tied to the main themes and arranged in a relatively loose manner. The modern feminist themes of the wife who is turned into a sexual object, the oppressive nature of marriage for women, challenging traditional gender roles, and female self-expression and fulfillment are all woven around the basic *commedia* themes of boy-meets-girl, boy-gets-girl, boy-marries girl. Yet they are simultaneously subverted and overturned. By the "improvisatory nature" of the play, I mean, not that Franca has created this play in performance, but that even as a written text it bears the signs of orality, and, in the way it is created, it allows the performer to have a certain freedom of expression, a certain flexibility of action and discourse, which Franca has always made the most of onstage.

The new feminist themes that Rame has developed in her theater have themselves become, like the commedia themes once did, recurrent topics, "movable blocks" which can be developed, arranged into a variety of forms: the woman dissatisfied with her sexual life, the woman who is afraid of getting pregnant, the woman who does get pregnant, the overworked, exhausted mother, the insensitive husband/lover who is focused on the gratification of his sexual desires, the revolt of the woman, the awakening of a feminist consciousness — all abound in the totality of Franca's theater and are treated in a variety of comedic forms. This play in particular gathers and develops all of them in a breathless, urgent rhythm, passing through the most important stages in women's lives and indeed justifying the generalizing note of the title.

The woman's irony toward the man's sexual ineptitude, the expression of her dissatisfaction and her worry about pregnancy are discussed and/or acted out also in *Sesso? Grazie tanto per gradire* (*Sex? Don't Mind If I Do*) and *Contrasto ad una voce* (*Dialogue in a Single Voice*); the frenzy of the overworked mother and the seeds of a feminist conscience in the famous play *Il risveglio* (*Waking Up*); the despair and the conflicted nature of the relationship of the couple in *Coppia aperta quasi spalancata* (*The Open Couple*) and *Una donna sola* (*A Woman Alone*). But only in *Contrasto ad una voce* and in *Abbiamo tutte la stessa storia* does Franca's carnival end in an explosive role reversal and a hopeful, altogether revolutionary position of the woman having taken possession of her destiny, body, sexuality and language. Similar to Isabella's *pazzia*, Franca's amalgam of stories, fairy tales, madness and carnival pulls together the strings of her theater and culminates into one tour de force of comedy and improvisation. As commedia scholars and as Dario Fo himself has demonstrated with the improvisation of commedia actors in general, Franca's improvisation develops and rearranges certain formulas. Hardly pulled from thin air, it is the result of rigorous, deliberate creation, which in performance depends on an extraordinary sense of timing.[108]

The oral and improvisational nature of this text is evident in its overall construction and syntax. Maybe more than any other text by Franca, this abounds in ellipses, parataxis, repetitions, the use of first and second person pronouns and verbs in simple tenses mostly in the present tense and some in the "imperfect," and the "basic rhythmic structure of parallelism"[109] that we have already noted in the improvisation of the commedia actresses. Throughout the play, particularly at key moments, such as the climax of the woman's partner (75), conception (76), pregnancy (77), and labor (78), certain formulas are repeated numerous times, almost in a chant-like style. The phrase "be careful" is repeated at least three times with variations of tone (75); the sentence "I'm pregnant," four times in a row, moving from despair to screaming. The expression "Yes, ma'am," adressed to the doctor or nurse, is repeated at least six times, in desperate, calm, and urgent tones; and at the point of the baby's delivery, the question "Where is he?" is repeated twice, followed immediately by "What is he doing?"

In the section where the narrator recounts the absurd fairy tales of the dwarf, the cat, and the engineer, certain formulas are used with variations in parallel narrative structures: "for as one knows, the urine of dwarves is a terrible poison for cats"(80); "for one knows that the leaks of electrical engineers are very venomous for dwarves" (81). That which Albert Lord, in his analysis of Slavic women's singing and storytelling in the study *The Singer Resumes His Tale*, has referred to as "tensions of associations" (49), the mixing of passages which give a "sense of textuality" (35) with various repetitive simple formulas which give a sense of ad-hoc creation, all carefully woven around "stable cores" and themes (62), make of Franca's texts brilliant examples of "composition in performance." But just as Lord and commedia scholars have warned us to not think of this process of creation as free-associating, so must we not fall into the error of believing that Franca's texts are the result of pulling lines out of thin air. The way she writes a dramatic monologue such as *Abbiamo tutte la stessa storia*, reflects to a degree the techniques of oral poetry and storytelling and the possibility of improvising together with a certain freedom of performance. They are both embedded within the text itself. As Cottino-Jones has noted, Franca is famous for the ease with which she breaks in and out of character, addresses the audience and goes back to her role, without missing a beat.

The general structure of Rame's plays, and all the formulaic, parallel, repetitive discursive and performative patterns woven around a number of recognizable themes, create a sense of fluidity and a freedom which would allow the performer to create variations on many of the lines, and to act the same play and yet a different one every time. Furthermore, in the places with most signs of improvised performance and orality the text is also the funniest and corresponds to points of tension in the representation of key women's issues. It is where she is most afraid of becoming pregnant that the female protagonist goes into almost mechanical repetitive discourse: "Be careful, be careful, be careful," or "Stop it! ... stop it! ... stop it!" Each repeated phrase is usually uttered differently or in a crescendo. It is when she is all nervous about having gotten pregnant and trying to decide whether to have the child or not and during labor that she keeps repeating "Yes ma'am, yes ma'am." And it is in the change of male partners that the sarcastic formula "As one knows, the urine of dwarves..." is repeated with a variation form one male to the next. The most ellipses are used during the performance of the sexual act which starts the play and during the labor scene. The simplest utterances occur in the scene following labor and represent the care of the new-born girl: "Breast-feeding. Injection! Vaccine! Another injection! Washing. Ploc, the beautiful big caca! Vomiting." (79).

Caring for a newborn, with its relentless repetitive gestures and actions, performed with an enhanced sense of urgency, is also one of the themes in Franca's famous play *Il risveglio*. Franca's performance is at its highest level of orality or improvisational modes of performance in key moments concerning those aspects of women's lives which have been most under the control of men or which have been most devalued by patriarchal structures: sexuality, contraception, reproductive rights, marriage. These are the aspects which would most benefit from the freedom and fluidity of improvisation and which also best lend themselves to female comedy: transgressive, at times angry, other times restorative, almost always carnivalesque.

While it is true that a part of improvisation, as seen in commedia and in this particular text, is based on a certain degree of repetition, this does not contradict the idea of freedom, fluidity and lack of fixity. On the contrary, the repetitions and parallelisms are also the performative and discursive elements which allow for the variations of formulas, for a certain interchangeability of textual structures. As most studies on oral poetry have shown, the art of creation in composition is based precisely on fixed structures, recurrent themes and variable formulaic structures, to which that which is entirely the product of inspiration in the moment is added. It is in the arranging and rearranging of all these elements that the beauty and spontaneity of each performance derives, be it singing, poetry, or storytelling. The fragmented and fragmentary nature of Franca's discourse, the rotation throughout this play of most themes important to women's lives, the moments of almost delirious repetition of certain formulas combined with variations on certain discursive patterns, the art of alternating very short, rapid phrases formed of a noun or a verb alone with longer sentences and more incantatory rhythms, and the constant oscillation in her acting between contrasting emotions (such as the sex scene, the pregnancy, the labor scene, the caring for the child) are precisely that which give her performance the spontaneity and brilliance of high quality improvisational comedy which illustrates in form the content she tries to convey.

The women of Franca's plays, whose lives are so often forced to fit certain oppressive molds, break through these molds with laughter, rearrange the formulas of their lives, create variations on known patterns, and, ultimately, as in the carnivalesque sexual reversals in the play, redefine and question altogether the authority of such "texts" as sexual politics, marriage, and traditional gender roles. Ultimately, the very title of the play *We All Have the Same Story* suggests simultaneously the ideas of textual fixity and improvisation, for the stories are similar in pattern, yet different in expression. The blurring of the distinctions between first-person female narrators in the play, the repetition of the stories of marriages or unions with abusive or insensitive male partners, with variations as striking as changing the species of the male partners from human to cat to dwarf to a wolf who turns engineer in the manner of fantastic tales, suggests that women of all walks of life and ages find common ground in the repetitive nature of their oppression, but also that their stories differ in the details and the tonalities of their voices. It is in the sharing of their stories more than anything else that the women gathered under the tree manage to "break up the law with laughter."

We now come back full circle to the observation, made at the beginning of this chapter, that it is largely the women in the audience who laugh wholeheartedly at Rame's plays. It is for two reasons: firstly, because we recognize all too well the scripts of our iniquities and, secondly, because we experience satisfaction at seeing these scripts subverted or altogether dismantled, into the multitude of variations and improvised movements that the lives of liberated women may take.

FOUR

"We feminist comedians can and should do whatever the hell we want." — Deb Margolin

Contemporary Colombinas
The Personal, the Public, the Political, the Intimate, and the Comical

Deb Margolin

Deb Margolin is an award-winning playwright and performance artist who writes and for the most part performs her own plays. She is also a founding member of the women's theater group Split Britches whose resident playwright she was for many years. She is the recipient of a 1999–2000 OBIE Award for Sustained Excellence of Performance, the Kesselring Playwriting Award for her play *Three Seconds in the Key* in 2005 and the Helen Merrill Distinguished Playwright award. Troublingly enough, in the anthology of Split Britches' plays edited by Sue-Ellen Case, Deb Margolin's role as the resident playwright and author of innumerable brilliant lines in the company's repertoire is dismissed and diminished almost to invisibility. She is mostly referred to in terms of her performance and not so much in terms of her artistic contributions to the company's bank of plays and dialogues. The book cover features the lesbian couple of the group, Peggy Shaw and Lois Weaver, in a gorgeous sensuous pose, while Deb Margolin is portrayed in thumbnail size on the back cover wearing binoculars. In the introduction, as Sue-Ellen Case tells the story of how the anthology came to be, Margolin is referred to in parenthesis in the following manner: "Although Shaw and Weaver would be in London much of that time (and Deb Margolin would be expecting her second child), they agreed to put their papers in order in their apartment for students to photocopy and compile."[1] While the two women were like bees hard at work in their poor, minimalist apartment sorting through tubs of plays and scripts, many of which had been written by Margolin, the latter would be popping yet another child. This sentence, and the positioning of Margolin's having her second child in parenthesis as a contrast to the other women being hard at work, reminds me of a department meeting in one of the schools at my university, in which the male department chair said with regard to a woman colleague as they were setting up the schedule of classes for the fall: "If she would stop having babies we wouldn't have to deal with [it]." Then they could actually get somewhere with the scheduling of classes.[2]

Isn't it sad and really not at all funny when members of groups that have been historically among the most marginalized end up perpetuating similar practices of marginalization onto others? When a certain group of feminists raise barriers and apply practices of exclusion that mimic pathetically the practices that have oppressed them or the group they claim membership into? A quick reminder to our readers at this point that Sue-Ellen Case was also the one who dismissed in half a sentence the entire tradition of the commedia dell'arte as dealing just with "fathers and sons."

I met Deb Margolin in Chicago at a panel of the Association of Theater in Higher Education where she performed a piece titled *Weapons of Mess Destruction*.[3] For the entire duration of the monologue I didn't breathe very much. I know I didn't move and my heart beat really fast. Her piece was about George Bush, about the obscenity of war, about the human condition and about a woman talking with her daughter and son in the bathroom about death and mortality. It was wrenching and funny in a way that made me gasp and quiver, and that made me think I had just found the other half of myself, a voice saying everything I had wanted to say for so long but couldn't find the words to articulate: about the obscene insanity of wars and about the fragility of our happiness, about my life as a woman walking on a tightrope across a moment in the abyss of history as I am trying to define myself, my language, my life, as I am being defined by my love for my children and their mortal bodies, about the impossible joy and horror of being a mother and understanding the idea of the transitory through the translucent and plump bodies of the baby you are nursing or whose diaper you are changing while there is always a war out there. It was as real and carnal and as related to my life as anything could ever be; it was ethereal, metaphysical, funny, raw and melancholy, political and philosophical.

At that same time in my life I was haunted, or should I say obsessed with my commedia actresses, the Isabellas and Colombinas who move through the pages of this book and whose lives and works have filled mine for almost a decade. Deb Margolin seemed to me then, and she does today more than ever, as the reincarnation of one of those brilliant, effervescent woman artists of the sixteenth and seventeenth century Italy and France, only also modern, postmodern, contemporary, speaking to us today about our anguishes and exhilarations, about the large existential questions and simultaneously about the things that are done, undone, said, unsaid in the small seconds that make up our days; about our human and female bodies with their array of joys and orgasms, miseries and frustrations, secretions and embarrassments in our capitalist/imperialist/global/war ridden/consumerist/climate-changing society. All that and more! Here in all its glory is the part of that monologue that retells the mother's conversation with her children in the bathroom:

All's Well That Ends Well (from *Index to Idioms*)

The woman is in the bathroom with her two children, Matt and Julia. All three in one smelly bathroom, the pink 50's tile, the tattered bath mat, the sink splattered with toothpaste droppings, the toilet exhausted from its sad receipts, the towels drooping like eyelids, oblique and damp. Two kids and a mother in a bathroom. Enough for a painting.

The girl is 6, and she's beautiful in that drowsy, preconscious way. Her lips are puffy, full of deep pink flesh, her eyes tight in her head as if in collusion with her mind and thoughts, her little feet exuberant with the floor. The boy is 8 and a half; his beauty is more obvious and easier to ignore, his hair is too long, his eyelashes are endless and curl up towards his forehead like those of a torch singer in an evening gown. He is very much the poet, out of step with the practical universe, richly attuned to invisible things. His sister torments him much of the time with the practicalities which elude him. She understands how to hurt anybody. She understands that different things hurt people.

The little girl has just realized that she's going to die someday, just realized this fully; for some reason, some unknowable reason, there's always just a moment in a young life when this dawns fully on a person, a person for whom death is generally very far away, but it dawns fully, like the soldier waking for his first day, a gun on his back, in a foreign country where he's been sent to fight a war. She's just realized she's going to die someday, here in this bathroom.

Everything is quiet for a few moments. Then she starts crying. She's yelling; this isn't a peaceful sorrow, not even a sorrow of any kind, really. It's an outrage, an insult. Like being called a dirty Jew. She's outraged. Her brother picks at a piece of soap stuck on the side of the tub. Mother is peeing.

I am not! she says.

Mother's pee sounds musical, jaunty, as it falls. They talk over this tinkling fountain.

I'm sorry, Julia, you are, her brother says. The piece of soap comes off under his fingernail. He tries to flick it into the sink. His sorrow rises with his eyelashes up over his head.

I'm not! I'm not going to die! And my brother's not going to die EITHER! she shrieks.

The mother looks at them. She's wiping herself, getting ready to stand up and flush. She tries an academic approach:

Everything dies, and when things die, they ready the earth for more life. It's a cycle, like in the Lion King, the great circle of life, remember?

My brother isn't going to die! I'm not going to do it! There isn't any circle! I'm not going to die, why do I have to do that! You can't make me do that, and I'm not going to!

Mother flushes.

Okay she says okay, that's fine. You don't have to do it.

What happens when you die, Mom the boy says, returning to his soap piece on the edge of the tub. Do you just see darkness, and lie there very still?

No the mother says You don't see blackness

What then? he says

Well, you just don't see. It's another way of being.

The girl has stopped crying and her eyes are ablaze. She's seen a piece of candy on the floor that she dropped there earlier, when she snuck in the bathroom to eat it secretly. Defiantly, looking her mother directly in the eye, she pops it into her mouth.

Mmmmmmm she says This candy is duh-LICIOUS!

She studies the mother, who does not respond. She swallows the candy, and then her eyes fill with tears again.

I can't do it, Mom, I won't.

Fine the Mother says don't ever do it

There's a silence. Mother opens the bathroom door, and sound from the house flows in like dammed water loosed.

Ma! Ma! The little girl says Can you talk when you're dead?

No. You can't talk! Says the brother sadly.

The Mother turns to the little girl, lifts her. I don't know the mother says.

But can you talk, can you talk? Is there any talking?

We can't hear the dead people talking, but that doesn't mean they don't talk the mother says.

The girl struggles down the mother's body, stands on her own. Says:

Well that means there's talking, and I'll just talk. If I can be dead and still talk I don't care that I'm dead. I'll talk and talk and talk and be dead and talk.

Daughter bursts out of the bathroom, relieved. Goes into her bedroom, pulls the head off one of her Barbie dolls and throws it up in the air. It hits the ceiling, falls down dully, rolls an instant and stops, nose down. The little girl puts the headless Barbie fully upright and says: I'm dead, and now I'd like to tell you a story! Are you listening boys and girls? Are you listening? Listen!

You stupid, stupid children! You have to listen!

Deb Margolin was sort of like Isabella of five hundred years ago in her "madness" scene when she talked about Aristotle's spirit in a bottle and about farting and peeing and the gods with their ridiculous thunders and an Egyptian caliph and the queen of England. She was also reminiscent of Franca Rame's women who tell their stories as they move about their daily chores, and in their domestic spaces. She mixed high philosophical existential ideas with the little, mundane details of a mother's life, with references to Americana popular culture such as the Barbie doll with her ridiculously unrealistic physique and size, with delicious children's discourse and wrenching musings about life, all in a roller coaster of emotion and thought that ultimately keeps us breathless in this moment, in this historical present. It also keeps us listening to a little girl's urgent ranting against death — a beautiful metaphor of theater's own claim at giving special weight to the present moment, and construed in a female voice. It is why I am devoting part of this chapter to Deb Margolin. She is a complete artist in the same way that Isabella Andreini or Franca Rame are, while also giving voice to something new that is only of our times, something that lucid women experience and want to express and want to hear: a wrenching melancholy about how small our progress has been in comparison to the progress of, say, technology or weapons of mass destruction, a shameless and raucous laughter that tries desperately to cling to hope, to the utopia of a better world for our daughters, and also to survive this moment with dignity while also inscribing it in history and while also living it to its desperate fullest. A laughter that says yes, we do want to devour our cake and also hold on to it just like men always have, but boy do we have to pay for that shameless greed.

The women of the commedia and Franca Rame found themselves on the cusp of new eras, of new movements and moments in history. Despite their innumerable obstacles and vicissitudes, such as having no birth control, traveling and performing all over Europe with children trailing behind them, or being arrested by the Italian police for "anarchy," they were moved by the motivation, energy and hope that things could only get better, that society was going through a radical change and they were part of the Revolution or even that they *were* the Revolution. The Renaissance, for all its wars of religion and lack of sanitation, must have been for those women artists a pretty exciting moment and place to be, particularly if you were a contemporary of Leonardo or Machiavelli or Michelangelo and most importantly if you were among the very first women to ever step in front of an audience on a stage. Franca's plays and performances, her theatrical activism in factories and deserted palaces, happened during and shortly after the women's movements of emancipation and liberation that swept all over Europe and America and gave us most of the rights we enjoy today; that mythic second wave of feminism that some of us are nostalgic for to this very day.

Deb Margolin's moment is a very different one, situated as it is on the

Deb Margolin in *O Yes I Will (I Will Remember the Spirit and Texture of This Conversation)*. October 2005, during the run of the show at Dixon Place in New York. Photograph by Janusz Jaworski.

cusp of a new millennium, with wars and genocidal events happening literally all across the planet, with the threat of overpopulation and climate change and with women still being paid less than men, being raped at a rate of one out of four — and that's in the "civilized world " — with sex trafficking going out of control, "honor killings" taking place in parts of the world even as this book is being written and most theaters and movies still portraying the same tired images of bitchy women when empowered and well paid, of sexy bimbos with no brains or of pathetic dying mothers who have sacrificed everything for their families and for that are portrayed as female role models. I am also talking about Deb Margolin because, like the *commedia* actors who always inscribed their comedy within their local and particular historical place and time, so does she always relate her philosophical musing about the human condition, her frustrations at gender injustices in this very historical moment with its huge mess and yet its glowing shreds of hope illuminating the rubble. Many of us identify with the mother who is multi-tasking even while on the toilet and tries to explain life and death to her children in a "smelly bathroom."

As a political refugee, working single mother, writer, teacher, scholar, playwright, theater director in twenty-first century America, I feel empowered and solaced by the many women stand-up comedians working today, by their art, their anger, their shamelessness, their stories and their laughter that resonate with mine and that "help me through the day," as Samuel Beckett's character Winnie puts it so poignantly in the play *Happy Days*. I feel exhilarated and renewed by Deb Margolin's art, her quivering stage presence, her unpredictable strings of multicolored words that unravel and tell stories which resonate with mine, that make me laugh because my own story meets hers in the process of telling it and performing it. Despite the pain, I feel like giggling when I meet her in the middle of her stories with myriad details that construe the life of a frazzled mother, or of an anguished patient under anesthetic, or that describe the carnal reality of our female bodies and souls in a world still hostile to us, to our creativity, to our bodily secretions and shapes. She makes me laugh because she does what Cixous urged women to do in "The Laugh of the Medusa": reclaim our bodies and our imaginations, "write with our bodies" by "flying" with language, by "stealing" language. Deb Margolin is such a cunning, startling thief of language that she makes me fantasize about a long series of celebrated canonical male playwrights remaining speechless across the centuries for one long moment to listen to her.

And let us listen to Deb Margolin now in the following interview about comedy, commedia, and her view of using humor even with the darkest topics:

Domnica Radulescu: What is in your view the role of comedy other than entertainment?

Deb Margolin: Comedy is an organic element in the continuum of human communication. It is a reflex, some miraculous combination of the autonomic and the voluntary. Babies laugh in their cribs at things! When something appears, then disappears, then reappears again; when a baby turns its head from side to side and sees everything swaying! Things are naturally funny! And there is, in the face of mortality, even if that face is in shadow or behind a curtain, a very profound impulse to use comedy as the delivery medium for messages of the absurd. The structure of so many of the jokes I know and love best leads the mind, in a sideways manner, towards recognition of the tragic flaws in the human psyche and the ultimate flaw in the human portfolio: the inevitability of death. Comedy decorates, annotates and becomes a source of deep pleasure and tenderness in the presence of death.

DR: Do you see comedy as a social force or as a force of social and political transformation? How? And is in your opinion women's comedy/humor different from men's comedy/humor? How?

DM: In answer to these questions, I would like to point to silence as one of the most pivotal aspects of delivering comedy, and to the feminist use of silence in particular when it comes to comedy. Timing is always talked about in regard to comic delivery, and timing has to do with silences, with waiting, with understanding how long to wait or not wait before speaking. And this critical aspect of comic anatomy is somehow a metaphor for what is feminist about silence as used in feminist comedy. Women are allegedly talkers, and talkers of nonsense. Women have been traditionally silenced because their speech has been considered to lack the gravitas, the logic, and the erudition attributed to men and to male speech. Thus there is something radical and reclamatory about female comedians who stand for long periods of time saying nothing. An example of this use of silence/speech as part of a whole pattern of expression is found in the work of Margaret Cho. I swear, she did this one HBO special during which she hardly said anything. She just came out and stood onstage in a very nice outfit and provoked waves of laughter just by insisting that she had the right to stand there, despite being Asian, being polysexual in some way, not looking like Nicole Kidman, not having a size 2 figure, all of that. This comedian just stood there, and a largely female audience just went nuts, laughing a laughter they'd been waiting to let out for years of sexism and suffering. The things she said were very, very funny: reflections on her parents, her culture, the world; various of the idiomatic human behaviors that drive her wild, but the richest matrices of her comedy were resident in her silences. She RECLAIMED silence. She went from being SILENCED to standing silent. This is just outrageous.

DR: What should feminist humor do or not do in your opinion?

DM: I have no prescription for feminist comedy, except that it not be self-objectifying and self-denigrating without somehow being a comment on the way women are traditionally seen. A woman standing onstage (or writing in a book and thus taking stage in the mind of the reader) is taking a radical step: arrogating to herself the right to speak, and to stand silent. As we do this with joy and self-respect, we feminist comedians can and should do whatever the hell we want. Personally, I love the use of everyday life and find in it the most profound sources of comedy.

DR: What do you think of treating grave, tragic, troubling subjects with humor?

DM: The only way to treat tragic and grave subjects is with humor. Otherwise, it's just black on black; you can't even see what you're looking at. Comedy is alembic; it purifies for our understanding the nature and texture of suffering. My friend Madeleine Olnek says it is immoral to write a drama when a comedy will do, and I agree. People cannot suffer visions of suffering undiluted. Comedy reaches deep into the psyche. Laughter is separated from weeping by something desperately necessary and indescribably small and exquisite.

DR: Do you see yourself in any way a descendent from the line of commedia dell'arte actresses like Isabella Andreini or the honest courtesans like Veronica Franco?

DM: As for the connection to commedia and its ravishingly beautiful subversions of the existing power structure, I most deeply and definitely feel that connection through the ages! Especially in my love of standing clownlike, and still, and stubborn, onstage! My way of making myself both articulate and ridiculous! Which as you know I consider a radical act! And that prostitute thing was so commedia! Truly! It was the merging of the virgin/tender-mother/whore in a way that just crashed the intellectual hard drives of all the men!

And when asked about the art of improvisation and whether her art ever relies on this practice, this is what she said:

DR: Do you ever improvise your own text onstage, or do you write your plays with the idea of a fluid transformation of the text while in performance, after the performance, do things come up during performance that you incorporate into the text afterwards?

DM: I write text that I mean to perform verbatim, with my body being the mediator between what I write and what the moment calls for that the act of writing could not possibly have known. When in performance, I sometimes feel an impulse to say something else, and act on it; some of my shows have invited this kind of impulsivity more than others. For example, in *Index to Idioms*, I stuck very strictly to the text as written, as the show was a series of tone poems that did not ask for nor welcome improvisation. In *O Yes I Will (I will remember the spirit and texture of this conversation)* I invited a more open state of mind in terms of deviations from scripted text, although those were rare and impulsive, and sometimes the result of forgetting the exact language of the text and opting instead for language of the moment. But as ever and always, the audience is my best editor, and if performance and its responses yielded information as to what worked and what seemed superfluous, I was always willing to adjust text to the deeper purpose, the more successful connection. I am a performer who pushes past the comfortable point, so I don't mean the audience had to feel perfectly comfortable with me or my body or my verbal overflows, but rather that I am able to see in performance what is working towards the purpose and what isn't; every performance is a kind of experiment, with results that can be felt and assessed for purposes of any adjustment.

This beautifully stubborn and elegant existence in the present and the respect for the shared moment with an audience, the generous willingness to not only talk to but also listen to the pulse of an audience and perform accordingly is one of the things that marks the ineffable beauty and the shimmer of

Deb Margolin in *Index to Idioms*, presented at The Culture Project in New York, April 5, 2006. Photograph by Jim Baldassare.

persistent irony in Deb Margolin's performances. Lynda Hart noted: "One of the many ways that I experience the beauty of Margolin's work is in the feeling she creates of waiting *with* rather than waiting *for*. A waiting without the anxiety of forward movement, without projection." And Jill Dolan notes, in response to this, that "Perhaps in these moments of communal, almost loving rest, when the flesh stops and the soul pauses, we come together, at attention and relieved, to feel utopia. In these moments, we feel the simultaneity of time; we revel in the 'now.'"[4]

Kimberly Dark

Kimberly Dark is a rising star performance artist who brings provocative issues to the stage, who speaks openly of LGBT life, relationships and issues, who boldly explores and crosses gender lines and gender divides in a mixture of high and low discourse, who blends academic gender theories with sultry, funny and intelligent storytelling. She envelops the audience with a sensuously poised stage presence and voice and with stories that break taboos about sexuality, notions of femaleness and the cunning negotiations with a world often hostile to women and even more hostile to women and people who defy heteronormativity.

I choose to include Kimberly in my book because she combines with great subtlety and courage a deftly humorous stand towards life's ironies together with an acute and lucid understanding of gender inequities and of inequities of all kinds. Most importantly, she is included in this study because she illustrates feminist humor in performance in ways that are both deliciously entertaining and empowering, because she writes, performs, directs and improvises her own one-woman shows, much like the other artists portrayed in this book. Dark is as much an activist as she is a skilled artist onstage, using the art of storytelling in cajoling, mesmerizing ways very much in the tradition of female storytelling as discussed in this book while also simultaneously shattering the fourth wall with a firm but feathery touch and confronting her audience with difficult questions about men and women, gender and sexuality, and violence against women. She never offers easy answers. A review of her performance in the *Salt Lake Tribune* notes, "Dark doesn't shy away from provocative, even incendiary statements. But don't expect a rant. Her shows, leavened with humor, are more likely to explore how small everyday moments can inform the arc of our lives." Most reviewers admire her art as a storyteller, the precision of her performance, and the combination of humor with social activism.[5]

I also interviewed Kimberly Dark about her stance on comedy, on the use of humor as a strategy of resistance and social change, and on the role of feminist performance and laughter. Her answers are as beautifully crafted and as honest as her performance art, filled with both emotion and critical thinking, while also connected to some degrees with some of the ideas expressed by Deb Margolin in her interview. With an intellectual agility reminiscent of the mythic Colombina she deliberately escapes definition, stereotype, or category, while also dealing with modern social and political issues.

Domnica Radulescu: What in your view is the role of comedy other than entertainment?

Kimberly Dark: Comedy is not just about entertainment — it's about life — and how we choose to live and create our world! Laughter has a physiological effect. The body relaxes and the parasympathetic nervous system is engaged. We don't experience the fight/flight response when we're laughing. It's just not possible. So comedy gets us ready, gets us fearless!

Everyone deserves pleasure. Pleasure is a sign that things are going RIGHT! Especially when there's oppression or pain or grief, we need to remember — in our bodies — that we have the power to create good feelings. And comedy is pleasurable. Think about a time when you were laughing and enjoying a story or a joke with others. Did you breathe more deeply? Sigh? How did you move your body? Was it a relief to relax?

When the body and mind are relaxed, we think more clearly. Some of my shows are very complex. I'm telling multiple stories at once. And the audience stays engaged; they stay with me. I don't think that would happen without humor. I deal with themes like sexism, racism, beauty and unattractiveness. Without humor, the themes would feel heavy — like the mind has to work too hard. When there's humor, thinking isn't a chore — it happens naturally. The mind wants to put together different story lines because there's going to be a pleasurable reward. Yes. I'll go so far as to say, comedy makes us sharper — more able to access our humanity and problem-solve.

DR: Do you see comedy as a social force or as a force of social and political transformation? How?

KD: Absolutely. One of the main reasons I started doing performance and humor writing was because of a desire to discuss social justice issues in ways that bring pleasure and allow us to access our wisdom and experiences. I'm a sociologist by training and we social scientists really discuss some amazing things about the world. But nobody cares because, as a group, we're crazy-boring! And let's face it; whether or not a comedy writer is a trained professional in social issues, we're all social observers. Truth and shared meaning are the ways something becomes funny.

Especially in performance, we feel the camaraderie of a group who also understands what we understand. There's shared meaning, and then there's laughter. Laughter gives us oxygen! And then we think more clearly. So, for me, if a story can reveal difficult social circumstances in a way that makes someone laugh and reflect on their own social position, that's the golden ticket. I'm not telling an audience what to think or do about a situation; I'm offering a place of pleasure and contemplation. I'm reminding the audience that we're all creating reality, here and now. How do you want it to look? What if we try to build in pleasure and social justices and clever, fun humanity? What's that like? Ah, a whole universe of possibility is there!

DR: Is in your opinion women's comedy/humor different from men's comedy/humor? How?

KD: Yes and no. Both men and women can take steps to reveal the other's brilliance. Both men and women can oppress others. We all have the responsibility to wake up! It's just easier, if one has gender privilege, to keep subjugating others without even seeing it — without questioning it. That part is very sad. (Hmm, someone should write a funny story to reveal the absurdity of humor that oppresses others. That's how we'd come to know more about the gendered nature of comedy...)

DR: What should feminist humor do or not do?

KD: Just as feminism seeks equality, feminist humor should too. Some humor looks for the joy of the shared experience by invoking common unkindness. Those can be funny too. Just because something's common and easily identifiable doesn't make it just. To my mind, feminist humor does not invoke oppression for a laugh. I'm very aware that everyone in the stories I tell — even the so-called villains — should remain human. Because I'm the storyteller, I can create the world where everyone's humanity remains intact. Sometimes that's rough. But I'm clever, so I figure it out. Even those who are oppressed can, in the turn of a head, become oppressors. We should never forget.

I often use re-created or remembered dialogue in my storytelling. It's important to me that I spend very little time (if any) re-inscribing oppressive language. While this might be funny — it might invoke a response of shared meaning — it can also retraumatize people and normalize language that has negative effects. I want to invoke the power of the imagination in positive ways — to allow people to laugh at the absurdity of something and then imagine weird or different ways to see that thing. That's pleasurable for the mind too. Rather than re-inscribing binaries like right and wrong, funny or serious, male or female, black or white, I try for stories that point out multiple interpretations. To me, this is one way feminist humor can work. It can be complicated, but neither self-deprecating nor other-deprecating. There are a lot of ways for something to be funny, and I think we need to choose wisely. Invoke and celebrate the complexity of the enlivened mind and spirit!

DR: What do you think of treating grave, tragic, troubling subjects with humor?

KD: It's the only way. I don't think we should be forced to laugh at things any more than we should be forced to cry about things. The human way is to oscillate between the two. And, let's be careful, compassionate. Some topics can only handle a little humor at a time.

Dealing with grave, tragic or troubling subjects can feel like drowning, unless we learn how to come up for air periodically. Humor is how we do that. Everyone's had these experiences in everyday life. Maybe you're at your uncle's funeral and it's so sad, but then someone notices that he's in the casket wearing jewelry he'd never have worn in life, or maybe there's a booger hanging out of his nose. And then people laugh. Those who can't laugh occasionally when something's tragic feel like they've been pushed under into the ocean of grief and may drown. We all need to come up and breathe, see the light of day. That gives us strength and the ability to use our mental clarity to tackle what needs to be handled.

DR: I was wondering if you could give a brief description of yourself as a feminist performance artist comedian of sorts, from an aesthetic and political point of view.

KD: I didn't set out to be a comedian — I'm a cultural critic — and yet, if that's not done with humor, it's a bit arrogant, right? Once, I was booked for an event at which I was to perform some new work, along with two other artists. I arrived to that city to find that the three of us had been billed as comedians. The show was titled *Laughing Matters*. I was horrified! The organizer was flabbergasted because she'd seen my work and thought I was hilarious. Well, that may be, but "comedian" is a very specific job description. Under that title, the audience expects a certain style, for the performance to follow a certain arc. That's not what I do — I tell stories and I want the interactions I have with the audience to be respectful — funny, yes, but meaningful. I don't insult audience-members and I don't desire heckling. And still, I understand the trouble this promoter was having. If I'm funny, I'm a comedian. Advertising often over-simplifies. (Indeed, my agent still comments that I'd be easier to book if I weren't so complicated!) Perhaps this is part of using feminist humor — I'm not interested in a laugh at anyone's genuine expense. From an aesthetic point of view, there is sometimes humor in the way I use my body onstage. When a fat person is publicly displayed, people are accustomed to laughing. (More specifically, people feel entitled to laugh — and often do.) Alternately, if it becomes clear that the fat is not the funny part, people want to ignore it. I try to offer a third alternative: in some of my work I "come out" as fat — that is to say, I let the audience know that it's okay to see me as a fat person. It's also okay for them to see me as a sexy person, as a smart person, as a tricky person, and so much more. And from there, we can laugh at the absurdity of putting anyone into rigid categories that don't allow for full humanity.

DR: What do you consider as the most radical or revolutionary gesture or action you have undertaken as a playwright performer in your career? I am thinking of radical or revolutionary mostly in terms of gender and of what Deb Margolin always says, that a woman standing on a stage in front of an audience is already a radical thing in itself.

KD: Each of us manages various identities, and yet we live in a culture that promotes dichotomous thinking: if you're not male, you're female, if you're not tall, you're short, if you're not thin, you're fat. On and on. Some identities are fairly invisible because they're the norm. This is how white people can get away with acting like they don't have a race — it's just plain "normal" to be white — no discussion is needed. Similarly, the male experience is the norm. I agree with Deb Margolin that a woman standing onstage in front of an audience is already a radical thing in itself. And then, if that woman also occupies other categories that disrupt dichotomous thinking — if she is not white, not thin, not pretty — wow, that's mind-blowing! But here's the really radical act: occupying multiple differences and still presenting a big, nuanced, fascinating life. It's amazing to me that people still think the woman should be talking about women's issues, the person of color should be talking about race, the lesbian should be talking about queer issues — on and on. I learned, from the audience back in the 1990s, that my physical presence onstage was a huge part of my work (and I don't even DO much onstage). I am a fat, queer woman talking about things like sexuality and parenting and peace and civic engagement and I'm making fun of my life without making fun of being fat or queer. It's not that I ignore those aspects of myself, but they're not my main focus. I don't put my humanity up for grabs onstage — and the show can still be funny. To paraphrase Heather McAllister — founder of the Fat Bottom Revue (the first all-inclusive fat burlesque troupe in the U.S.) — the idea of a fat woman being onstage and NOT being the object of someone's joke is revolutionary.

DR: And I am wondering, if you were to see yourself in a continuum or sisterhood across the centuries with other women performers and theater artists, you would consider as part of this sisterhood the first actresses of the commedia dell'arte who created and performed those sassy roles of women standing up to tyrannical fathers, husbands, structures and had the last laugh, with performing courtesans and poets such as the Venetian courtesan Veronica Franco and other such complete and highly irreverent artists of the stage?

KD: I definitely identify my work in the lineage of writers and performers such as Veronica Franco — women who learned the deft manipulation of words and presence in order to bargain for their lives and statuses. I must also place burlesque performers in my feminist performance lineage as well. Though I've never revealed much of my body in my solo shows, I am always conscious of the story as an act of alternating revelation and concealment. Humor is one of the ways that painful truths can be concealed with a bright-feathered fan until the time is right for a deeper knowing.

DR: Do you ever improvise your own text onstage, or do you write your plays with the idea of a fluid transformation of the text while in performance, after the performance, do things come up during performance that you incorporate into the text afterwards?

KD: I am constantly learning from audience. I solicit feedback in a number of ways and I also reflect on audience personality during a performance in order to create a successful flirtation, seduction. Most of my shows follow a format that includes tightly scripted storytelling (often poetic storytelling) interspersed with loosely scripted monologue and interaction with the audience, and punctuated with occasional improvisation. The show I'm currently working on (working title: *Good Fortune*) really pushes me with audience participation by allowing audience members to choose images from a deck of

Kimberly Dark, promotional shot. Photograph by Roni Galgano.

tarot-like cards (assembled according to my themes and specifications). Each image corresponds with a story or poem from my past ten years of work. I then assemble a performance for the audience on the spot, using those cards and stories. I'm still workshopping it, but it's been such a gift to work with the 7 visual artist collaborators, first off, but also to push the boundaries of how I use radical presence and audience interaction, along with scripted work. (Scripted work is important for a whole different set of reasons — I can't imagine giving up the tight use of language, metaphor and the ability to weave a complex scene, but improvisation has its place as well.) One of the things I realized in the first workshop performance of *Good Fortune* was that I had lost some control over how much humor the show would have. This is uncomfortable — but I'm looking forward to learning from the unfolding...

And here is in its elegant "unfolding" is a recent story/mono-

Kimberly Dark, in *The Butch/Femme Chronicles: Discussion with Women Who Are Not Like Me (and Some Who Are)* which toured between 1998 and 2004. The promotional shots for that show included a series of neck-up photos of Kimberly Dark with the question "Butch or Femme?" beneath, prompting the viewer to question what cues to gender identity are expressed just in a person's face, a person's subtle comportment. Photograph by Kate Mayne.

logue/performance piece written and performed by Kimberly Dark, quoted here in its entirety and in the poem-like shape shared by the author herself[6]:

The Story He Can Understand

"Let me talk to him," I said to her
as the officer walked around to her side of the car.
A busy road on a hillside —
the kind that would wash out in a bad storm,
send little tin shacks tumbling,
foul people's drinking water for weeks.
To our left, the ravine and barbed wire fences

that separate the nation and city of my birth
from the nation we are in.

We were driving too fast.
Though offense is not entirely necessary
for being stopped in this border city
by notoriously corrupt police.

Who will he be?

Police are people.
I watch his face, his jaw, his stance.
He is looking at our car — a good sign.
This is not personal.
He is trying to decide
based on the age, condition and worth of the car
what our bribe will be.
"Buenos Dias!"
I lean across the seat and begin in a cheery tone.
He will get money
but I will try to maintain control of this interaction.
She sits beside me
And I send her a telepathic message:
Please stay quiet
take no offense
make no offense.
Let me handle this.
[...]
He wants to speak English — ask questions.
Talk is good and I am warm, friendly, apologetic —
still speaking Spanish because she doesn't.
She must not join this conversation
reveal herself as a threat to his fragile gender.
I long for men to be stronger so we are all safer.
[...]
I am managing.
He is managing.
She is sitting quietly
and this is not always so.
She is a great storyteller!
And a big presence in the room
She lives boldly — when we're on our home turf, at least.
In the city, never hesitates to offer me her arm
when we are walking on the street.
She opens doors for me and holds my purse when asked
and publicly accepts a quick kiss of thanks
for her common chivalry.
She is good at managing things too —
the glances of onlookers, the reinterpretation as man and woman

no, woman and woman.
Dyke and woman? No. Man? No.
She knows how to manage a situation too, no doubt.
[...]
Next to me, in Tijuana, the officer staring in the window
I am the woman with the story he can understand.
And she is still big and strong and powerful
and I'm grateful that she is not acting that way now.

I'm not sure she knows that this negotiation
could turn at any moment
And I would be out of this car
and letting him press against me, cop a feel
as we negotiate my payment.
To protect her I would let him put me in my place
if it came to that.
Because my desire to protect her is at least as fierce
as her desire to protect me.
I love her
and I will not end up in a Mexican jail today
watching her beaten and gang raped
because she is a threat to maleness
and I need to be shown the error of my ways.
Women like her get the worst of it
but I have survived abuses,
avoided many others,
by managing the situation.
[...]
She's never learned of countries,
such as this one,
where being gay is not defined
by the gender of the person with whom you have sex
but by the role you take in the fucking.
And women never do the fucking.

I understand that this man's identity is a fragile glass bauble.
I can see right through him and
I will be careful with him
because we are not getting cut today.
God help you if you seem to take male privilege unduly!
And oh, my lover, you take it so well....

As she offers the Spanish word for firefighter—
a male-only job in this country, nearly so in our own—
I chuckle and
(still speaking Spanish so that her machismo remains intact)
I reframe her as a paramedic
explain that in our country the two travel together
and that women aren't paid much anyway.

I am steering us back to the cost of the bribe
and she does not know that I have just insulted
her profession and accomplishments.
And he does not have any idea,
as I haggle the bribe, pay the money, drive away
that she is my lover
and she fucks me harder and longer and satisfies me more
than someone like him ever could.

That evening, safely at home in bed, she was gallant once more,
back in her element with me
she took me a little more aggressively than usual —
joyful at being back in a position she could command.
As she started to form the clever and funny story of the event
as she is wont to do,
I stopped her and said "Thanks for letting me do the talking today."
To which she replied, somber for a moment.
"I was scared."
I nodded and then made light of the situation again,
because I couldn't stay with my own fear.
I love her bigness and would not diminish her for anything.
Masculinity is too fragile, no matter who's wearing it, it seems.
And the truth is, we keep each other safe
even though she's the one who walks by the street, as she offers me her arm.

As Kimberly herself noted in her interview, the humor in her story is subtle. It comes and goes in fleeting sparks but mostly bubbles in the telling and in the performing. Her style is mellow yet confident, sassy and intelligent, and defies placing in any specific category, be it that of storyteller, performance artist, or comedienne. But maybe it is most worthy of the larger frame of feminist artist who makes use of feminist humor, just like all the other artists in this book. The delicious line "Masculinity is too fragile, no matter who's wearing it" seems to beautifully crystallize one of the recurrent themes of this book as well as offer glimmers and echoes of that female "chuckle" at the real and imagined power of the phallus and the masculine noted from the very start.

FIVE

The Heritage of the Commedia dell'Arte for Today's Feminist Theaters, Comedy and Activism, and Radical Acts by Women Artists

The performance art and strategies of the commedia dell'arte, and, more specifically, the comedy of the performers I have discussed in this book, have the potential of being excellent models and sources of inspiration for performers of comedy, for female performers and for women in society. Recently, theaters in Europe and the United States have seen a rebirth of commedia style performances, and theater events such as the Avignon International Theater Festival offer an increasing number of productions attempting to emulate the commedia style, yet for the most part, this rebirth is only at a superficial level. For instance, plays by Molière or Jarry are produced with masks or accentuated makeup, include a lot of acrobatics and physical comedy in their productions and often leave some room for improvisation and interaction with the audience. And famous directors are known to have made use of the *commedia* style acting techniques, such as Ariane Mnouchkine in her Théâtre du Soleil performances. Mime, pantomime, buffoonery and physical comedy of all sorts are often seen in the street, at fairs, carnivals and theater festivals in Europe and the United States. However, the spirit of the commedia and the more profound aspects of the theatrical aesthetics and the philosophy of production of this genre fail to be brought to life and to be properly explored. Furthermore, most Western conventional theaters are still based on a hierarchical system of production, in which the writer and the director hold most of the artistic power and the actors are generally interpreters of a given script, with given directions.

On the other hand, feminist and women's theaters of the past several decades as well as feminist performance theory have kept an uncanny silence with regard to commedia dell'arte theater techniques and modes of production, although quite a few of the performance and production strategies they advocate or practice bear striking similarities to this form of theater. And a brilliant performer like Franca Rame, a pioneer who for almost half a century has successfully combined her knowledge and experience of commedia dell'arte with feminist concerns and performance techniques, is blatantly left out of most feminist performance theory as an outstanding illustration of it. Occasionally, she is mentioned in passing, as an actress who mocked the blonde bombshell stereotype by the use of exaggerated makeup[1] and mimiced "the gender signs of heterosexual femininity."[2] And only one of the feminist theaters of the seventies and eighties, Monstrous Regiment, translated and performed several of her monologues.

A detailed listing of the commedia techniques in general and of the particular performative and comedic strategies used and created by the artists I have studied might urge feminist performers and theoreticians to include such techniques in their practice and theory, and to recognize its sources when indeed using similar methods. Interestingly, the Split Britches company first started out under the name Punch and Judy, and acted in parks and cafés, with the Wow café in New York as their headquarters. The two characters Punch and Judy are precisely modernized versions of commedia type buffoonish characters, with Punch sounding like a short form of the Puncinella character of traditional commedia. The unconventional nature of acting spaces of feminist theater troupes, from regular theaters to cafés, to outdoor spaces, art centers, community centers or schools is also much like the commedia's itinerant theaters.[3] The commedia troupes carried their properties in a wagon and acted as often in palaces or theaters as they did in the street and in parks. The eighteenth century idealized representations of the Italian actors, as seen in Watteau's or Fragonard's or Walter Pater's paintings. All depict idyllic love and humorous scenes in gardens and parks. Sketches and drawings of commedia actors from the sixteenth and seventeenth centuries portray commedia troupes building rudimentary stages in city streets.[4] Similarly, feminist performance is generally subversive of realist and mimetic representations, the space and the set usually defy the material conglomeration of objects found in realistic theater, and their choices of space are unconventional.

Consistently, as Vivian Patraka points out when she talks about Split Britches, the group's technique is to create an "unstable space onstage," which is "made up of a series of impulses and moments that keep shifting, not only in performance, blurring the boundaries between performer and character."[5]

The same could be said of virtually all of Franca Rame's repertoire of female monologues. Her acting space is always fluid and shifts with the voices she creates onstage. At the same time she mixes her own voice with that of her characters, be they the confused overworked working mother, the cunning lover, or the abused woman turned revolutionary in *We All Have the Same Story*.

The performance of monologues and dialogues by the Split Britches Company is also based, much like Rame's performance, on the "staging of routines" and the inclusion of "popular forms of entertainment."[6] As Fo has shown in his writings on the revival of the commedia tradition in his theater, the inclusion of and reliance on popular forms of entertainment has been one of the most revolutionary moves of his and Rame's theater, as they departed from the conventional bourgeois theater. As for the "staging of routines," most of Rame's one-woman shows involve at least one such example: from the routines of the isolated housewife going sadly about her chores as she is telling her life story to a neighbor (*Una Donna Sola*), to those of *Il Risveglio*, in which the frantic working mother is getting ready for work, desperately looking for her keys while thinking in horror she has placed the baby in the oven, as those of the women in *Abiammo tutte la stessa storia*, as in her lesson of sexuality in *Sex? Don't Mind if I Do*. And like Rame, Split Britches creates a multilayered performance with meta-theatrical dimensions as their characters' actions or routines or "labor" point to the performative act in itself, to the "labor of performing and improvising."[7] We have seen that not only Franca but within the commedia tradition itself, the female characters like Colombina mix and blur the distinctions between theater and life, and often their commentaries on life, marriage, sexuality and women's lives apply equally to their actual performative art of improvisation. Finally, the female carnivalesque in which women's sexuality is performed, described, and talked about openly, drawing attention to "the mentioned 'unmentionables': women's otherwise invisible physicality, their urinary and sexual organs,"[8] is theatrically explored by Split Britches as it is in abundance by Franca, not just in her actual plays, but, as we have seen, even in the prologues to her plays.

All feminist theaters engage at least to some extent in cross-dressing and the representation of gender is fluid and unconventional. In women-only companies such as Split Britches and Siren, women played all male and female parts. We have seen that in the commedia troupes, the most ingenious actresses, like Isabella Andreini and Caterina Biancolelli, turned cross-dressing and acting in disguise into a real art. Furthermore, Isabella Andreini played male roles in earnest and not only as a comic device, as for instance her role in Tasso's *Aminta*. As Isabella herself writes in her letters, playing in disguise or cross-dressing was part of the tricks of the trade of the commedia actors, men and women alike.

However, like the millennium-long Western tradition of exclusively male theater troupes and of male and female parts being played exclusively by male actors has rightfully been subject to significant criticism by feminist theorists and theater practitioners, the women's theaters that insist on a no-male policy risk opening themselves to similar criticisms. Although I am myself supportive of such projects, and I have in my theater practice worked with all-female casts (more often than not out of necessity),[9] upon lucid consideration, I can see both the advantages and limitations of all women or of mixed troupes, from the vantage point of the female performer. Theater groups that are adamantly against including men are opening themselves to the rightful criticism that they are mimicing or reversing the same structures they have been critical of. Although the work of the many feminist theater groups of the seventies and eighties has shown that, in fact, they are engaging in a theater that is *far* from being a female version of the traditional Western theater run and played by men, problems of power, control and even stereotypical portrayals of men do occur. Feminist troupes such as the Women's Theater Groups, Monstrous Regiment, Siren, and Split Britches have had extraordinary artistic achievements, which have been indispensable to the raising of a feminist consciousness as well as to the creation of a feminist theater aesthetic.[10] It was high time that theater broke away from all conventional representations of women and modes of production and brought to their audiences women's issues, women's stories and women's creativity. The seventies, eighties and nineties having passed, and feminist performance theory and performance having reached a plurality of voices and orientations, as well as having increased their confidence and healed to some extent their bruised egos as a result of centuries of marginalization, feminist and women's theaters could afford and even benefit at this point from mixed groups and productions. In theaters with an openly lesbian orientation such as Split Britches, the decision to not accept men is a politically understandable one, as the whole point of such theaters is precisely to destabilize uniquely heterosexual views and representations.

Speaking, however, strictly from the viewpoint of comic performance, which is the focus of this book, just from a purely practical standpoint mixed companies may have an even wider range of possibilities as well as of subversive modes of performance. Take cross-dressing, for example. Having myself worked in the theater and directed plays with students for almost two decades, I have worked quite often with exclusively or almost exclusively female casts. My experiences with them have been equally exciting and inspiring. The groups with at least a few male students however, offered, in my experience, a wider range of comic possibilities in terms of cross-dressing, even as far as destabilizing conventional and uniquely or compulsory heterosexual structures and representations. In my shows, I have often had both the women and the men play both male and female parts, much in the way that it was done in the commedia troupes. In those instances, with a cast of, say, ten or twelve women and one or two men, I have in fact cast the one or two men in women's roles and many of the women in men's roles. I staged, for instance, Alfred Jarry's *Ubu Roi* with a cast of ten women and one man, with the man playing the part of Mother Ubu and several of the women taking turns in playing Father Ubu. Besides the comic possibilities in such casting, this created a fluidity of gender lines that was highly beneficial for my students. Not being fixated on what was conventionally male or female in the characters, they had to focus on what was the human or the grotesque or the inhuman core of the character. Furthermore, they saw male and female stereotypes being equally exploded, as for instance, Mother Ubu's stridence and cunning were taken on by a male actor while Father Ubu's cruelty and machismo gone bad were portrayed by a female actress. It is what was going on in the commedia dell'arte plays where Arlecchino played in disguise as a marquise or a coquette, or when Isabella or Colombina took on a multitude of masculine attires and poses, from soldiers to old fathers to lawyers. While not entirely devoid of some risks of enforcing certain gender stereotypes, such mixed and equal cross-dressings do point inevitably to the social construction of gender and to performance as a means of both enforcing and dismantling constructions of gender altogether.

Another important aspect of the commedia dell'arte theater and of the commedia female performers' acting style is the relation to audience. We have seen, not only from the criticism and reports about the commedia theater, but actually built in many of the texts in the Gherardi collection, for instance, that the interaction with an audience, taking in the audience as accomplice, as player, and as intrinsic part of the show, was crucial to the art of the commedia actors. As so much of the commedia shows went on in the street, drawing the attention of the audience and keeping it for a certain amount of time was of the essence for these troupes. On the other hand, when the commedia shows were given for a more select audience, such as the Medicis at Isabella's famous performance in 1589, the actors adapted their text to fit the occasion and the audience, and, as we have seen in Isabella's mad scene, often alluded to events in contemporary politics. As Allardyce Nicoll has pointed out, upon entering a city, the troupes proceeded immediately to draw their audiences and, more often than not, it was the female actresses often dressed as amazons who signaled, in a most theatrical manner, the arrival of the troupe.

Not only does Colombina speak to her audience, she also reprimands them (the Marquis in *La Fille de bon sens*) or urges them to take her side and gives them the responsibility of judging and deciding the outcome of a plot (*Les Chinois*). For Franca Rame, the contact and the dialogue with the audience is indispensable to her theater and, as she notes, it is precisely at the point where she started thinking seriously about her audience and about including them, that her theater was revolutionized. Franca declares that it is "only when Dario and I decided to abandon the official theaters circuit, did I find myself compelled to learn to hold an audience by speaking directly to the stalls."[11] Women's and feminist theaters also make an important point in addressing and interacting with their audience or establishing a variety of relations with their audiences, real or imagined. The Women's Theater Group, for instance, "consciously performed for an imagined feminist spectator, perceiving each member as 'an acting partner.'"[12] When it comes to comedy, Franca Rame noted in several interviews, its most important role should be that of "planting the nails of reason" in the heads of the spectators.

One other crucial aspect of commedia theaters, which has been redis-covered and brought to great aesthetic and political heights by feminist the-aters, is that of collective creation. Michelen Wandor from Siren declares, as she speaks about her company's goals:

> They share one common intention: in different ways they have sought to democ-ratize the social division of labor in the theater by developing flexible and collab-orative work methods, by introducing theater to new audiences, and by representing the experiences and interests of groups of oppressed and exploited people.[13]

Interestingly, the method of collaborative creation in the theater is men-tioned together with the general democratization of theater and of exploding traditional modes of representation. The system of collaborative script writing and directing, though often presented in feminist studies as an innovation of women's and feminist theaters, has, as we have seen, a history of five centuries. Furthermore, it was the commedia dell'arte theaters that democratized enter-tainment during the European Renaissance and that reflected, in their work ethic, much of what they were presenting onstage: servants, the simple people and women always laughed last as characters and, as performers, men and women contributed and benefited equally in the production process and the division of shares. The shows were for everybody, but quite a bit more for the great masses of people. That which was usually portrayed onstage was sub-versive and critical of various forms of injustice and exploitation. The female jesters, tricksters and buffoons of the commedia in the style of Isabella, Colom-bina or the modern *giulliaressa*, Franca, have often tricked the tricksters. With regard to patriarchal structures and the condition of women in society, they have used satire as a vehicle against the violence, cruelty, hypocrisy and injustices performed unto women.

It would be of great benefit to feminist performers and theoreticians to recognize their ancient sources, since, as the studies of Kathleen McGill have shown, it was largely through the participation and contributions of women performers that the commedia troupes developed these successful forms of collaborative script creation and production, and also because women played such an important role in establishing the very modern roots of Western theater.

Feminist theater groups have used very similar methods of show production, based, for instance, on "a conflation of the scripting and directorial processes." The script is usually the result of teamwork, and one or more members of the group are often assigned the responsibility of "scribing the process," taking notes to document the ideas, images, and lines that come forth in rehearsals.[14] The Split Britches company stores all this information in what it calls "banks," much like the *zibaldone* kept by the ancient *commedia* troupe leaders, in which one of the actors, usually the troupe leader, wrote down script ideas, lines and possible dialogues, *lazzis* and various acting techniques. Examples are the acting notebooks kept by Pietro Maria Cecchini in the sixteenth century and those of Domenico Biancolelli in the seventeenth century.

In her study *Feminist Theater Practice*, Elaine Aston offers several examples of collaborative script or play writing and categorizes them in three different types of creative endeavors: play or script written by a writer together with the group, entirely "collective writing," and writing by a writer "emerging from the group" (33). As examples from various women's groups demonstrate, the most difficult to achieve is exclusively collective writing. However, we can see from the documentation and accounts of the system of artistic creation within the *commedia* troupes that collective script writing was *precisely* how the troupes functioned, particularly with the participation of women.[15] The key difference here is the fact that the commedia troupes did not actually write plays, but composed scenarios which became part of the artistic "bank" of the troupe. These were kept in the commedia families and handed down from one generation to the next, and each actress/actor was largely responsible for the creation of her/his lines. Thus the final product, namely the show, was the result of various forms of improvisation, individual and collaborative creation.

One problem with modern women's theaters and one reason why they may have become less and less visible (if not altogether disappeared during the nineties) may be the fact that they have not freed themselves of at least one of two things: the text and/or the director. Even the most experimental feminist theater groups that have produced plays entirely by collaborative script writing still rely on a written text to be memorized and on the artistic direction of one person. With the text, of course, comes the literary value of the production, but much of its freedom and authentic theatricality is lost with it as well. The scenarios of the commedia troupes, it has been said many times, lacked literary value, but, on the other hand, they contained the potential for the most explosive and comic theater experiences. They also gave great freedom to the actors and in particular to the actresses who flourished and amazed all of Europe with their improvisational talents. Isabella Andreini and Caterina Biancolelli would not have had reason to complain as a twentieth century actress does: "I have always felt the difficulty of having to play a character that someone's written for me and that I have not been able to create myself. No matter how much we talk about a story and a plot, to have a character sketched out and given lines, ways, and relationships that haven't been created by myself— that has always been an imposition."[16] Inversely, as even some of the more traditional commedia critics have shown, the female roles in particular, more so than the male ones, which often derived from ancient traditions, were significantly the creation of the actress herself and often reflected and emerged from the actress's own experience and personality. Therefore, for the most part they did not have to suffer such "impositions."

Furthermore, someone like Isabella wrote stage dialogues in abundance, wrote plays such as *The Mirtilla* in which she played the main part and improvised, created her own roles and her own lines with gusto in all the plays whose scenarios are gathered in the Flaminio Scala collection. Analogously, Caterina Biancolelli acted in many of the plays written by French authors for the troupe, but her roles were largely of her own creation and a result of her improvisational creativity, as my analysis of texts from the Gherardi collection demonstrates.

As for Franca Rame, the system of collaborative writing and directing she has initiated with Dario Fo follows much in the line of the commedia system and offers a positive example of collaborative creation that *does* work. All of these are examples of "actors' theaters" in which the actors have the first and last word about what will be played onstage and how. The same stands true for the director, whose role, as Aston notes, "can often be one that comes to dominate group work" (37). This was not a problem for the *commedia* troupes either for, according to documents, they functioned in a sort of well-timed orchestration of movements, ideas, gestures and dialogues, with no one in particular directing the shows but everybody in the troupe bringing their contribution to its general outcome. Nor is directing much of a problem for

Franca's theater, as she directs most of her shows or creates the direction in collaboration with Fo and the rest of the troupe.[17]

I believe the key element for this freedom from both the authority of the text and that of the director is the unique training and skill of improvisation that was typical of the commedia tradition in which Franca was raised. More than any other European theaters, including Shakespeare's theater, the Italian troupes of the commedia were unique in their art of improvisation. As Kathleen Lea has remarked, what all the other troupes may be lacking by comparison with the Italian ones is "the discipline of co-operation which was the secret of the improvising comedians."[18] Beyond just the problem of the women's marginalization in the theatrical project, Western theater has ultimately marginalized all actors, men and women, in the creative process. Colombina has a point, after all, in defending with such passion the integrity of the Italian theater together with the Italian marriages of the actors of those times, for that model of collaborative creation through improvisation and in almost complete freedom from text and director was somehow in tune with more egalitarian relations between men and women.

As is obvious in Aston's many accounts of collaborative endeavors by feminist theaters, either at the level of script writing or directing, many are fraught with tension, and the problems of control and power existent in mixed companies seem to appear as well in the all-women companies, where hierarchies of power are often built with the writer or director being on top. Invariably also, whenever male directors were assigned to women or feminist theaters, the same structures of power and control that women performers tried so hard to free themselves of were put back in place. Sarah Daniels complains about it and states she will only work with women directors. In Aston's words, "Like Daniels as a writer, many women practitioners feel strongly that it is not possible to have a man in the position of director" (38). Franca Rame herself has openly expressed her complaints with regard to her lifetime theater partner and husband, Dario Fo, and in an interview with Serena Anderlini, she downright declares that she is "through" with Dario, precisely for reasons of control and power.[19]

Admittedly, it is tempting and easy for us today to idealize the work style, improvisational skills and "discipline of collaboration" of the commedia dell'arte troupes. We may be tempted to criticize the efforts of modern women's and feminist theaters to build new forms of theatrical production which reject conventional hierarchies and power structures. The fact of the matter remains that, based on the knowledge we have about the Italian companies and their work style, they were doing something right and that something is worth emulating today.

David George has noted in his introduction to *Studies in the Commedia dell'Arte*, "Chameleon-like, the commedia tradition has adapted to the needs and moods of each succeeding epoch, receiving new sustenance in the process" (11). However, with regard to the aspects of collaborative creation, it was really almost exclusively in its golden age that the commedia shone with unequaled brilliance. But the fact of its "chameleon-like" dimension is to be retained, as more than anything, *commedia* has bequeathed to us a certain model of authentic theatricality combined with democratic forms of production, which is worth pursuing in any historical period and which easily lends itself to adaptations that fit the needs of a certain epoch.

The paradox is that the lack of texts, scripts, and dialogues from that period, with the exception of some collections of scenarios and collections of scenes such as the Gherardi one, may just be proof of the success of collaborative theater. As there were no directors, and, with some exceptions, no assigned writers, the actors were in full control of their performance. But with the actors in full control and strongly emphasized performance, there is no text from which to reconstruct their performances. We sense only a certain "spirit" of the commedia. This may not necessarily be a bad thing. While troupes such as the Women's Theater Group have attempted and succeeded at collective writing, performers did complain that the task was difficult. One of the actresses in the group notes that "writing was a long and often painful business, inevitably there were disagreements and compromises."[20] Again, from what we know about the *commedia* troupes, this doesn't seem to have been a problem for them, mostly because they really did not care much about having a fixed text in the first place. If a text did come along — for instance, the plays or stage dialogues written by Isabella Andreini — they gladly took possession of it and produced it. But for the most part, the authority of the text was really nonexistent and they cared little about agreeing on "every comma" as one of the actresses in the WTG declared in speaking about their collaborative writing.

While I am in no way advocating that feminist theaters and playwrights should stop producing fixed plays and texts, I am advocating, as a form of experimentation in theatrical collaboration and in the interest of a certain creative freedom at the level of performance and pure theatricality, that women performers, theaters, students of theater, *try* the commedia model of relinquishing at least some of the attachments to a certain text and learn a wide variety of methods of creating shows by using improvisational techniques built up around a basic scenario. What I am suggesting is to embrace, at least for the sake of experimentation with a new model, the primacy of the performative and of orality, at the expense of the text and the written. As I pointed out at the beginning of the chapter on Isabella Andreini, Western thought, having been so fixated on the importance and the virtues of the written word, has often disregarded the beauty and artfulness, evanescent as that may be, of the spoken word and of a performance which lives fully in the present, which is not necessarily based on a text or which is based on a fluid text, with openings for improvisation and change, as are many of Franca Rame's plays. Linking this to the central point of the present study, namely the comic, such freedom and fluidity, based on a strong model of collaborative creation and performance, is also more resourceful in the production of humor. For as noted earlier, there is something in the very unpredictable, slightly unordered quality of that which is improvised that lends itself more easily to laughter and to the comic.

Humor Can Be Learned: A Practical Guide Toward a Feminist Revival of Commedia Techniques and Toward Reviving the Commedia in Modern Context

In this concluding section, I would like to propose several models for improvisational comedy for women, taking my cues from the commedia tradition and from the performers whose stories I have traced in this study. These methods can be used in theater workshops, drama classes, and, ultimately, in theaters, as finished productions.

The sexist humor theories against which feminist critics have raised their voices during the past several decades are most often essentializing theories based either on the notions that women are "natural" objects of humor because they are inferior creatures[21] or that women are "naturally" devoid of humor and incapable of producing any,[22] and, in general, that humor is "naturally" a masculine attribute, although really the mark of humanity par excellence — that which distinguishes humans (men) from animals, and obviously ... from women. As I have shown in my study, feminist theorists and critics have successfully dispelled this most offensive myth and proven quite a bit of the contrary. In its modest way, the present study has also attempted, by analyzing the work and telling the stories of several female performers in the commedia tradition, that women are extraordinary creators of humor, often in pioneering and revolutionary ways.

In this concluding section I will take this notion even further and show that, not only there is no such thing as a "natural" gender distinction in terms of humor and comic abilities between the two sexes, but humor and comedy can actually be learned and created with deliberation and lucid discipline or practice, that comedy may not always be something that descends upon the writer or performer miraculously, from the "grace" of the comic Muse. In what follows, I suggest twelve different techniques that I have drawn from the example of the commedia performers, some of which I have myself experimented with successfully in my own theater practice. The following is a list of the suggested methods; I will discuss each in some detail.

1. The creation of fluid scenarios which reverse conventional comedy plots such as "boy gets girl type"; keep a notebook of the troupe with a "bank" of scenarios. Write all important stage actions, entrances and exits in the scenarios.

2. The research and creation of roles by each individual actor (write blocks of lines, quotes).

3. The creation of stage dialogues by groups of two performers acting complementary roles, such as lovers, friends, father-daughter, etc.

4. If the company is mixed, cross-dressing for both men and women, disguise and rich costume changes.

5. The creation of "mad scenes" à la Isabella, Colombina, Franca or Deb.

6. Engage in carnivalesque discourse and acting.

7. The women in the cast play the conventional male roles by mimicry and caricature.

8. The women in the cast have men onstage dress up as women and present them in a variety of roles but particularly in roles where women are victims.

9. Take women's issues (sexuality, motherhood, contraception, abortion, day care, work and mothering) and create scenes with short dialogues.

10. Re-create known fairy tale or myth plots by introducing feminist and women's issues.

11. Create simple dialogues based on: parallel structures, parataxis, repetitions with interchangeable or shifting phrases.

12. Address and discuss with the audience, ask questions of the audience, listen to their responses and incorporate them in the show.

1. Gathering, creating and "banking" a set of comic scenarios in the style of the commedia dell'arte troupes can be a refreshing and efficient theatrical work method for a theater group, a theater class, a series of theater workshops, or even, in everyday life, say as a parent, for storytelling. The basic plotlines and scenarios that belonged to the *commedia* troupes and of which we have only very few remnants are quite simple in terms of pure theatricality and comic effects, and the stage directions, stage actions, entrances

and exits are all rigorously notated. One of the basic plots of the commedia appears to be the "boy gets girl" or "boy meets girl" plot. An anecdote about Franca Rame's family tells how Dario Fo was invited to dinner at the Rames' and he suggested that Franca's father improvise on the "boy meets girl" scheme. It was minutes before the whole family was into it, with lines, roles and actions distributed to everyone and various versions of the scheme being played around the dinner table.[23]

Other schemes or plotlines of the commedia theater may be: father opposes marriage of young lovers; lover is unfaithful; two men are in love with the same woman/maid; father forces marriage upon daughter. Flaminio Scala's collection is actually a gold mine for comic plots. These simple plotlines that account for much of classical comedy all the way through the twentieth century lend themselves to rich overturns and reversals in which, for instance, say a cast of women or a feminist cast could indulge in an indefinite number of possibilities. In fact, even the traditional commedia scenarios or collections of scenes themselves, in which the two star female performers, Isabella Andreini and Caterina Biancolelli, excelled at the art of improvisation, already offer quite a few possibilities and openings for reversals of traditional schemes. In Scala's scenarios, a better title for many of Isabella's plots would be "girl gets the boy of choice"; "girl tricks father"; "girl tricks old husband"; "girl gets her way in marriage."

The commedia was a revolutionary form of theater for its time, both politically and aesthetically. It offers, even in its most ancient forms, plotlines and themes which present positive female models: strong women, cunning maids, female tricksters who usually get their way. In the Gherardi collection, Colombina reverses several times even the early traditional commedia plot-lines, of the kind found in the Scala collection. In Gherardi's scenarios, boy doesn't always get girl, and girl often finds happiness in *not* marrying, or even in divorcing. Invariably, fatuous lovers or old husbands are tricked or punished. Add to all this the tricks and disguises used to escape unwanted marriages, the tyranny of unreasonable fathers or to punish unfaithful lovers, that both Isabella and Caterina richly engaged in, and you have a simple, efficient start for a show, a class, or a workshop.

Write in the scenario description all the stage actions, such as disguises, fights, quarrels, chases, and reconciliations, and all the exits and entrances of the characters. You now have a "bank" of possible shows for all ages and for many circumstances and spaces, from traditional theaters to classrooms, parks, or your own home. Some possible examples of feminist plot schemes for the creation of scenarios could be: two boys are in love with same girl, girl gets away from both and goes to college; boy meets girl, but girl falls in love with another girl; girl finds out husband is cheating and teaches him a lesson; strict Catholic father of rich suburban family forces daughter to marry lawyer in father's company, girl disguises as man and runs away, gets accepted at Harvard Law School.

Ultimately, the possibilities are unlimited. In fact, many of Hollywood's romantic comedies rely on similar plot schemes, with the exception that, in the end it all ends up in marriage of boy and girl. These plots can be created in collaboration by the entire cast, or maybe even better, each cast member can come up with his or her own idea for a scenario and place it in the troupe "bank." Ultimately, more than anything at this point in the theatrical production, what matters most is the idea of keeping a set of plot schemes the way the commedia troupes did. It does not matter much what kinds of plots they are going to be, as that can and should be decided jointly by the troupe. What matters is that the plot schemes and scenarios are invented and written with openings for comic possibilities and for physical comedy, that they are divided into scenes, and that stage actions, possible exchanges between the characters, as well as props and costumes all be written in the scenario and pinned on each side of the stage. I believe this system allows both the freedom and the discipline for a troupe to work creatively in collaboration, and without the authority of a fixed text.

2 and 3.   Once you have gathered, say, a dozen versions of scenarios on different schemes, each performer in the troupe or the class should spend some time working alone, writing possible lines and dialogue for their respective roles, collecting poetry, quotations, and jokes, and memorizing them. Then performers can meet in groups of two and put their lines together, work them out in dialogues, combine the lines they have created for themselves with those of their partner and make as many combinations as possible. An excellent model for this is the stage dialogues in Andrea Perrucci's *Dell'Arte Rappresentativa*, in which he gives examples of possible dialogues and combinations of lines for the lovers, the servants, the matchmakers, and the old men. Once each actor has memorized a set of lines that represents his or her character, and has worked out combinations of lines with a partner, they can practice improvising, combining and recombining their lines.

For example, say a woman playing the role of "girl in love with another girl" thinks up two or three different lines in which she tells the boy who loves her that she is not interested in him Version 1: "Don't you understand, I like you as a friend, but not as a lover. I don't love, *love* you!" Version 2: "I have to be frank with you: I like men as friends, but not as lovers. Women, on the other hand ... do you get it?" Version 3: "I have to tell you, I want you as my friend, but really, I'm in love with Jennifer." The male character, whether played by another woman or a man, should, on her/his own create his own lines. Version 1: "But I love you. I can't live without you." Version 2: "Can't you have both a boyfriend *and* a girlfriend?" Version 3: "Yes, but maybe it's just a phase. I'll wait for you." The two partners can then recombine each version of their own lines with each version of their partners' lines for an entire dialogue or scene. The choice of versions could be left to the actual performance moment and not made in advance. This way the stage dialogue will have a fresh, spontaneous quality in performance and all sorts of other lines may come up spontaneously onstage, once the two performers have acquired a certain ease at these kinds of exchanges. These examples are of course rudimentary, but if you are working as a group leader, say with a class of undergraduate students, you can ask your students to add poetry to their lines, to make them sensuous, intellectual, playful. They can, as the commedia actresses and actors did with Petrarcan verses, create a repertoire of love verses from classical or modern poets and add them to their lines. Or, of course, there is always wrapping. Once they have these lines up their sleeve, they can play and experiment with various versions onstage during performances, rehearsals or class time. Imagine the fun and the sense of freedom when you and your group of actors find yourselves ad-libbing, creating dialogues and scenes without worrying about remembering your exact lines, but knowing you have created those lines and your own role, and that, furthermore, some of it may even have been created directly onstage.

My own experience with such experiments with undergraduate students has been particularly fulfilling. Following the model of the scenarios in the Flaminio Scala collection, my students in an advanced seminar on women and comedy prepared short scenarios on a set of themes, such as the mirror, the jealous lover, and Colombina's two lovers, and presented them in an end-of-the-year performance, all in French. We also worked on internalizing a set of actions and learning to let the language emerge from the actions, in a sort of reversed Stanislavski method, and going more in line with the techniques of Jerzy Grotowski or Eugenio Barba. "On stage, the body speaks, so let the body speak," I often told my students. I stressed the principles of the body being "decided," "alive," "present" in the moment.[24] For instance, in a scene titled "The Mirror" I asked the two actors/lovers to mimic each other's gestures first with no words and to let the words emerge naturally after a few such routines that turned out to be quite funny each time. I asked each student to connect with the other person as if talking to themselves, then to surprise each other, to move very slowly or very fast. They had internalized throughout the semester several basic plot schemes, and gathered a certain number of props and costumes, which we placed in a large box onstage. At the beginning of the show, they picked out their props and costumes in front of the audience, and performed their mini-plays. The dialogues were slightly different with each rehearsal, but the plotline remained the same, and that gave the students the confidence to improvise and make up lines in performance. They had the story line, they had certain actions their bodies had internalized, and the dialogue often emerged in startling ways. At other times, they relied very intelligently on memorized lines that fitted the situation. The final performance was a treat of improvisational comedy and the students had a great sense of accomplishment, because they felt they were the creators of the entire show. Their language skills and ease in talking in front of an audience, even for the shyest of them, were dramatically improved. To say nothing that they did all this in *French*.

4. Isabella Andreini, Caterina and Isabella Biancolelli, Vitoria Piisimi, Orsola Cortesi, Patricia Adami — most of the actresses of the commedia used disguise and/or cross-dressing in their shows, in order to advance, entangle or disentangle the plot, and for performative, comic reasons. Isabella and Colombina beat the record in terms of disguises. Colombina created a dizzying carnival of appearances. Their disguises most often carried also a social or political message, usually on behalf of women, as they took on the prerogatives and social freedom of each kind of dress. Other than cross-dressing, their disguises represented marginalized classes and social or ethnic groups, such as Gypsies, foreign women, Moorish slaves, and peasants. Isabella, who, as an inamorata represented a nobler class than the *zannis*, often played in disguises that represented lower social classes, such as servants; inversely, Colombina, a maid, often dressed up as or acted roles of the inamorata, or noble women.

Disguises and cross-dressings destabilized both gender and social boundaries and allowed the performers to develop and exhibit a wide range of improvisational and performative moods and strategies. If you have a mixed cast, the possibilities for disguises and cross-dressings are even more complex. Try having men and women play both male and female parts, both in earnest and in exaggerated or caricature drag. Women are so easily, so often fixated on a certain dress which usually has certain connotations about their social, professional status, age, marital status. Isabella and Colombina consistently subverted the persona that was conveyed by their main role within the company, and one creative and comic way in which they did that was by frequent changes of dress.

You should try within your group as many forms of dress, disguise and "cross-gendering techniques" as possible.[25] I have many times successfully used this technique with my students. For instance, one actress may layer a variety of dress styles: wear a long ball gown with a man's blazer on top, with a baseball cap on her head, or a leather mini-skirt with a turn-of-the-century hat with flowers and fruit, with army boots; she can wear one kind of dress on top of another and gradually take them off onstage; or, she can quickly change dress and outfit from one scene to the next. In real life, it is liberating for women to change often and radically their dress style, just so one can never actually label, frame, box or pin you in any particular kind of persona. As we have seen from Isabella Andreini, social life is much more of a constant performance for women than it is for men. Isabella, for all practical purposes, given the age and times she was living in, had to perform her virtue, her innocence, her ideal femininity socially, in order to subvert it all onstage and be the buffoon or the trickster that she was. Today, we can do both: subvert and explode our expected personae, our "good girl" personae, onstage and socially. The choices we make in terms of our physical appearance — our clothes, hairstyles, general demeanor — can be important forms of negotiation between our private and social persona, and have the potential of both reinforcing and exploding fixed images of femininity and gender stereotypes.

5. As I have pointed out several times throughout my study, the relation between women, madness and performance has a longstanding tradition. The mad scenes used to be one of the most important tours de force and steppingstones for actresses of the commedia dell'arte. Feminist critics such as Sandra Gilbert and Susan Gubar[26] or Shoshana Felman have elaborated exciting theories with regard to the relations between madness or hysteria and female creativity, and have demonstrated at length that a poetic or narrative discourse or a set of behavioral patterns which bear the signs of what traditionally has been labeled as insane has often been for women a method of breaking through the limitations set by patriarchal rules and discourse.

It is significant that the first actresses on the European stages acquired some of their acting fame and praise due to scenes in which they represented and acted out madness. Although the *zanni* characters could at times, in their buffoonery, verge on the insane, it was the female performers who introduced the full-fledged mad scenes, as "theatergrams" and as an important unit of their shows. As I discussed in the chapter about Isabella, the mad scene reveals the full complexity of her performing and improvising skills, as well as the full extent of her comedic talents. It allows her to break through her idealized persona of the innocent inamorata, and it gives her the freedom to be funny, subversive and carnivalesque. It is within the framework of madness that she can trick, mimic, and impersonate the buffoons. The creation, insertion and performance of mad scenes or of hysteria, within the development of the plot or the creation of your show, can prove a very fruitful and powerful strategy of feminist performance.

The creation of mad scenes has the potential of being a satisfying artistic experience, as it can offer women a practically unlimited range of discursive and performative forms of expression. It can be the place where female performers can experiment with almost pure, spontaneous improvisation. The performer preparing her role and her mad scene could, for instance, choose certain aspects of patriarchal discourse or male behavior, and give herself free range to mimic, reverse and mock them. As Isabella mocked the other male characters in the commedia and spoke derisively of classical, ancient and contemporary philosophers, kings, writers, so a modern female performer can take, for instance, male characters of traditional epic poetry or drama, such as Achilles, Hamlet, or any male character of modern drama or film, even political personalities of our times, and mimic or parody them. The female performer can take one area of specialized discourse, let's say legal or political discourse, and parody it in ways that illustrate the "premeditated art of improvisation," with its combination of well-prepared scenic and verbal techniques, and spontaneous expression in the "stream of consciousness" style illustrated so brilliantly by Isabella. Deb Margolin does this masterfully in her piece *O Yes I Will! (I Will Remember the Spirit and Texture of This Conversation)* in which she moves with acrobatic linguistic and physical dexterity between the specialized medical language used during the surgery her character is undergoing and the "mad" flow of emotive, sensuous, voracious language that her character produces under the anesthetic:

(V.O.): YOU KNOW, WE REALLY SHOULD GET STARTED.

Oh, forget it! Just tell me: why did you decide to become an anesthesiologist!? When you could have been any kind of doctor, why did you choose that? I think of the word *aesthetic*
And then the prefix *an*
and it means
getting rid of beauty getting rid of feeling
and it means bringing an end, bringing relief from feeling
Is that why you chose this? This whole thing is unbearable, isn't it, like watching something inevitable and being unable to stop it and when you put me down, will you bring me up? Beloved man, mumbling man older man, will you bring me up? From deep, where you send me? Will you? If you do, I'll make you happy. I'll spend the rest of my life making you happy. You won't remember my name or face, even though you put tubes in my teeth and down my face, but I'll spend the rest of my life making you happy, I will. You feel for me already, I know it, I know you love me, I know it. You've caught love from nearby things, from trees that are balling up to blossom the way little babies go quiet and tight when they're about to shit, you've caught love from the order in this room, from the pigeon-toed lights and the clean instruments, that mirror a psychedelic sliver of the hand that passes over them, you've caught love from me, from the way I looked at you when I realized, when I realized I love you.

Couldn't you imagine having sex with me, very slowly, couldn't you?

I'm trying to think: What is language, anyway, what is speech? Does it just float, like smoke from fire, away from the speaker, signifying rather that being the thing that caused it? Is speech, like smoke, a byproduct of some burning rather than the burning itself? It is that, isn't it, my speech is like smoke and my body is the burning, can't you see that, I'm sure you can see that, be gentle with this eternal flame as you extinguish it be mindful of its eternity, and bring it back dear gentleman dear older older gentleman who speaks to me and touches me like the Mediterranean sea.

I watch birds, do I have time to tell you about that? I know you're very busy! I watch birds outside my window, and honestly, one of them, one of them, I love him as much as I love you, his head is red, so pure flaming red, and his wings are black and white polka dots, it's just beyond chic, it's an apotheosis of organic fashion! His beauty! If I had wings, beloved, you'd never see me again, forgive me, you'd never ever see me again! And watching these birds, I watch them fly, I watch the mechanics of their flying, and flying is graceful and lovely in the telling, but the mechanics of it are awkward, and the wings squeak sometimes, or creak, it's quite an effort really, and I watch it carefully, the listing take-off, the steadying, the sudden dizzying loft, the work! The body at work! I watch that, and sometimes dearest handsome older gentleman of mine, all mine, always mine, I am beginning to feel that I could do that, that I could! That I see how that is done, and that, someday, when alone, I will do that!

Of course not everyone can master the intricacies and meandering paths of language to the degree that Deb Margolin does, but one can learn from the freedom she allows her voice, syntax, word choice, rhythm, as if constantly and voraciously avid for language like Cixous's female thief.

The use of hysteria, mimicry and parody of patriarchal lines of discourse and/or sociopolitical structures in performance is precisely one of the ways that Luce Irigaray suggests for the subversion of the status quo. Torrie Moi notes that "Irigaray's undermining of patriarchy through the over-miming of its discourses may be one way out of the straitjacket of phallocentrism."[27] Feminist critics such as Elaine Showalter, Torrie Moi, and Anna Furse[28] have elaborated in theory and in theatrical practice the notion that hysteria can be used as a form of "feminist protest" against the signs of the feminine imposed on women by patriarchal societies. Five centuries ago, Isabella Andreini and other commedia actresses were giving their full talents to the representation of female madness, or of what today we have labeled as hysteria, in ways that seem strikingly subversive and transgressive for their times. Colombina also, though not specializing in mad scenes as the sixteenth century actresses did, took the art of mimicing both the signs of femininity and masculinity to its highest comic form. And Franca Rame uses with gusto discursive and performative strategies which are kin to hysteria and engage in an over-mimicing of the signs of femininity or which parody male behavior, as in the piece about faking orgasm, as in the play about the woman frantically trying to get ready for work on a Sunday (*Il risveglio*), and in the play *Abbiamo tutte la stessa storia*.

The insertion of full-fledged mad scenes in which Aristotelian logic, reason, conventional syntax and "normal" behavior are reversed and altogether exploded in the form of unexpected combinations of discursive levels, unusual behaviors, free associations on a theme, and dreamlike sequences, can be a liberating form of artistic expression for women, and can offer female performers the opportunity to develop and experiment with a variety of improvisational techniques. And invariably, mad scenes, whether concluded with a return to that which is considered "sanity," as in Isabella's plays, or whether they are used to take the performance to a different level and establish madness or hysteria as the "norm," have an unlimited potential for comedy, exactly due to their unpredictable nature, to their incongruous associations, to the overlap between the "elasticity of life" and rigid linguistic or behavioral structures. The performance of madness in theater, with its rich potential for comedy, with its reversals and subversion of logic and order, and, yes, with the laughter that it can produce, may just be a fruitful and creative way to gain expressive freedom and, indeed, sanity. Isabella's lesson of negotiating sanity and madness onstage, her improvisational skill, and her carnivalesque performance, embedded within what was recognized as an admirable social persona, remain valuable lessons for us today, not only in the history of theater, but at all levels of social life with its myriad performative dimensions.

6. Madness and hysteria are directly related to and feed well into the carnivalesque. The aspects of carnivalesque discourse and reversals have been regarded by several feminist critics as excellent forms of subversion and disruption of patriarchy. The "political effectiveness of the aesthetics of carnivalesque" and the relations between carnival and the construction and/or deconstruction of gender have been brilliantly explored by Dale Bauer and Judy Little. For Mary Ruso, "Carnival and the carnivalesque suggest a redeployment or counter production of culture, knowledge, and pleasure. In its multivalent oppositional play, carnival refuses to surrender the critical and cultural tools of the dominant class, and in this sense, carnival can be seen above all, as a site of insurgency" (17). It has also been noted that "Carnival suspends discipline — the terror, reverence, piety and etiquette which contribute to the maintenance of social order. The carnival participants overthrow the hierarchical conventions which exclude them and work out a new mode of relation, one dialogic in nature."[29]

Furthermore, besides its disruptive function in terms of social norms and political structure, the carnival is also crucial in the theorizing and practice of theater because of its revolutionary relation to the body. As feminist critics have shown and as I stress in the present study, in the carnivalesque mode, much attention is given to the "lower bodily stratum" and its regenerative powers in the cycles of life. The grotesque body, the naked body, the openness of the body and the discourse about the body take a central position in narrative and performance. Much of the comedy of Isabella's madness derives from carnivalesque behavior and discourse: the use of scatology and obscenity, as well as cross-dressing, the exposure or the disguise of the female body in transgressive ways (male attire, partial nakedness). Isabella's mad "rantings" mix the high and elevated discourse, philosophy with scatology with politics, with culinary elements. Franca Rame never cross-dresses, but she carnivalizes radically the discourse about female sexuality, taking it out of its forbidden or sanitized zone and legitimizing the naming of and discussing about the female anatomy. Her female voices talk openly about their sexuality, their sexual organs, their physical likes and dislikes and engage in scatological humor, as in the scene when the engineer drinks the urine of the midwife. By combining the performance of madness or hysteria with the carnivalesque, modern performers as well as women in society and in everyday life transgress conventional lines of behavior in a liberating laughter. They assert themselves in their unadorned physicality and establish alternatives to phallocentric discourse and to behaviors dictated by male established lines of reason.

To carnivalize the performance of your theater group members, practice speaking openly and in unadorned ways about sexual issues and sexual anatomy; do not shy away from what may be perceived as obscene discourse. The buffoons of the Middle Age farces or carnival market culture, as well as the *zanni*-buffoons of the commedia, based most of their comedy on scatological and sexual humor, gestures and behavior, and many of the *lazzis* were obscene.[30] Such behavior and discourse, while totally accepted and encouraged for men, were of course considered highly inappropriate for women. When they did occur, they were associated with prostitution. The commedia, however, gave women the opportunity to break those taboos at least partially.

Today's performers, stand-up female comics and playwrights, women like Karen Finley,[31] Eve Ensler (*The Vagina Monologues*), Roseanne Barr[32] and Franca Rame, skillfully combine the hysterical mimicry of feminine signs with the carnivalesque discourse and body. In preparing original feminist shows or in creating feminist theater workshops, you can try to have each member of the cast or the workshop create scenes and write dialogues or short narratives in which they discuss an aspect of female anatomy or sexuality, the way Franca discusses and performs the acting out of female orgasm, real or fake. You can guide your students or cast members to use uninhibited language and, like Eve Ensler in her *Vagina Monologues*, or like Franca Rame in the prologue to her series of female monologues, to experiment with the creation of new names, metaphors and adjectives to talk about and describe female sexuality and anatomy.

The over-feminization and objectification of the female body, added to the arbitrary creation of certain norms of feminine physical appearance and behavior in the history of Western representation and in particular in classical art and literature, have been a great detriment to women. It has trapped them within idealized notions of female beauty, behavior and discourse at best and has reduced them to their anatomical and biological functions at worst. "The modern West," notes Judy Little, "has deployed a notion of power and law that has also defined a counterpart in the 'hysterization of women's bodies.'" The response to this deployment of power has been, according to Little, "'the creative hysteria' of women's discourse," in which "a comic tension frequently emerges between the (male) heritage of power and a rebellious 'hysteria' that carnivalizes or mocks both itself and the phrases borrowed from a language of power."[33] One such example of carnivalized discourse is a dialogue between two women in Megan Terry's play *Calm Down Mother*: "You had better. You had better. Carlyle said that you had better. You had better. You had better. You bet your butter. Carlyle said that you had better. You had better. You bet your butter. Carlyle said that you had better."[34]

Isabella, Caterina, Franca — they all carnivalized their discourse and their performance by incorporating in their speech and/or act a borrowed language of power which they simultaneously mocked. Isabella's incorporation of Aristotelian philosophy within her mad discourse and mixing it with scatology and food, Colombina's mimicing of male behavior and discourse and her spell-like threats to Arlecchino, Franca's ironic use of political language during intercourse ("I know, it's not your fault, it's the fault of society, of selfishness, of exploitation, of imperialism, of the multinationals," *Abbiamo tutte*, 75) or the delirious caricature of a female faked orgasm, all are brilliant examples of carnivalizing discourse and performance by reversals of power language, caricature and parody of linguistic commonplaces or expected norms of behavior. The practice of carnivalesque discourse, reversals, and acts by a feminist theater group, a feminist theater workshop or a theater class can be an excellent form of empowering through humor, of liberating through irony, of gaining self-confidence through subversion of the languages of power. You can start with simple exercises such as taking various formulae of authority that are commonly used by fathers with their daughters, husbands with their wives, male employers with female employees, and reverse them, humor them, carnivalize them. You can take behaviors of male superiority and authority, act them out mockingly, and add the carnivalesque discourse to the behavior. And you can start humoring and carnivalizing your sentences in real life when you are treated and spoken to in authoritative or inappropriate ways by the men in your life.

7 **and 8**. The following two feminist performance strategies are also a derivation of the carnivalesque and continue to illustrate the theme of the "woman on top," but with precise specifications with regard to cross-gender dressing. One of the most powerful examples of angry and subversive female humor in the commedia dell'arte plays is the one where Colombina has the boorish Marquis, who is pestering her, dressed and made up as a coquettish woman onstage, by a group of women in order to compromise all possibility of marriage. Once dressed up as a woman and presented to the father, the Marquis is rejected and taught his lesson, while Colombina is happily free. In the case of a mixed group, the cross-dressing of both male and female performers can have a powerful effect and message, as it points blatantly to the social construction of gender by dress and behavior. Male performers dressed in overtly feminine and sexual clothes, paralleled by female performers dressed in clothes which bear the signs of male power, can unmask the disadvantages of each and point to how we associate the power or the lack thereof with these constructions of gender. Even if the male impersonation of females risk enforcing stereotypical images of femininity, as Ferris has pointed out, the actual dressing onstage in front of an audience might divert that danger.

As I noted in the discussion of Colombina, since it is the women in the performance who are staging or directing this cross-dressing in front of an audience, its deliberate and overtly ironic dimension would have the power of the mimicry of the feminine signs advocated by Irigaray in the second degree: the men would have to experience the exaggerated signs of the feminine which have been imposed on women by patriarchal societies. This technique has an enormous revolutionary and political potential as well. Imagine that, as in the Gherardi play, a group of women creates onstage a *mise en scène* in which one or more men dress in women's clothes — only the scene is set in an Islamic culture: the women, at first dressed in black gowns and burkas, disrobe onstage, revealing themselves in men's clothes underneath. Then they dress the men onstage in the black gowns and veils that have only narrow slits for the eyes. The overt role reversals performed openly this way, in front of the audience, precisely due to their blatant and direct quality, reveal the arbitrary nature of the construction of gender in the first place. Because the stage is both a real space and a virtual space of all possibilities, it lends itself to the deconstruction and reconstruction of accepted norms, conventions, dress codes and roles. The stage is the place where revolutions can begin. As Augusto Boal so beautifully said it, "Theater is a rehearsal for Revolution." It is said that Beaumarchais' *The Marriage of Figaro* gave a real impetus to the French Revolution, not just because of its denunciation of the social and class inequalities, but also because of the powerful women portrayed in it. It is Suzanna, Marcelina and in the end the Countess Almavira who, through their many disguises, tricks and rebellions against the tyranny of men and their arbitrary rules, are the greatest revolutionaries in the play. The Suzanas, Marcelinas and women of all walks of life had an extraordinary input in the French Revolution. After the Revolution was won, a series of backlashes against women followed throughout the nineteenth century.[35] History repeats itself and, sadly, each period of women's emancipation has invariably been followed by periods of backlash. We are living in one right now. But subversive art, theater, and transgressive humor have the power to break, once in a while, through the monotony of oppressive structures.

9. Many of the plays of the early commedia, most of the plays of the Comédie Italienne, and all of Franca Rame's monologue plays represent or treat with humor and irony the problems and issues confronting women's lives. It is, of course the number one goal and accomplishment of women's and feminist theater groups. Whether dealing with the oppressive nature of marriage arrangements and marital relations, with the infidelity of lovers, the hypocrisy or fatuousness of husbands and lovers, the financial and economic freedom of women or the lack thereof, the double standards in the imparting of justice to men versus women, unsatisfying sexual relations or the capitalist patterns of oppression of women, Isabella, Colombina and Franca, all three, weave into their performance art issues pertaining to women's lives. Quite often, their own voices and concerns are entangled with the voices and the larger concerns of the women of their times. Always, they treat these issues with various levels of humor, varying from burlesque forms, to irony, to biting sarcasm, to playfulness, to angry comedy. They all "break up the law with laughter."

Following their example, experiment with your group in creating scenes which represent the widest possible gamut of problems and issues confronting women's lives today, differentiating some of the issues according to age, social class, race, sexual orientation, education, line of work, and marital status. Franca Rame deals widely with the problems confronting the lives of working and nonworking women and mothers. Colombina voices the frustrations of middle-class women in a society entirely run by men. Isabella acts out the dilemmas of young women of relatively elevated social status in oppressive family situations. Deb Margolin voices the wrenching struggles of mothers, of violated women, of women struggling with illness, of intellectually vibrant and sexually voracious women who are often endearingly confused by the insanity and violence of the world. They all turn the tables on tradition in ways which are relevant to their own times, both in terms of the aesthetics of their performance and the content of their plays, dialogues, or monologues.

The point has been made over and over again by many feminist critics, theoreticians and artists that "the personal is political."[36] "We need to find ways of 'taking people's lives seriously,' or rather 'women's lives seriously,' as a subject for theater making and academic study," urges Aston (171). Four hundred years ago, Colombina/Caterina Biancolelli was weaving abundant details of her and her sister's personal histories with the stories of their fictional characters. Franca Rame has openly combined information and stories from her own personal experience as a woman, wife, and mother into her plays and exchanges with the audience. Performance artists like Bobby Baker, Claire Dowie, Kate Clinton, Deb Margolin, and feminist theater groups like Split Britches, and the Women's Experimental Theater have all illustrated in their art that the personal is political by bringing to the foreground their own stories and blending the autobiographical with the fictional. Caryl Churchill's plays have often derived from workshops in which she has drawn actual information from people and used it in her plays (*Mad Forest, Cloud Nine*). And Ariane Mnouchkine has made use of interviews, letters and personal stories of women in some of her plays (*The Trojan Women, Le Dernier Caravansérail [Odyssées]*).

However, the staging of personal women's stories which derive from or use elements from the very experience of the actual performers, as Colombina, Franca or Deb engaged in, is still not a very common theatrical practice. Much has been written about the fact that the commedia actors' stage personae coincided significantly with their social personae and vice versa, that they brought to the stage what they were in real life and back to real life what they had become onstage. This fluid exchange between on- and off-stage personae in a continuous recreation of each of the two sides of the performer's identity is something worth experimenting with. Yes, stand-up comedians, male and female alike, indulge a lot in autobiography when creating their acts. But for many it remains at the level of juicy details revealed onstage by a famous comedian. The work of someone like Deb Margolin or Kimberly Dark, on the other hand, while delicately or boldly delving into autobiography from the recounting of a terrifying surgery under general anesthetic in the case of the former to that of an incident with police while traveling through Mexico with her lesbian partner, in the case of the latter, illuminates the biographical detail with a deep awareness of the simultaneous individuality and commonality of experience and transforms it under our very eyes into a work of art that becomes independent of the author and is generously given to us the audience to possess and embrace.

In the context of a theater workshop or a women's studies class, or the preparation of a show, the cast members can share personal stories and dramatize them, then act their own or each other's stories. Try experimenting with the epic theater method used by Franca Rame, or simply turn your story into a short play or a scene. Fictionalizing, dramatizing, performing your story in front of an audience can have powerful political and aesthetic consequences, as it legitimizes and validates the personal in a public setting.

10. The use and re-creation of myths, fairy tales, and nursery rhymes has extraordinary comic and revolutionary potential in terms of women's and feminist concerns. As I noted earlier, parodies of canonical and classical plays were part of the standing repertoire of the commedia troupes and Colombina's troupe made extensive use of this resource. Her recreation of the character of Medea in the play *Jason ou la Toison d'or* is comical as it is revolutionary in its message for women. Colombina turns the character of Medea into a powerful, independent female character who gives Jason and many of the men in her society a good lesson and a warning against the mistreatment of women, with the use of tricks, cunning and irony. She re-creates her character to make it relevant for her time and personal experience, as when she presents Jason with her list of conditions, among which are that he stop going to the tavern, stop running after young girls and stop being jealous "à l'italienne." The character and myth of Medea have also been used by the British feminist theater group Monstrous Regiment and re-created to reflect the concerns of modern women. Franca Rame also has used the story of Medea to reflect on the condition of women and in particular on the drama of mothers who, once the children are gone and their physical appearance is touched by old age, lose the affection and respect of their husbands.

As we have seen, Franca has brilliantly used, with extraordinary comic release, fairy tale motifs in the play *Abbiamo tutte*. She has mixed them up and given them a feminist and surrealist twist. Isabella took a traditional dramatic form, the pastoral, and gave it a new twist, in which it is the female trickster who ends up victorious and laughing. Turning fairy tales or myths into modern stories that reflect women's concerns and in which traditional gender roles are reversed can be a truly invigorating experiment to engage in with a group of students or actors. The possibilities are unlimited, the material extremely rich, and the potential for comedy enormous, for you have the entire Western tradition at your disposal to subvert, parody and overturn. Furthermore, this narrative and performing strategy blends harmoniously with the method of carnivalizing or "humoring" the sentence explored in the second point of the list, as it is based, on a larger scale, on the simultaneous incorporation and reversal or parody of Western narrative lines, plots and themes.

11. As noted many times in this study and in most studies about the improvisational techniques of the commedia actors, the most successful improvisation is the one that combines a component of preparation and deliberation with freedom and spontaneity. Andrea Perrucci in his seventeenth century study refers to *l'arte premeditata* (premeditated art) of the improvisation. And Franca Rame has noted that her improvisation does not equal "pulling lines out of thin air." The great improvisational art of the commedia female performers, abundantly illustrated by Isabella's stage dialogues and plays, Colombina's plays, and Franca's monologues, emerges from the use of certain linguistic techniques and prepared dialogues which, once they become second nature to the performer, can be used freely, changed, and interchanged during the actual performance.

Following the model of the commedia performers, try preparing with your group of students dialogues which follow certain discursive rules and which allow the freedom of improvisation onstage. Firstly, in terms of syntax, the use of parataxis is an important device: create and think up sentences which are parallel and use simple, short sentences, as well as ellipses. Secondly, create dialogues that use mostly the first and second person personal pronouns and verbs in the present or simple past tenses. Create parallel and repetitive formulae and phrases in the dialogue, and use as many mnemonic devices as possible when thinking up the dialogue: alliteration, assonance, onomatopoeia, and repetition. Work the lines so that you end each one with a clue that can be resumed in parallel by your partner.

Let's say you are working on a scene between two lovers who are on the brink of separating. You could have as a starting point a dialogue based on the following phrases and linguistic structures. Character 1: "I am not happy with you. My heart aches." Character 2: "Why are you not happy? My heart aches for your heart's ache. I grieve for our lost love." Character 1: "Our love is lost indeed, for I love you no longer. Another, better, more interesting, more sensitive and more accomplished person has entered my heart." Character 2: "You have no heart then. Who can be more interesting and more sensitive and more accomplished than I?" Character 1: "The prince from the kingdom next to ours is, and he is certainly more humble than you." Note that each reply resumes on a different footing, words and syntactic structures of the previous line.

By creating "discourse level cues"[37] such as using certain words more than once, ending the sentence in a word or line which can be continued, by either phonetic or lexical associations, or creating "a constant rhythmic doubling of words and ideas,"[38] the commedia performers built up a solid base for their improvisation. Once these techniques and a set of lines appropriate for different kinds of stage situations and scenes are assimilated in the knowledge and conscience of the performer, the freedom to change, shift, re-create, and add can be more easily explored and enjoyed. Study of the commedia has shown that women were crucial in the development of the improvisational techniques of the genre. This is because of their knowledge of certain popular, oral forms of storytelling or short humorous dialogues recited at weddings or other festive occasions

The *contrasti*, short humorous dialogues on a theme, of the kind gathered in Isabella Andreini's collection, can be an excellent method of developing, creating and producing full-fledged improvisational shows by female performers or by mixed companies for that matter. We have seen Franca Rame use this genre creatively, with deliberation, and turn it into a monologue, a one-woman show, in the play *Contrasto ad una sola voce*. The play is written to give a sense of the improvised and to leave openings for improvisation, changes or shifts in the discursive line. The phrases of endearment, inspired by love poetry, become funny as they are changed to unexpected varieties such as "my lotus" and "my flower," and could, during performance, change indefinitely. Similarly, the many varieties of mock cries of love that Franca gives her female audience in her fake orgasm lesson can be experimented with and changed in various ways. Or Colombina's famous vindictive incantation, "Perfido, traditore, se non m'hai negli occhi m'avrai nel cuore!," could shift or change its adjectives and be used in many scenes of the same type. As long as a certain formula is well assimilated, a seemingly indefinite number of changes can be achieved.

Les Essif, in an article on reconstructive methods of staging classical plays with undergraduate students, and in a theater workshop I hosted at my own university, has developed an exciting method of improvising or re-creating shows from a given canonical text by taking lines from the original text, keeping in mind the main themes and story lines and then elaborating from there.[39] What arises is a variety of staging and improvisational possibilities for the production of the one play. While his method is based mostly on the use of a classical or canonical text to start with, the methods I advocate do away with a fixed text altogether and use as a foundation only a story line or a scenario, created together by the group, and the assimilation, in the repertoire of each performer, of a set of dialogues, lines, verses, and formulae, that may be interchanged and used in a variety of scenes and theatrical occasions. Furthermore, the use of storytelling or of a feminist version of Brecht's epic theater, developed quite a bit by Franca Rame, lends itself to innumerable and exciting possibilities for improvisation and for comedy. In the very use of fairy tales, and in their re-creation from a modern feminist perspective, certain formulaic structures and phrases with great comic potential are inscribed. Start, for instance, by playing with the most formulaic fairy tale formula, the famous ending line "and they lived happily ever after." Most likely, you'll come up with many comical versions, and most importantly with versions which subvert, as did Colombina, the comedy's conventional ending in marriage.

12. As I have noted many times, in the discussion of both modern feminist performance and commedia dell'arte style performance, contact between performers and audience is crucial. Furthermore, both the commedia dell'arte performers and many feminist performers today include the audience in the show to the point of actually blurring the distinctions between performers and spectators. Colombina depended on the audience to give the verdict on the ending of certain plots; Franca Rame actually takes questions or asks questions of the audience during her shows. For modern female improvisers and performers, it is even more important than for traditional performers to establish a connection with the audience, as an important aspect of women's or feminist performance is to initiate change and start revolutions at the levels of personal and social relations and of the mentalities that govern much of gender behavior.

More than four hundred years ago, Colombina spoke to her female audiences and taught them the art of survival in a man's world, while giving warnings to the male audience about the great potential for violence and vindictiveness in all the mistreated women. Franca speaks directly to her audience of women and establishes, through the humor and irony of her performance, a special complicity of laughter with her female audience. Try creating shows or theater workshops in which you address portions of the audience differently, or direct your performance unapologetically toward the women in the theater. Inviting audience members onstage to take part in the show, dressing up male audience members in female dress, for instance, can be a powerful, subversive performative method. For women, "acting out," making a spectacle of themselves, performing in front of an audience has an even more profound political dimension than for male performers, for, as we have seen, women historically have been much more tied to the private sphere and forbidden from the public sphere than have men. On the other hand, once women were allowed onstage, Western drama fixed them solidly as objects for the audience's avid gaze, to the detriment of their acting, improvisational skills and creativity. By establishing various ties with an audience and even shifting or destabilizing altogether the lines between audience and spectator, female performers subvert the history of their own objectification on the Western stages and break through the distinctions between the private and the public. By creating complicity with portions of the audience, such as the female portions, they can have a profound revolutionary impact on the lives of women outside the theater.

Comedy as "Rehearsal for Revolution"— A Contemporary Example of Commedia for Social Justice

Norma Bowles and her theater group called Fringe Benefits are a living example of the use of commedia techniques and humor meant to raise consciousness about social inequities based on gender, race, class, sexual orientation and to incite to social change. Bowles is the artistic director of the group and has worked with diverse populations, sometimes to sensitize them and raise awareness about their own set of prejudices and at other times to empower the most marginalized, those truly on the fringes of society and to endow them with strategies with which to fight their own marginalization. From homeless gay, lesbian, and transgender youth who had been thrown out of their homes by their own families, to rich members of Rotary Clubs, to homophobic Latinos, to middle school and high school children, to sorority and fraternity members at universities across the United States, Norma Bowles comes in with commedia masks from different parts of the world, Mardi Gras beads, and an inexhaustible array of comedic strategies and energies to empower the disempowered, sensitize the insensitive, and transform communities. Almost as an improvisational commedia trick I bring in the work of this group at the end of my study to root it strongly in our own times and to prove that commedia still lives, that humor can be learned and taught, that comedy and theater can and should be used to not only create "intimations of a better world," as Jill Dolan beautifully puts it, but to actually bring about "a better world," or better worlds at different local levels of our society, in different communities and pockets of social and human interactions.

The following interview with Norma Bowles illustrates the richness of the commedia techniques and the chameleonic ways in which they can be successfully used to tackle difficult issues of discrimination productively and creatively.

Domnica Radulescu: From your experience do you think comedy, humor and comic strategies can be learned or developed? If so, what has proven to be the most effective way of developing comedic timing or humorous situations or dialogue?

Norma Bowles: I *absolutely* believe that comic technique — especially comic timing and the ability to use satire and parody to good effect — can be taught.

The most rigorous and transformative pedagogue of *comic performance technique* I have ever had the excruciating pleasure of working with is Philippe Gaulier. Over the years, I've adapted a number of the techniques I learned from studying commedia dell'arte and Clown with Gaulier to help students develop an ear for the music of comedy, the point/counterpoint of lively repartee, and a heightened awareness of how to exploit the full comic potential of *everything* fellow actors say and do, every word in the script or "offer" in an improvisation, every single item, the set, properties and costume designers have placed on the stage, even every giggle, groan or cell phone sound from "the house." Some of the techniques I use include asking students to speak gibberish when they are working on comic timing so that they can concentrate on the melodic, rhythmic and dynamic aspects of their utterances, rather than on how clever they can be. I have also found that the use of character masks can help liberate performers to work in a bolder, freer, more fully-embodied way. Often I will take on the role of an inner demon provocateur and side-coach my students, goading them to go further, to break the rules, to devour the scenery. But more important than employing any specific exercise or strategy, I believe that it is crucial when teaching comedy to create an environment in which the students feel giddy, virtually intoxicated, with the pleasure of playing!

When considering how to dramatize various manifestations of sexist discrimination, one group developed a montage of darkly comedic sketches, including a *CSI* parody of chauvinistic "Walk of Shame" attitudes towards women who return "suspiciously" late from their dates; a commercial for "Bud-Dumber: Pick-Up Lines in a Can!" satirizing drunken cat-calling and sexual harassment; and a "Martha Stewheart" episode in which she shares her "Friday Night Home Run" cocktail: "This is great for those dates who are really sweet, and really cute ... but REALLY not into getting down to business! Just garnish with a bit of mint and serve! You're in for a night *you'll* NEVER forget ... but *your date* will never remember!" Whether one uses television shows, sports metaphors, Carl Orff's *Carmina Burana* or *Alice in Wonderland*'s "A Mad Tea Party" [sic] as springboard for creating a satire, it's helpful to find a concept that promises to be fun to work with, feels like a wickedly good "fit," and sheds light on a central irony in the situation.

DR: Why do you think comedy is a good strategy for raising awareness about social inequities and inspiring people to become agents of change?

NB: Comedy is an ideal strategy for raising awareness about social inequities and inspiring people to become agents of change.

Throughout the world, since long before Aristophanes sent his protagonist Trygaeus to Heaven on a dung beetle to fight for peace, theater artists and comedians (as well as jesters, clowns, *bouffons*, satirists, etc.) have used humor to raise our awareness, tweak our consciences and spur us to act, to rebel, to transform ourselves and the world around us.

DR: You have had so much success in your career using comic techniques to deal with some of the most taboo and hardest issues confronting our society, from homophobia to sexual violence, to racism and various forms of hate speech. Could you give a few examples about how you and your group use humor and comedy to bring about social change and raise consciousness about various forms of social inequity.

NB: In the early years, 1991 to 1993, Fringe Benefits worked with homeless LGBT youth to create and perform plays addressing homophobia for Highways Performance in Santa Monica, California. The audience was hip, pretty far to the left of center, and mostly LGBT.... So, the humor we used in those plays was camp, heady, sharp and queer, queer, queer! We used the humor in these shows to reinforce our connections with the audience, as well as to provide some relief from the powerfully affecting, often harrowing stories about fag-bashing, predatory adult chicken-hawk behavior, child abuse, child molestation, teen suicide, and attempted lynchings.

The plays also show how many queer youth use humor as defensive armor — as a shield. In "Perseus Mirror," a scene from our first play, *People Who Live in Glass Houses,* the "faggot" hero Perseus uses the figurative mirror of camp humor to deflect the oppressive, reifying condemnations of Medusa — heterosexist society. In *Street Dish,* the young writer/performers play "Truth or Dare" with the audience to level the playing field and help make transparent the prurient interests of the audience: "You want us to talk about the sex work we do.... Well, just ask us! But then we get to ask you some intimate questions, too." In *Friendly Fire* Maurice, fully decked out in professional wrestling attire, reenacts a typical weekend "smack down" with his mother as a wrestling match in which over and over again his mom, dressed in curlers and a robe, sipping coffee and smoking a cigarette, effortlessly pins him down.

Over the years, the homeless youth with whom we worked told us — and statistics confirmed it — that one of the biggest problems they had faced was endless harassment, bullying and isolation in their schools. So, we decided to go into those schools and try to stem the flow of youth onto the streets.

With *90210 Goes Queer!* our high school tour show, humor became even more important as a road in for the audience. We decided we needed a central character who could be a cross between our "Moveable Middle Target Audience Member," basically a fun-loving, well-liked jock, and the gay youth to whom we wanted this target audience (straight, male jocks) to begin to relate. So we created CJ, the captain of the Football Team and Homecoming King. From the moment CJ enters he is making jokes about "Wide Receivers!" and "Tight Ends." At first many of his fellow students laugh along, but as his anti-gay joking grows darker and more relentless, he starts losing friends. Eventually, the audience finds out that CJ has been using this homophobic humor as a way to hide his own sexual orientation. We used this character and his joking as a way to connect with the audience, to get them to drop their defenses against "Oh God, not another preachy school assembly," and laugh along with us and enjoy the show. We also portrayed CJ as a "Regular Joe," fun-loving jock as a way to get the audience to identify with, even care about a gay character. (To be fully honest, we also had a more cynical reason for putting anti-gay humor in the mouth of a character who we later find out is gay: if we couldn't persuade our target audience to stop their homophobic behavior for any other reason, we hoped we could at least get them to stop if only out of fear that their peers might think they were gay, just like CJ!)

Our strategy for transforming anti-gay attitudes worked pretty well. In show after show, the students in the audience laughed along with CJ's "fag" jokes at the beginning, but less and less as the play went on. In the post-show discussions, they applauded how some characters had stood up against his and others' homophobic behavior. They noted how hard it must have been for CJ to deal with all the anti-gay pressure they saw him getting from his parents, and how much "cooler" the accepting parents of the bisexual cheerleader seemed to be. Most impressive, however, was the impact our show had at one Catholic middle school. The administrators at the school had decided it was important for their students to see *90210 Goes Queer!* (titled *Turn It Around!* for our school performances). They had heard the students frequently using "Fag!" as a put-down on the playground, and had tried to introduce them to some anti-bias lessons. In response to a survey question following those lessons, 80 percent of the students wrote that they would prefer having a terminal illness to being gay. After our show, however, only 20 percent of the youth indicated they still felt that morbidly afraid of homosexuality.

Another time, a group of thirty Latina mothers asked Fringe Benefits to work with them to create a show to help their husbands understand how harmful machismo and homophobia are to all children. After a few hours of

Theater for Social Justice with Commedia Masks. Undergraduate students on an American university campus in a commedia dell'arte style performance directed in 2007 by Norma Bowles of Fringe Benefits. The topic of this skit was date rape. Photograph by Norma Bowles.

story-sharing and discussion, the mothers decided that the best way to reach their husbands and other men like them would be through a humorous, Spanish-language video they could watch in the comfort of their own homes. We then worked with the mothers to create that video, which we titled *Mitos, Ritos y Tonterias* (*Myths, Rites and Silliness*). In *"Super Cortes"* ("Super Cuts"), a *telenovela*/soap opera–like segment of the video, a macho father comes home and finds out his daughter wants to get a haircut — and HE IS FURIOUS!! "Only *putas* and *tortilleras* — [prostitutes & dykes] — get their hair cut short!" The only ally he can find is Abuelita, the grandmother whose hair is so long that even though she immigrated to the United States decades ago, "most of her braid still hasn't crossed the border — great-nieces and nephews are still combing out the split ends in Chihauhua!" Basically, we wanted to destabilize our male audience members' attachment to macho ideas, by putting a lot of their old-fashioned, sexist behavior and discourse into the mouth of someone the men would want to distance themselves from: a cartoonish, silly grandmother with an absurdly long braid in which she ends up entangling her entire family throughout the scene.

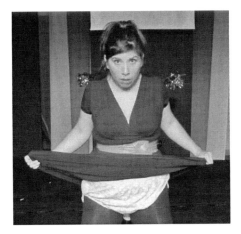

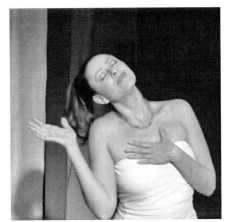

Slip of the Tongue— Chicana performance group. Sara Guerrero, top left, in "The Tale of CALZONES CAGADOS" (a stolen bike and one's journey into early dysfunction), Cristina Nava, top right, in "Rocks in My Salsa" (somewhere between Chicana and Mexican. You hold a rock while grandma held a Bible and self discovery happens at the bottom of a dirty martini glass), and Elizabeth Isela Szekeresh, right, in "When Song Leaders Go Bad aka the Lighter Side of Crazy" (tragicomic exploration of race, sexuality and mental illness). Photograph by Apolonio Morales.

And here ends the interview with theater activist Norma Bowles, which I hope has proven to some degree the power and potential for social change that comedy and performance can have in a variety of communities and social environments.

Women's and feminist theater groups that work collaboratively and create all components of their shows, that weave comedy with issues of social justice, are proliferating in the United States and a wonderful thing it is. Some emerging groups, such as the Los Angeles–based Latina Breath of Fire Theater Ensemble, much like the Chicago-based theater group Teatro Luna, deal with issues of Chicana identity, sexuality, ethnicity and the immigrant experience. The women artists of Latina Breath of Fire, Sara Guerrero (the group artistic director), Christina Nava and Elizabeth Szekeresh, create shows that emerge directly from their personal experiences and stories as

Latinas in the United States, and that boldly use comedy to explore a variety of difficult and taboo subjects such as sexual abuse and violence, mental illness, delinquency and drug addiction, but also celebrate healthy sexuality, solidarity among women, and the colorfulness of the ancestral heritage. They do all this with explosive, irreverent, fiery humor à la Colombina and Franca Rame while also incorporating aspects of Latina lore and culture. They present their shows in their own theater space in Orange County, California, but also across the state and the country for a variety of audiences from school-children to university students, to local community members. They manage to be all of the following at once: activist and consciousness-raising, hilarious, provocative, wrenching and poetic — a pretty tough act to balance. But this and other such rising theater groups are topics for another story, for another book.

I would like to refer to all such bold performative endeavors, not only as a modified version of Boal's line "rehearsals for revolution," but also in the inspired words of Jill Dolan, as "rehearsals for utopia, in a gesture, in a way of living, in an address to an audience that converts strangers into community."[2]

Being Funny about Tragic/Sad/Embarrassing/Taboo Topics

The entire range of comedy discussed in this book emerges largely from difficult, oppressive, sad or even tragic situations. From dealing with humor and images that are degrading to women, to violence against women, to forced marriages, to deteriorating marriages, to discrimination and inequality, to the revelation of one's mortality or a life-threatening surgery, the funny women in this book churn humor out of tears and survive with dignity and sassiness. Some theater artists go even farther with their use of comedy and break what we thought were unbreakable taboos about, say, illness or disability. Joan Lipkin is a feminist playwright and theater activist, the artistic director and founder of That Uppity Theater Company in St. Louis. She works on theatrical projects dealing with disability, homophobia, and reproductive freedom, and thus engages in powerful gestures that "convert strangers into communities." She noted in the interview I had with her, when asked about the social power of comedy:

> Of course comedy is a force for social and political transformation. As dire as their current situations may be, it is highly likely that there is comedy percolating in Egypt, in Libya, in Iran. It has to do with sharing a vocabulary

or an experience as well as the physical and psychic need for release. Not unlike music, comedy has probably been involved with every social movement throughout time. And comedy can become a point of reference that unifies and energizes people as they find healthy ways to respond to their situation.

Think about it. Women. Jews. Italian Americans. African Americans. Slavs. People with disabilities. Gays and lesbians. Latino/as. All of these groups of people have had humor developed by and about them that has enabled survival and has helped to identify what is particular to their shared experience in a positive way and what is oppressive. Through recognizing shared realities, culture is developed. Most importantly, comedy has the potential to move from beyond the individual to the group, which is essential for laying a foundation for social change. Laugh and cry, cry and laugh. And then organize.

Joan Lipkin's theater and various projects function according to the principles of cultural diversity and innovative theatrical practice in order to promote civic dialogue. They specialize in working with underserved populations including LGBT youth, adults and their families, people with disabilities, women with cancer, urban youth and adults with Alzheimer's disease and early onset dementia to develop their voices, create performances and foster community. When I asked her about what she thought of treating grave, tragic, troubling subjects with humor, her response was similar to Deb Margolin's: "It is often necessary. Laughter lives next door to tears. Humor can be a form of psychic survival for both marginalized people as well as individuals. Despite certain social mores, sometimes the more desperate the circumstances, the more humor is needed, often the humor of the absurd."

Here are a couple of examples from two of her plays that prove just that. They are excellent examples of ways to create laughter that emerges from pain and embarrassment, and they show how breaking such taboos actually sensitizes audiences to a variety of difficult life issues and situations as well as offers intimations of a more inclusive, tolerant world. Lipkin actually works with the groups that the plays are about: LGBT people, disabled people, and men and women of all colors and sizes, thus embodying her political messages and realizing true performative utopias. I am keen on including the following short pieces from her work on health care and disability because these topics are not commonly used in feminist theater or comedy and they illustrate the intersectionality of feminist humor with a variety of issues other than gender inequity. Just like the Latina Breath of Fire or Norma Bowles' theater activist work, Joan Lipkin's feminist comedy encompasses diverse kinds of inequity, marginalizations, social injustices, and human suffering, and is as biting as it is soothing through its empowering laughter.

Club Med

Characters:

Male Speaker

MALE SPEAKER

So I just flew back in from vacation and man are my arms tired! Ahh.... Club Med — St. John's white sandy beaches, lazy breezes, reggae mon, beautiful women everywhere, kind of like here, am I still on vacation?

Alright, so it wasn't the Caribbean. But I couldn't really go on vacation with a urinary tract infection. It was actually Club Med ... icine. And it wasn't St. John's the virgin islands. It was St. John's Mercy Medical Center.

But when I think about the fact that it's been two wives since my last vacation, it wasn't such a bad idea.

It starts out exotically enough. I just call my favorite travel agent, an easy number to remember, 911. Then, suddenly, I'm transferred into a gurney and I find myself in the back of a warm van with a woman in uniform.

She says, "What's your name," and begins touching me in different places, "How does this feel"? "Here? Here? ... Now do you have insurance?" OK, so that bubble bursts.

Before I know it, we've arrived at St. John's, the doors slide open, and I'm whisked — like royalty — to my semi-private room. And I find almost everything a guy could hope for: my personal TV remote, and my favorite — the call button. One touch and a lovely nurse is at my service! And room service: three almost-edible squares a day, no tipping necessary.

But even I need a change. I remember getting three showers over my nine days there. Just me and another luscious nurse! I even got a shampoo after I convinced her I couldn't do this:

(He demonstrates trying to raise his arms above his head)

I feel like a pampered pooch. And the whole time, at least one of us was naked!!

Just when I think this couldn't get any better, we vacationers are offered day trips! As I lie in my trusty gurney, we head down the hall, and by the signs I can see my entire health history pass by. MRI — got it; X-rays — got 'em; CT scan, urodynamic torture — check, check; kidney stones — no, thank God; maternity — what are you trying to do, kill me? Men can't survive that level of pain.

Then we arrive at physical therapy, where a sexy PT demonstrates some stretches. "Oh, I'm not sure I've got that one," I ask, "could you show me again?"

But suddenly my stay is over all too soon. I must get some other infection, and go on another trip. Maybe this time to the Sinai — okay, Cedars-Sinai Medical Center? Or St. Joseph's? Okay, St. Joseph's Hospital in Kirkwood.

And next time, I'll bring pictures. Okay, they're called x-rays. But that way you'll be able to know me from the inside out.

You Going to the Show?

Speaker #1: Are you going to this thing today?

Speaker #2: What are you talking about?

Speaker #1: This "Disability Show"?

Speaker #2: Yeah, I was thinking about it.

Speaker #1: Really? I can't imagine that watching a bunch of handicapped people hobble around or use wheelchairs is gonna be entertaining.

Speaker #2: Hey! My grandma uses a wheelchair!

Speaker #1: Yeah, but she's old, that's different. Besides, Granny isn't trying to do shows that our Bosses/Teachers are making us go to.

Speaker #2: My Boss/Teacher isn't making me go.

Speaker #1: Then why would you go?

Speaker #2: I don't know, I guess I feel sorry for them. I'd be terrible if nobody showed up. Plus, I don't really know any disabled people. I guess I'm a little curious.

Speaker #2: Hey, THEY found partners, so maybe they should feel sorry for you. Speaking of sex, when was your last date?

Speaker #1: Why don't we leave my sex life alone?

Speaker #2: I think YOU already have. Snap!

Speaker #1: Hey folks, we're not what you expected are we? I'm (NAME).

Speaker #2: And I'm (NAME). Welcome to a guilt-free show. Sit back, relax, and feel free to laugh with us, because if you don't have a good time, ...

(Speakers #1 & #2 together): *We* don't have a good time. And we LOVE a good time! So, let the show begin!

Maybe one of the most wrenching and at once uproariously funny (particularly when performed), pieces of feminist comedy of the artists mentioned in this book is the monologue of the Latina Breath of Fire performer Elizabeth Szekeresh about mental illness, sexuality and mixed race, masturbation and the Catholic Church, all of which derive from the artist's own story. It is another powerful example of the use of comedy in treating taboo and painful subjects in ways that are cathartic, healing, empowering and also destablilizing of stereotypes and the fixation on a specific racial or sexual identity. Here is a precious bit of it:

Stage Left sits an easel with chart papers. First chart paper says, "GO TEAM!" outlined in many colors. Stage right sits a chair with a cheer bag.

(Music Up: "Ya All Ready for This")
(Enter Song Leader in Song Leader uniform)
If I were a superhero my magical weapon would be pom-poms.

(Music Out)

Ready! OK! *(Cheer)* "B-I-P-O-L-A-R! Bipolar, polar, polar, yeah!" A few months ago I was diagnosed with bipolar disorder. Not Bipolar type I, but type II — kinda like the lighter side of crazy. But I prefer the term manic depressive — much more dramatic. It's taken 10 years to get this diagnosis. First it was depression. Then depression with ADHD and finally bipolar disorder; either way undiagnosed mental illness doesn't exactly make you the most popular kid in class. I'm not sure if it was because I'm brown or that I have a mental illness or that I'm obsessed with sexuality or that I'm weird, but being different in the way I was different was not good in Huntington Beach, California. *(Cheer)* Surf City!

(Change to new chart paper and reads it) *Bipolar Disorder:* A major affective disorder marked by severe mood swings (manic or depressive episodes).

In retrospect the depression is easy to spot: the poem about the end of the world in 3rd grade; the "I can't get out of bed" depression episodes; and the thoughts of suicide. But I think I was just born with default feeling of worthlessness. The Catholic Church didn't help. I'm a halfie. Half Manic. Half Depressive. Half White. Half Brown.

(Cheer*)* "W-H-O-R-E. God doesn't like brown girls, like me!"

(Kneels and makes the sign of the cross) At the age of six I knew I was a whore. Abuse. Not abuse. Who knows? But I was sexualized young.

My first day of catechism I knew it was over — too dark of soul and skin to be saved. *(Gets up)* I knew I didn't belong. White church. White God. White everything! I would beat myself up for being brown, dirt brown, shit brown.

God, why did you make me brown and not white like my dad or at least give me blue eyes like my grandma and my cousins? You must hate me to make me brown. I envy people who had a brown Mary. Fuck the Virgin/Whore complex; it would have been nice to know my choices were both brown.
(Changes to a new chart paper and reads) Some symptoms of manic episodes include: grandiose thinking, racing thoughts, distractibility, and decreased need for sleep, rapid speech, taking big or unusual risks.
(Cross to cheer bag) For some reason manic was harder to see: the uncontrollable spending sprees, the episodes of rapid speech that overtook me and the short-lived hobbies: **(goes through cheer bag and throws out ballet shoes, books etc)** playing bass, growing roses, soap making, ballet ... **(holds up**

coin belly dancing scarf) the usual stuff. And then there is stimulus seeking behavior.

(*Cheers*) "If you feel the need to escape/Masturbate/It feels great!"

I started masturbating young, like five/six years old. Hiding in the bathroom, selfloving and feeling intense shame afterward — *(sign of cross)* the Catholic way. In Jr. High I discovered every girl's answer to porn: romance novels. By high school I couldn't keep my hand out of my cheer skirt. I didn't know about vibrators. I only knew the old fashioned way *(hand motion)*; yup, just me and my books.

As this book is coming to an end, let many such shows begin all over the world. But let this book not end before we have seen a few radical acts performed by some of the Colombinas gathered at this virtual reunion. I asked Deb Margolin, Kimberly Dark and Joan Lipkin what has been the most radical thing they have done as theater artists. There is spontaneous improvisational, revolutionary and uproarious comedy as well as moving, wrenching soul-searching in their actions and radical performances:

Some Radical Feminist Theatrical Acts

Domnica Radulescu: What is the most radical thing you have ever done onstage?

Deb Margolin: One of the most radical things I think I have EVER done onstage was with my show GESTATION. It was a show about pregnancy, and specifically the insomnia that I experienced during both my pregnancies, and I did the show while in my ninth month both times. In this solo piece I portrayed a pregnant woman reading about the birthing process from a very out-of-date book on the subject, a genetic counselor talking about the process of sperm and egg conjunction while suppressing some kind of unnamed hysteria, and finally, the most outrageous and uncomfortable thing I did: after having gained about 50 pounds, with my rear end the size and width of an economy car, my huge belly and thighs, my popped-out navel, I put on a skin-tight black spandex dress and spike high heels and tried, as a character who was a prostitute, to pick up the various men in the audience. I would run my hand salaciously over my vast and untameable belly, saying: Does anyone want to party? And, spotting a man, would tell him: You look very nice tonight, would you like to party? Pointing to my belly, I would say things like: Oh, don't worry about him! He loves to meet new people! Or, it'll be like a ménage à trois! and things like this. I insisted on my body in a way that delighted and amused the women and HORRIFIED, I mean, HORRIFIED, MORTIFIED, the men. They would look away, cough, scratch their necks, check their watches. There was something sexually confusing and frightening and violently upsetting for them in this that I would finally address, shrieking:

Is it HIM? (referring to the fetus) Is THIS the problem? WELL, WHAT DO YOU THINK SEX BRINGS? THIS! Then finally, I just said: Okay, fine! I'd rather watch TV alone than look at it over your shoulder anyway! And marched away, promising the baby within my body that I'd eat pizza right away, since I knew he loved it.

Domnica Radulescu: What do you consider as the most radical thing you have ever done in your theater career?

Joan Lipkin: Sometimes, I think just daring to put my voice out there has been radical. As poet Muriel Rukeyser wrote: "What would happen if one woman told the truth about her life? The world would split open."

Almost everything I have done throughout my career has been radical. I have spoken about subjects that were and sometimes are off limits such as daring to make a musical comedy out of a teenage boy getting pregnant and contemplating an abortion in "He's Having Her Baby." The piece has been produced throughout the U.S. and Canada and infuriated some people. We had pickets and a bomb threat. I don't know if it is because we questioned the sacrosanct issue of reproduction, or that we dared to do it with humor, or that we challenged male audience members with having to contemplate the experience for themselves. But some people were pissed.

Other people liked it very much. I remember one woman, a journalist who was not much of a theatergoer, saying to me. "It's very funny. It's so funny, I don't know why I feel like crying." And I said to her: "The humor makes it bearable to look at the reality: young, poor women getting pregnant and having no say in what happens to their bodies. It is painful to realize that we don't have freedom in this country. After all, what is a most basic precept of freedom if not the ability to make decisions about our own bodies?" Then she started to cry, this journalist who was an editor at a major alternative weekly newspaper. A minute earlier, she had been laughing. Laughter and tears, tears and laughter. They live next door to each other.

Probably one of the most radical things I have done was to oppose our administration by organizing the largest interdisciplinary arts event in St. Louis to protest the war in Iraq. We had over 100 artists participating: actors, dancers, poets, visual artists. To call attention to our opposition to the war and the event, I also organized and participated in a photo shoot of a peace sign of about 60 nude women on the roof of a museum for a weekly newspaper.

I was happy to publicly strip for peace to make a point. People take off their clothes for much lesser stakes. In some areas where the publication was distributed, the law enforcement agencies did not agree. The paper was either turned upside down, presumably to hide the offending image of nude women of all ages, races, shapes and sizes united in a statement for peace, or it was confiscated.

Domnica Radulescu: What do you consider as the most radical thing you have done onstage?

Kimberly Dark: There's one story I'd like to share here regarding radical acts onstage. Before each show — really, right before I walk onstage — I say a quick prayer that all those in the theater will get what they need from my presence. (Really, my presence, because I've learned that it could be just watching me move and talk that gives someone something important.) What I try for onstage is radical presence. Sure, I'm telling some stories that are scripted; I'm doing things mostly as I've planned them.

And yet, no two gatherings are the same — how could they be? So, I was performing my show *Stripped and Teased: Scandalous Stories with Subversive Subplots* at Pontine Theatre in New Hampshire in 2008. It was the opening night of the run and the house was packed. Right after the show, there was to be a wine and chocolate reception and the mood was merry. I said my little prayer and walked onto the stage to perform this show that I'd been touring, at that point, for four years. I must say, I felt fairly merry myself — everything was comfortable, great crowd, nice night ahead. And the show fit like comfortable shoes. About fifteen minutes into the show, there's a story about my experience as an eighteen-year-old job seeker, applying for a job as a stripper and a job as a waitress within the same week. The story juxtaposes the position of women in service professions where tips are the mainstay of the income. It's a social commentary, sure, but the story also includes some funny characters — especially "Dan the cook" and "Rose the head waitress" at Uncle Sam's Pancake House. There are also some painful moments in the story — just the sort of arc I often relish. So, about 15 minutes into the show, I was speaking the lines about my eighteen-year-old self, and suddenly I was overcome by emotion. Really, a genuine welling-up occurred in me and I still don't understand its origins. First, I couldn't speak, and then I started to cry. I have speculated that this emotion had to do with my eighteen-year-old vulnerability in that story, alongside my son's eighteen-year-old vulnerability in 2008. He had recently been in an accident and while he was recovering well, the event had shaken me. Whatever the cause, there I was onstage, suddenly unable to speak. And I remembered my commitment to radical presence. I took a deep breath and whispered, "Excuse me," and took a few sips of water from my onstage glass. And I started into the story once more. Again, I choked up and started crying. This time, I told the audience that I was feeling emotional and asked them to take a few deep breaths with me. They did this and I stopped the show and discussed the idea of radical presence with them. This calmed me and I was able to resume the performance.

I resumed the show with some fear in my heart. Perhaps the rest of the performance wouldn't "work out." The audience relies on me to keep them emotionally safe, after all, through some difficult material. There is also a moment in that show when I invite a man onto the stage to try on the gigantically tall stripper shoes and I interview him about his experience. This is always a very funny portion of the show, but I worried that this time, they could have lost trust in me. Thankfully that wasn't the case. The rest of the show went well and the audience felt as "with me" as in any other packed-house performance. Afterward, however, at the reception following the show, individual responses were tremendous. Rather than feeling like they had to comfort me — perhaps this is the fear we all have, should we "lose control" onstage — many felt they'd received something they wouldn't have imagined getting at the theatre. They felt they'd witnessed human emotion — not an actor recreating human emotion — real emotion.

Although there were a few moments where I did want to run sobbing from the stage, I didn't do that. I asked for their help (by breathing with me) and I recovered. Showing strength and vulnerability is a radical act in a woman's body for sure.

Conclusions

I am ending the book with these stunning examples of radical acts by women theater artists to make, one last time, the point that women's performance as social revolution implies a courageous yet deliberate gesture of putting one's body on the line, of embodying feminist ideas in space and time in a way that defies and by incremental degrees eradicates centuries and millennia of exclusion of women's bodies from public spaces, that resists and denounces centuries of violence against and degradation of these bodies and voices, of the intellectual and artistic expression of these embodied women. In their bold and holistic approach to the theatrical stage and to the larger world stage, these artists are reinventing our world and making it into a safer, more joyful, richer, more complex and definitely more bearable place to be, even as their laughter and ours arises from or is mixed with tears or even because of it.

Isabella, Franca and Colombina, Deb and Kimberly, Norma and Joan are creators in performance in the full sense of the world. Each in their own time has continued and developed the carnivalesque comedy of the mythic Baubo. They have shown us the magic as well as the revolutionary power that can emerge from the freedom of improvisation and the complex ways in which women's lives and creativity best thrive under such freedom. They have taught us to steal and fly with language. They have deliberately and successfully blurred the distinctions between their stages and social personae, and they have created unprecedented forms of subversive comedy, while creatively making use of the alternative tradition of women's humor and oral forms of expression.

Their art, their plays, their performance and their voices make us laugh with an empowering laughter. Gay Gibson Cima has expressed hope that "we may be able ... to rediscover, from the theatrical past, female directors who give our work in the present a sense of history as rich as our sense of the future."[40] Writers of comedy, improvisers and directors of their own roles, tricksters and militants each in their own way, all the gutsy Colombinas portrayed in my book do precisely this not only for female directors but for female comedians and creators of comedy, and for women in general: they give us a sense of history, while also providing us with rich examples of well-rounded female creators, in the tradition of the multi-dimensional Renaissance artist. More than the female stand-up comics, they create a great variety of female voices, as they embody, impersonate and tell the stories of women from many walks of life caught in a variety of dramatic circumstances, which they always work out to their advantage, by cunning, intelligence, trickery and humor. More than actresses, they not only interpret and act out the roles they themselves have created but they improvise on these roles, fluidly change and recreate them. They are mostly responsible for the direction and the performance choices of their stage presence. Their humor unfolds at a variety of linguistic and performative levels, as it is expressed in gesture, stage action, speech or deliberate silence.

Together, I see all the performances, the roles, the stories acted out and created by the female artists portrayed in this book like a modern female-authored version of Boccaccio's *Decameron*, as they reflect the lives of women in a multitude of colors, tones, and shapes, and as they engage in humor from its subtlest to its most unbridled, even crudest forms. Their humor is bold and incites social change, it resists and denounces sexist and other forms of degrading humor, it is empowering and soothing to women and marginalized groups such as racial minorities, people with disabilities, gays and lesbians. It is at times melancholy, at times angry, at other times subtle and ironic, at other times bawdy and unleashed. It lives and emerges from the body and in the moment, it honors the present and it honors us, the greedy audience. It creates communities and utopias of joyfulness and freedom from pain even as it often emerges from pain. It is a multi-layered creation as it simultaneously draws from experience, destabilizes traditional histories, subverts definitions and stereotypes, reveals the cultural construction of gender, merges theory with practice. Through the example of such women theater artists as Isabella, Caterina, Franca, Deb, Kimberly, Joan and Norma, we women can keep having our own Renaissance, and we can keep laughing, chuckling, cackling, grinning, smiling or roaring with laughter.

Chapter Notes

Preface

1. Jill Dolan, *Utopia in Performance: Finding Hope at the Theater* (Ann Arbor: University of Michigan Press, 2005), 61.

2. Dolan, *Utopia in Performance*, 3.

3. Dolan, *Utopia in Performance*, 61.

4. Anne Beatts, quoted by Philip Auslander in *Acting Out: Feminist Performance*, ed. Lynda Hart and Peggy Phelan (Ann Arbor: University of Michigan Press, 1993).

5. Melissa Vickery-Bareford, Isabella Andreini: Reimaging "Woman" in Early Modern Italy. Dissertation. University of Missouri, Columbia, 2000. Discussed later in this study.

6. Also derived from a doctoral dissertation, Anne MacNeil's *Music and Women of the Commedia dell'Arte in the Late Sixteenth Century* (Oxford: Oxford University Press, 2003).

7. See Domnica Radulescu, "Caterina's Colombina: The Birth of a Female Trickster in Seventeenth Century France." *Theatre Journal* 60 (2008): 87–113.

8. The French edition edited by Charles Mazouer, referenced later on.

Introduction

1. For discussions and analyses of the mythic figure of Baubo, see Froma Zeitlin, Frances Gray, and Franca Rame. They all point to the image of Baubo as the first female creator of comedy for women and about women, breaking taboos and bringing solace to suffering women. You will find interesting comments by Franca Rame on this topic in Dario Fo's book entitled *Le gai savoir de l'acteur,* trans. Valerie Tasca (Paris: L'Arche, 1990). See Frances Gray, *Women and Laughter* (Charlottesville: University of Virginia Press, 1994) and Froma Zeitlin, *Playing the Other: Gender and Society in Classical Greek Literature* (Chicago: University of Chicago Press, 1996).

2. See the article by Olender, called "Aspects of Baubo," in David M. Halperin, John J. Winkler, and Froma I. Zeitlin, editors, *Before Sexuality: The Construction of Erotic Experience in the Ancient Greek World* (Princeton, NJ: Princeton University Press, 1990), 86–88.

3. See Mary Unterbrink, *Funny Women: American Comediennes, 1860–1985.* (Jefferson, NC: McFarland, 1987), 5.

4. See Annette Lust, *From the Greek Mimes to Marcel Marceau and Beyond.* (Lanham, MD: Scarecrow Press, 2000), 23.

5. See Allardyce Nicoll, *Masks, Mimes and Miracles: Studies in the Popular Theatre* (London: George G. Harrap, 1931), 96.

6. In the Theodosian codex, any man who would "take an actress on his own horse and keep her there so that she could not appear in public" was punished with a fine of five pounds in gold. And Justinus, Emperor of the East, had passed a law concerning the marriages of the *mimae* and legitimizing their children. See Nicoll, *Masks, Mimes and Miracles*, 92. This shows that the female performers were trying and to some degree, under Theodora, managing to gain some dignity in their profession.

7. See Franca Rame's interview in Dario Fo's *Le Gai savoir de l'acteur*, 277.

8. See the article by Constance Jordan, entitled "Feminism and the Humanists: The Case for Sir Thomas Elyot's Defense of Good Women," in Margaret Ferguson, Maureen Quilligan and Nancy Vickers, editors, *Rewriting the Renaissance: The Discourses of Sexual Difference in Early Modern Europe* (Chicago: University of Chicago Press, 1986).

9. Rame in Fo, *Le Gai savoir*, 277.

10. See Peter Burke, *Popular Culture in Early Modern Europe* (New York: Harper & Row, 1978). With regard to the creation of humor by women in a variety of societies and cultures, see Mahadev Apte, *Humor and Laughter: An*

Anthropological Approach (Ithaca, NY: Cornell University Press, 1985).

11. Cesare Molinari, *Theatre Through the Ages*. Trans. Colin Hamer (New York: McGraw-Hill, 1972) and *La Commedia dell'arte* (Milano: Arnoldo Mondadori, 1985); see Ferdinando Taviani, "La Fleur et le guerrier: les actrices de la *commedia dell'arte*." Trans. Eliane Deschamps-Pria; Ferdinando Taviani and Mirella Schino. *Il segreto della Commedia dell'arte*. (Firenze: La casa Usher, 1982). For a study of the way in which the first commedia companies functioned in relation to their patrons and of the relations within companies, see Winifred Smith, *Italian Actors of the Renaissance* (New York: Benjamin Bloom, 1968); and also Winifred Smith, *The Commedia dell'Arte: A Study in Italian Popular Comedy* (New York: Columbia University Press, 1912). For the most revolutionary perspectives on this topic, see the articles by Kathleen McGill about the role of women in the development of the art of improvisation in the commedia dell'arte: "Improvisatory Competence and the Cueing of Performance: The Case of the *Commedia dell'Arte*." *Text and Performance Quarterly* 10 (1990): 111–122; "Women and Performance: The Development of Improvisation by the Sixteenth-Century *Commedia dell'Arte*." *Theater Journal* 43 (1991): 59–69.

12. See Ferdinando Taviani and Mirella Schino, *Il segreto della Commedia dell'Arte*. In this study, Taviani and Schino argue at length that the great "secret" of the commedia is that women performers had a crucial role in precisely that aspect of the genre which accounted largely for its "mythical" quality, namely improvisation.

13. See Gustave Attinger, *L'Esprit de la commedia dell'arte dans le théâtre français*. (Paris: Librairie théâtrale, 1950). See also Richard Andrew, *Scripts and Scenarios: The Performance of Comedy in Renaissance Italy* (Cambridge: Cambridge University Press, 1993).

14. See also the recent study about the tensions between literature and performance in the commedia dell'arte and the modernity of this form of theater by Robert Henke, *Performance and Literature in the Commedia dell'Arte* (Cambridge: Cambridge University Press, 2002) 1.

15. See the study by Pierre-Louis Ducharte, *La Commedia dell'arte* (Paris: Editions d'Art et Industrie, 1955). See also the Introduction, by Kenneth McKee, to Flaminio Scala, *Scenarios of the Commedia dell'Arte: Flaminio Scala's Il Teatro Delle Favole Rappresentative* (New York: New York University Press, 1967), for a description of the history and sources of the commedia dell'arte, as well as for a description of the influences of the commedia in classical comedy.

16. McGill notes that the courtesans were also professional improvisers and the first actresses of the commedia.

17. See Burke, *Popular Culture in Early Modern Europe*, for an excellent exploration of the various cultural constructs and the roles of the marginalized groups, particularly women, during medieval and renaissance Europe.

18. The studies by McGill, Margaret Rosenthal, and Leanne Shemek offer important information and insights into the lives of courtesans, actresses and women in general during early modern Europe.

19. "La faccia femminile della *Comemdia dell'arte*, oggi la piu dimenticata, rappresenta, con ogni probabilita, il fattore determinante di quell proceso per cui I teatri espresso dale compagnie italienne della fine del XVI siecolo sono ancor oggi ricordati come un genere a parte e quasi un archetipo di teatro. Ed infatti all'inizio sono loro, le attrici, ad incarnare il livello piu nobile di quel che presto diventera il simbolo della Commedia dell'arte: l'Improvvisazione" (339).

20. Many of Isabella's ideas — about art, performance, comedy, love, women, the relations between men and women — are articulated in the letters she wrote to many of the personalities of her time. See *Lettere della Signora Isabella Andreini Padovana comica gelosa, e Academica Intenta, Nominata l'Accesa*. (In Venetia, MDCXL VII, Alla Minerva) 3.

21. A superb study on the commedia dell'arte and the Comédie Italienne during the second half of the seventeenth century in France is Virginia Scott, *The Commedia dell'Arte in Paris*, 1644–1697. (Charlottesville: University of Virginia Press, 1990).

22. In the nineteenth century, the writer George Sand produced with friends at her country estate commedia-type shows which tried to re-create precisely the art, the style and the dynamics of the earlier commedia troupes. Her son, Maurice Sand, wrote a valuable study on the commedia dell'arte.

23. Frances Gray, Regina Barecca, Philip Auslander, Anne Beatts, and Judy Little have all written substantive and valuable studies on women's humor in general, the cultural differences between men's and women's humor, the marginalization of women's humor in the sphere of mainstream comedy, and women's humor and comedy as forms of resistance to and subversion of oppressive social structures.

24. See Lisa Tuttle, *Encyclopedia of Feminism* (New York: Facts on File, 1986).

25. See the studies by Little, Barreca, Gray, and Apte.

26. In Hart and Phelan, in *Acting Out: Feminist Performance*, 316–317.

27. Quoted in the article by Philip Auslander, "'Brought to You by Fem Rage': Stand-up Comedy and the Politics of Gender," in Hart and Phelan, *Acting Out*, 315–337.

28. See the excellent study by Judy Little, *Comedy and the Woman Writer* (Lincoln: University of Nebraska Press, 1983).

29. Gray does articulate the idea that the Eleusinian mysteries are very likely the origin of comedy, together with or even before the Dionysian cults, usually considered as the source of Western comedy.

30. Rosalind Miles is quoted in Gray, 30.

31. Luce Irigaray in *This Sex Which Is Not One* (Ithaca, NY: Cornell University Press, 1985).

32. This view is shared by critics such as Apte, Barreca, Beatts, Gray, and Little.

33. See the article by Patti Gillespie, entitled "Feminist Theory of Theater: Revolution or Revival?," in Karen Laughlin and Catherine Schuler, *Theater and Feminist Aesthetics* (Madison, NJ: Fairleigh Dickinson University Press, 1995).

34. In *Upstaging Big Daddy*, edited by Ellen Donkin and Susan Clement (Ann Arbor: University of Michigan Press, 1993).

35. Quoted from Linda Gordon by Jill Dolan, in *The Feminist Spectator as Critic* (Ann Arbor: University of Michigan Press, 1988), 3.

36. In Robyn Warholl and Diane Price Herndl, *Feminisms* (New Brunswick, NJ: Rutgers University Press, 1997), X.

37. Jill Dolan, *Utopia in Performance*, 4.

38. See Richard Bauman, "Verbal Art as Performance," *American Anthropologist* 77 (1975): 290–312. See also Linda Pershing, "There's a Joker in the Menstrual Hut: A Performance Analysis of Comedian Kate Clinton," in Linda Morris, *American Women Humorists* (New York: Garland Publishing, 1994).

39. In *Feminisms*, on "Women and Madness."

40. Sue-Ellen Case, *Split Britches: Lesbian Practice/Feminist Performance* (New York: Routledge, 1996), 4.

41. Aristotle, Hobbs, and Freud stressed that humor emerges from a feeling of superiority of the spectator toward the "inferior" doings or characters of certain types of human beings. Of course the long and disturbing history of sexist humor is based precisely on the dynamics of one class of people taking another as the butt of jokes. See also Gray on the notion of "the butt of jokes," particularly developed by Freud.

42. Stierle, Kant, and Bergson developed theories according to which humor emerges either from incongruous juxtapositions, such as, in Bergson's words, "the overlapping between the human and the mechanical," or when an action is taken out of its habitual context. These theories are more gender-blind, and would offer fruitful ground for some analysis of feminist humor.

43. Hegel and Bergson also believed that humor is a form of liberation from anxieties and inhibitions. According to Hegel, comedy is supposed to have a "reconciliatory" effect reflecting the movements of consciousness in surpassing its own inner conflicts. This view contrasts with that of many feminist theorists who believe that women's humor is not only not "reconciliatory" but that the "reconciliatory" happy ending in marriage, for instance, is in itself a form of reenforcement of the status quo of patriarchy.

44. Offensive and disparaging views of women's ability to create humor have existed for centuries and they persist today. Two examples of such views, often quoted by feminist humor theoreticians, are the statements made by William Congreave, with regard to "women's inability to be witty," and Reginald Blyth's idea that women, being "natural," can only be, like the monkeys in the zoo, "the undeferentiated laughing at which man laughs" (Quoted in Gray, 7). See Reginald Blyth's *Humor in English Literature: A Chronological Anthology* (Folcroft, PA: Folcroft, 1959).

45. See Auslander, "'Fem-Rage,'" in which he points out the connections between humor and power, and the analogy between humor and power and sex and power. The same analogy is discussed by Gray as well. Auslander's article is in Hart and Phelan's collection *Acting Out: Feminist Performance*.

46. Gray, 13.

47. Ibid, 36.

Chapter One

1. For comprehensive studies on the lives and condition of women in early modern Europe, see Vickery-Bareford, Joan Kelly Gadol, and Mary-Beth Rose. Critics such as Gadol and Rose have discussed at length the various layers of the marginalization of women during the Renaissance. In the article provocatively entitled "Did Women Have a Renaissance?" in the collection *Feminism and Renaissance Studies*, Lorna Hutson, ed. (Oxford: Oxford University Press, 1999), Gadol (then Joan Kelly) gives a negative answer to the title question. Rose discusses at length women's levels of marginalization and of resistance at different levels of social and cultural life during the Middle Ages and Renaissance in her edited collection *Women in the Middle Ages and the Renaissance: Literary and Historical Perspectives* (Syracuse, NY: Syracuse University Press, 1986).

2. Critics such as Anne McNeil, Pierre-Louis Duchartre, Ferdinando Taviani, and Melissa Vickery-Bareford are among the few commedia critics who have explored and analyzed at some length the life, works and performance art of Isabella Andreini.

3. On the history of commedia and the first female performers, see the studies by Pierre-Louis Duchartre, *La Commedia dell'arte*; Cesare

Molinari, *Theatre Through the Ages* and *La Commedia dell'Arte*; Ferdinando Taviani, "Attori e attrici della commedia dell'arte" and "La Fleur et le guerrier: les actrices de la *commedia dell'arte*"; and Fernando Taviani and Mirella Schino, *Il segreto della commedia dell'arte*. For a study of the way in which the first commedia companies functioned in relation to their patrons and of the relations within companies, see Winifred Smith, *Italian Actors of the Renaissance* (New York: Benjamin Bloom, 1968) and also Winifred Smith, *The Commedia dell'Arte: A Study in Italian Popular Comedy* (New York: Columbia University Press, 1912).

4. See the article by Janice Kliendest Joplin, entitled "The Voice of the Shuttle Is Ours," in the collection *Rape and Representation*, Lynn A. Higgins and Brenda R. Silver, eds. (New York: Columbia University Press, 1991).

5. Even critics such as Taviani, McNeil, and Vickery-Bareford, who explored the revolutionary role that Isabella's improvisational techniques had for her time and the development of the art of performance, still insist upon and attribute too much to this proverbial virtue.

6. Giuseppe Pavoni, Niccolò Barbieri and Tomasso Garzoni praised Isabella's art in exuberant terms. See Pavoni, *Diario Descritto da Guiseppe Pavoni. Delle feste celebrate nelle solennissime nozi delli serenissimi sposi, il sig. Don Ferdinando Medici, and la sig. Donna Christina di Loreno gran duchi di Toscana. Nel quale con brevità si esplica il torneo, la battaglia navale, la comedia con gli intermedii, and alter feste accorse di giorno in giorno per tutto il di di 15, Maggio, MDLXXXIX* (Bologna: Giovanni Rossi, 1589); Niccolò Barbieri, *La Supplica, doscorso famigliare di Niccolò Barbieri detto Beltrame diretto a coloro che scrivendo o parlando trattano dee'comici trascurrando I meriti delle azzioni virtuose* (Venice: M. Ginammi, 1634); and Garzoni, *La Piazza universale di tutte le professioni del mondo, nobili e ignobile* (Venice: Gio. Battista Somasco, 1585).

7. An example of such "hystera theater" would be the retelling and staging of Freud's story of Dora by Cixous and Benmusa in their play *Portrait de Dora*. The performance is a combination of sounds, dreams, and images, following Cixous' urging women to abandon all notion of plot and action, and instead tell their story, rely on gesture, on their own language, and on their laughter, akin to the laughter of Medusa, who is not "deadly," but "beautiful." In Elaine Aston, *Feminist Theater Practices*, 71–72.

8. See the article by Elin Diamond in Hart and Phelan, 372.

9. Mikhail Bakhtin, *Rabelais and His World*. Trans. Hélène Iswolsky (Bloomington: Indiana University Press, 1984), 9 and 19.

10. Quoted in Gray, 37.

11. See the writings of Duchartre and the preface written by McKee to the Scenarios of Flaminio Scala with regard to the nature and sources of the commedia.

12. McGill points out that the actresses' stage presences were highly idealized and/or eroticized during the period of the commedia.

13. In "Women and Performance," 64.

14. "Ne riso fè, che non beasse un core." In *Vite et ritratti delle donne celebri d'ogni paese* (*Lives and Portraits of Famous Women from Every Country*).

15. "Avendo ella fatto profondo studio del cuore umano, sapea toccarne le piu occulte fibre ed eccitare come piu gli piacesse l'amore, la pietà, la tenerezza, l'ira, la disperazione, l'orore, lo spavento, il giubilo et l'esultanza," 246.

16. "Women and Performance," 63.

17. Critics like Molinari, Nicoll, Duchartre, and McGill all stressed that the improvisational art of the commedia would not have been what it was without the presence of women.

18. Vickery-Bareford and Duchartre discussed the fact that the female roles emerged from the lives, personalities and imaginations of the actresses who played them.

19. McGill is the only critic who has developed at length the argument that one of the main sources of the improvisatory art of the commedia was the oral culture of women.

20. McGill discusses at length the fact that women brought with them collaborative work practices and creation, which became the working style of the commedia troupes.

21. Louise Clubb and Duchartre have noted that the commedia plays, precisely because so much depended on the highly collaborative practice of improvisation, were based on a generally egalitarian division of parts and of stage presence, without encouraging the prima donna style of monopolizing the stage.

22. See Clubb, *Italian Drama in Shakespeare's Time* (New Haven: Yale University Press, 1989), 260.

23. See McNeil's summary of criticism about Isabella Andreini from the sixteenth century to the present, 11–25.

24. "Essendo per avventura questo desiderio di sapere nato in me più ardente, che in molte alter donne dell'età nostra." *Lettere della Signora Isabella Andreini Padovana comica gelosa, and Academica Intenta, Nominata l'Accesa.* (In Venetia, MDCXLVII, Alla Minerva) 3.

25. The "honest courtesan," in Taviani and Schino, 340.

26. Taviani and Duchartre have pointed out how the actors playing Arlechino or Pantalone were often called by these stage names in real life and how their stage persona often merged with their social and real life personae.

27. See Gray, 20.

28. See the studies by Robin Lakoff, *Language and Woman's Place* (New York: Octagon Books, 1976), and Deborah Tannen, *You Just Don't Understand: Women and Men in Conversation* (New York: Morrow, 1990).

29. Pietro Mattei, *Histoire de France, et des choses mémorables, advenues aux provinces estrangères Durant sept années de paix. Du regne du Roy Henry IIII, Roy de France and Navarre. Divissé en sept livres.* (Paris: Chez I. Metayer Imprimeur du Roy, and M. Guillemot, 1606) ; Antonio Maria Spelta, *La curiosa, et dilettevole aggionta del Sig. Ant. Maria Spelta, cittadino pavese, all'historia sua; nella quale oltra la vaghezza di molti cose che dall'anno 1596, fino al 1603, s'intendono, sono anco componimenti arguti, da quail non poco gli elevati spiriti potrano prendere* (Pavia: Pietro Bartoli, 1602).

30. Louise Clubb notes: "Through the bombast of Francesco Andreini's baroque evocation ... relentlessly histrionic and tumid with crocodile tears, those turned to the history of this famous theatrical couple may hear accents of genuine heartbreak." In *Italian Drama in Shakespeare's Time,* 257–60.

31. McNeil, Taviani, and Molinari all discuss the importance of mad scenes, or *desperatione*, which were stepping-stones and necessary tours de force in the actress's career.

32. Quoted in McGill.

33. Salerno and McKee in Scala's collection xvi, Andrews in *Scenarios.*

34. See Molinari, 1985, 37–47.

35. In Zannetti, 246.

36. Vickery-Bareford comments on Isabella's place in the balcony.

37. Tommaso Garzoni, *La piazza universale di tutte le professioni del monde* (Venice: Somosco, 1585), 737.

38. See Jean Howard, "Cross-Dressing, the Theater, and Gender Struggle in Early Modern England," in Lesley Ferris' collection *Crossing the Stage: Controversies on Cross-Dressing* (New York: Routledge, 1993).

39 See Deanna Shemek, *Ladies Errant: Wayward Women and Social Order in Early Modern Italy* (Durham, NC: Duke University Press, 1998).

40. See Shemek, "From Insult to Injury: Bandello's Tales of Isabella Luna," in her *Ladies Errant.* Isabella Luna was apparently a formidable woman who had achieved a certain degree of wealth and notoriety as a courtesan and also as a soldier, the courtesan or prostitute soldier being a not uncommon phenomenon during the Renaissance in Spain and Italy.

41. Howard in Ferris, 25.

42. Fletcher, "Planché, Vestis and the Transvestite Role," 31, quoted in Vickery-Bareford.

43. In Ferris, 26.

44. See Howard, in Ferris 26. Howard discusses the radical symbolism of a woman leaving the house, and the freedom that came with cross-dressing with regard to women leaving the domestic sphere for the public one.

45. See Susan Glenn, *Female Spectacle: The Theatrical Roots of Modern Feminism* (Cambridge, MA: Harvard University Press, 2000), 41.

46. Henri Bergson, "Laughter," in *Comedy,* ed. Wylie Sypher (New York: Doubleday Anchor Books, 1956), 85–87.

47. Luce Irigaray, *This Sex Which Is Not One,* 76.

48. See Mary Beth Rose, XIV; also see Hanley and Neuschel, in Wolfe, *Changing Identities in Early Modern France.*

49. See also the pages about the carnival and social reversals in Peter Burke's study about popular culture in early modern Europe.

50. In *Speculum,* 26.

51. Gray, 6.

52. "La laideur, c'est a dire la non-conformité au code actuel du beau, dont se sert telle comedienne, come l'indice non seulement d'une violence subie dans sa féminité, mais aussi d'une révolte contre toute féminité convenue." As noted in Anne Ubersfeld, *Lire le théâtre II. L'école du spectateur.* (Paris: Belin, 1996), 140.

53. Shemek discusses aspects of this culture of the gaze during the Renaissance.

54. Margaret Miles, in her book *Carnal Knowing: Female Nakedness and Religious Meaning in the Christian West* (Boston: Beacon Press, 1988), discusses at length these two antithetic forms of representation of the female body.

55. See the excellent article by Elisa Weaver on "convent drama."

56. See Winifred Smith's *Italian Actors of the Renaissance* (New York: Benjamin Bloom, 1968). Smith speculates on Andreini's Venetian origins.

57. "Il risultato piu pieno dell'arte scenica italiana del Rinascimento" and that it has the value of "una summa, oltre che dei modi teatrali, anche di una complessa, articolata e contradittoria visione del mondo." "L'altra faccia del 1589: Isabella Andreini e la sua pazzia," *Firenze et la Toscana dei Medici nell Europea del 500* (Firenze: L.S. Olschki, 1983), 573.

58. See the article by Gay Gibson Cima, entitled "Ways of Subverting the Canon," in the edited collection called *Upstaging Big Daddy*, on the interaction between theory and practice in theater.

59. See the article on "hystera-theater" by Elin Diamond in Hart and Phelan, 376.

60. Quoted in Barreca, 28.

61. See Rose on the role of marriage and women's resistance to it during early modern Europe. Also see Gadol and Rose on the subject of women and marriage during the Renaissance.

62. See the book by Robert Mouchembled entitled *Passions de femmes au temps de la Reine Margot 1553–1615.* (Paris: Seuil, 2003).

63. See Diamond's article in Hart and Phelan, 364.

64. Ibid, 365.

65. See Elaine Aston, the chapter about hysteria and the discussion of Charcot's experiments with Augustine.

66. She has in fact been compared to Ophelia by both Clubb and Henke.

67. Critics like Gray, Finney, Glenn, Auslander, Barreca, and Beatts all start discussions of women's humor by trying to contend with this oppressive cliché of women's supposed lack of humor.

68. Quoted by Philip Auslander in his article "'Brought to You by Fem-Rage" in Hart and Phelan, *Acting Out*, 317.

69. Quoted in Clubb, 259.

70. "Il suo sano e dotto intelletto," Pavoni, 46.

71. "Mormorio et meraviglia," Pavoni, 46.

72. "Mentre durera il mondo, sempre sara lodata la sua bella elloquenza e valore," Pavoni, 47.

Chapter Two

1. Duchartre, Attinger, Virginia Scott, Charles Mazouer — all point out the presence of Colombina as part of the repertoire of the Italian troupe in France under Louis XIV.

2. Silvio d'Amico and Sandro d'Amico, *Enciclopedia dello Spettacolo* (Roma: Casa Editrice Le Maschere, 1975); and Luigi Rasi, *I Comici Italiani: Biografia, bibliografia, iconografia* (Florence: Fratelli Bocca, 1897–1905) vol. I, 425.

3. François Parfaict, *Histoire de l'ancien Théâtre Italien depuis son origine en France jusqu'à sa suppression en l'année 1697*. See also Delia Gambelli, *Arlecchino a Parigi: Dall'inferno alla corte del re sole* (Rome: Bulzoni Editore, 1993). Gambelli provides ample information about the Biancolelli family and their theatrical activities throughout the seventeenth century in France. She mentions the moving anecdote, related by Thomas Simon Gueullette, that Caterina decided to play the role of Colombina when as a child she saw in her father's house a portrait of her grandmother Isabella carrying a basket with two doves ("colombe"), a symbol of Colombina, 256. See also Thomas-Simon Gueullette, *Notes et souvenirs sur le théâtre italien au XVIII siècle* (Paris: Droz, 1938), and Silvio d'Amico and Sandro d'Amico, *Enciclopedia dello spettacolo* (Rome: Casa Editrice Le Maschere, 1975), 425. It is to be noted that Caterina's mother, Orsola Cortesi, was also a playwright besides being a consummate performer, as were other actresses in the seventeenth century. For more information on the Biancolelli family see also the article by Sergio Monaldini, "Arlecchino figlio di Pulcinella e Colombina: Note sulla famiglia Biancolelli, tra

Bologna e Parigi," *L'Archiginnasio* 91 (1996): 83–161. In this chapter I will use the French and Italian versions of Catherine/Caterina, Columine/Colombina interchangeably to point to her double citizenship and cultural identity. The same stands true for Arleguin/Arlecchino.

4. See Bruce Griffiths, "Sunset: From Commedia dell'Arte to Comédie Italienne," in George and Gossip, *Studies in the Commedia dell'Arte* (Cardiff: University of Wales Press, 1993), 93–94.

5. See Virginia Scott's study *The Commedia dell'Arte in Paris, 1644–1697* (Charlottesville: University Press of Virginia, 1990) and the introduction by Charles Mazouer to the modern edition of Evaristo Gherardi's collection of French plays on the contributions of the French writers and the collaborations with the Italian troupes during this period.

6. Griffiths, 93–94.

7. In *The Commedia dell'Arte: A Study in Italian Popular Comedy*, 202.

8. In *Evaristo Gherardi: Le Théâtre Italien*. Ed. Charles Mazouer. (Paris: Société des Textes Français Modernes, 1994) 22.

9. In Rasi, vol. I, 440.

10. Griffiths and Scott have both commented on the possible influence of Molière or crossover between the two troupes.

11. See McKee's preface to Flaminio Scala's scenarios on this point.

12. See the studies by Elisa Weaver on convent drama: "The Convent Wall in Tuscan Convent Drama," in the collection edited by Craig Monson, *The Crannied Wall : Women, Religion, and the Arts in Early Modern Europe* (Ann Arbor: University of Michigan Press, 1992); and "The Convent Muses: The Secular Writing of Italian Nuns," in the collection edited by Lucetta Scaraffia and Gabriella Zarri, *Women and Faith: Catholic Religious Life in Italy from Late Antiquity to the Present* (Cambridge, MA: Harvard University Press, 1999).

13. In Mary Beth Rose's collection *Women in the Middle Ages and the Renaissance: Literary and Historical Perspectives* (Syracuse, NY: Syracuse University Press, 1986) 181–83.

14. In Margaret Rosenthal's *The Honest Courtesan* (Chicago: University of Chicago Press, 1992), 2.

15. "In consequence of the agreement of the king obtained by Mademoiselles Françoise and Catherine Biancolelli, sisters ... to enter into the said troupe and continue to play there each of them the character which they have already begun.... " Quoted in Scott, 253.

16. Translation in William Howarth, *French Theater in the Neo-Classical Era, 1550–1789* (Cambridge: Cambridge University Press, 1997) 364.

17. See Campardon, *Troupe Italienne*, vol. II, 109–12.

18. Howarth, 323.
19. See Burke and Rose on the subject of women's access to books, writing and the problem of illiteracy among women during the Renaissance.
20. Quoted in Scott, 257.
21. The story of the misfortunes of Françoise Biancolelli is recounted in detail in Parfaict's *Histoire du théâtre français*.
22. Scott, 103.
23. See Susan Glenn's book *Female Spectacle: The Theatrical Roots of Modern Feminism* (Cambridge, MA: Harvard University Press, 2000). Glenn brilliantly connects performance to the beginnings of modern feminism.
24. Glenn, 59.
25. In particular, Scott and Duchartre.
26. See Duchartre's description of Arlecchino, 118–122.
27. On the history and origins of Arlecchino, see Duchartre and Molinari.
28. See the already mentioned studies by McGill, Lust, Griffin, and Rosenthal, which all point out the importance of the courtesans in the development of theatrical entertainment and their particular improvisational, comedic, poetic, and acting skills.
29. See Rame and Lust on female mimes, acrobats, and dancers.
30. McGill points out the wedding songs, jokes, and poems as part of the repertoire and oral culture of women during the Renaissance.
31. See Burke on female alternative forms of entertainment.
32. In her book *Ladies Errant*, Shemek analyzes in detail the phenomenon of the prostitute soldiers, in particular that of the legendary Isabella Luna, a striking example of female independence and emancipation.
33. *Enciclopedia dello spettacolo*.
34. Both the drawing and the poem are reproduced in Duchartre's book on the commedia dell'arte.
35. Both Griffiths and Mazouer suggest this possible influence, but without any clear evidence.
36. As McKee has suggested in his preface to Flaminio Scala's scenarios, the reverse influence is more probable: that of Molière and, before him, as pointed out by McKee, Shakespeare himself, taking plots from the commedia repertoire and reworking them in their own plays.
37. Shemek, 161.
38. See Duchartre on all the characters and the performers who played them in the various troupes.
39. As, for instance, in *Les Souhaits*, in the scene explicitly entitled "Contre les hommes."
40. Hélène Cixous and Catherine Clement, *The Newly Born Woman*, translated by Betsy Wing (Minneapolis: University of Minnesota Press, 1986), 33.

41. The interesting pun here is that "linnet" in French also means "scatter brain."
42. See Frances Gray's critical analysis of different theories of humor in her book *Women and Laughter*.
43. Auslander, Gray, and Beatts have noted that much too often women have been historically used as objects of male humor, rather than seen as subjects capable of humor themselves.
44. As Hobbes does in his treatise *On Human Nature*. In W. Molesworth, ed., *The English Works of Thomas Hobbes*, Vol. IV (Bohn: 1840), 46.
45. Aristotle, *Poetics*, Trans. T.S. Dorsch, in *Classical Literary Criticism* (New York: Penguin, 1965), 37.
46. See *In Stitches: a Patchwork of Feminist Humor and Satire,* edited by Gloria Kaufman (Bloomington: Indiana University Press, 1991).
47. Burke entertains this theory. However, this is all arguable as it is undoubtedly better to at least have that "valve" and the suggestion of a liberation, or the glimpse of social reversals, however briefly, than not to have it at all. According to French theater theorists like Patrice Pavis, humor and comedy imply a certain degree of enhanced lucidity of one's condition. It is also the opinion of the playwright Eugène Ionesco.
48. See Scott, 257, and, as mentioned earlier, Parfaict, under the entry for Françoise Biancolelli.
49. The Norma Gravely quote is given in Gray, 34. For the comments on the coquette see also Natasha Sajé, "'Artful Artlessness': Reading the Coquette in *Roderick Hudson*," *Henry James Review* 18, no. 2 (1997): 161–72.
50. Griffiths, 101.
51. Quoted in Barreca, 14.
52. Both Scott and Attinger discuss in some detail the holding of shares and the financial and administrative dynamics of the Italian troupes.
53. See also Scott on the issue of the Italian versus French troupes with regard to maintaining the reputation of the women and of the acting families in general.
54. See Griffin with regard to the actress-courtesans of the nineteenth century, as well as Glenn about the collapsing of the personal and the public or the performative with nineteenth century actresses.
55. Griffin discusses several cases of extravagant and strikingly rich courtesans, particularly during the Belle Epoque, and discusses them in terms of their "legacy of virtue." As I have pointed out in my comparison between Colombina and Machiavellian ethics, so Griffin notes that the courtesans were "virtuous in a moral sense," in the sense "once applied exclusively to men," which refers to "the strengths and attributes that characterize as well as distinguish a person" (10). By this she means precisely the art of

surviving and prevailing over social and personal vicissitudes.

56. See the chapter called "Satirizing the Courtesan" in Margaret Rosenthal, *The Honest Courtesan* (Chicago: University of Chicago Press, 1992).

57. See Cixous and Clement, 34.

58. In *Rereading Aphra Behn: History, Theory, and Criticism*, edited by Heidi Hutner (Charlottesville: University of Virginia Press, 1993).

59. This is Howarth's and not my translation; he discusses this practice in his book on the commedia dell'arte, 371.

60. Translation mine.

61. See Griffiths, 97.

62. See the introduction by Lesley Ferris, as well as the article by Jean Howard in the same collection.

63. See Julia Kristeva, *Histoires d'amour* (Paris: Denoel, 1983).

64. Griffiths, 100.

65. Griffiths, 100.

66. Winifred Smith comments on Colombina's many disguises.

67. "Oh, ça coquins, je suis Colombine, et voici Arlequin. Vous avez joué a croix et pile, a qui m'epouserait, je vous ai fait jouer au roi de Coeur, a qui serait pendu, et je me marie avec Arlequin. Cintho et Octave se mocquoient de ma maitresse, elle s'est moquée d'eux" (vol. IV, 198).

68. See the article by Bonnie Marranca, Elinor Fuchs, and Gerald Rabkin, "The Politics of Representation: New York Theater Season," 1990–1991," in *Performing Arts Journal* 13:3 (1991), 39, 14.

69. Ferris, 41.

70. See Mazouer's preface on this point.

71. Mentioned in Barreca, 7.

72. Barreca, 8.

73. Keir Elam, *The Semiotics of Theatre and Drama* (New York : Methuen, 1980).

74. Perrucci, 256.

75. See Mel Gordon's book *Lazzi: The Comic Routines of the Commedia dell'Arte.* (New York: Performing Arts Journal Publications, 1983).

76. See Gordon.

77. The following studies on orality are pertinent to theories of improvisation. Albert Bates Lord, *The Singer Resumes the Tale* (Ithaca, NY: Cornell University Press, 1995). Lord coined the term of "creation in performance" when discussing the improvisational art of oral poets and storytellers, referring to the notion of the spontaneous creation of lines, images, and verse while performing a song or telling a story. See also John Miles Foley, *The Singer of Tales in Performance* (Bloomington: Indiana University Press, 1995).

78. McGill, 119.

79. McGill, 119.

80. See N. M. Bernardin, *La Comédie italienne en France et les théâtres de la foire et du boulevard (1570–1791)* (Paris: Editions de la revue bleue, 1902), 19.

81. "L'action qui rate son but," *Dictionaire du théâtre,* under "le comique."

82. Barreca, 16.

83. Barreca, 15.

84. Clement and Cixous, *The Newly Born Woman.*

85. As noted in the discussion of the comic dimensions of Isabella's performance, according to Bergson, one of the sources of laughter is the "overlapping of the mechanical over the human."

86. See Hélène Cixous, "The Laugh of the Medusa," in E. Marks and T. de Courtivron, trans. and eds., *New French Feminisms* (Brighton: Harvester Press, 1981), 249.

Chapter Three

1. Franca Rame and Dario Fo, *Récits de femmes et autres histories,* trans. Valerie Tasca (Paris: Dramaturgie, 1986).

2. Palazzina Liberty is also the site of a revolutionary act by Rame and Fo. They initiated, followed by thousands of people, the occupation of a cluster of buildings in Milan, which had been condemned by the municipal government. Rame and Fo performed on a regular basis in the abandoned gardens and buildings. But, as Ron Jenkins has noted, it was Rame who "has always been the driving force behind the couple's political activism. She is the one who organizes events that reflect their joint commitments to theatrical artistry and social causes." In Ronald Scott Jenkins, Dario Fo and Franca Rame: Artful Laughter (New York: Aperture, 2001).

3. See Joseph Farrell, *Dario Fo and Franca Rame, Harlequins of the Revolution* (London: Methuen, 2001), 26.

4. See the article by Antonio Scuderi, "Improvisation and Framing in the Fo-Rame Collaboration," in Walter Valeri, *Franca Rame, A Woman on Stage* (West Lafayette, IN: Bordighera, 2000), 176.

5. Ron Jenkins' article in Valeri, 59.

6. Scuderi's article in Valeri, 177.

7. Luciana d'Arcangeli, "Franca Rame Giullaressa," in Valeri's edition, 160.

8. Cotino-Jones' article in Valeri, 9.

9. In Valeri, 175.

10. As Serena Anderlini D'Onofrio has demonstrated in her article titled "Rame and Fo's Theater Partnership" in Valeri.

11. Cotino-Jones, 9.

12. Farrell, *Dario Fo and Franca Rame, Harlequins of the Revolution,* 74.

13. In Fo, *Le Gai savoir de l'acteur.*

14. Cotino-Jones, 10.

15. Cotino-Jones, 11.
16. See d'Arcangeli in Valeri, 161.
17. In *Acting Out: Feminist Performance*, 373.
18. In Farrell, 27.
19. Vol. I, "Avertissement."
20. Farrell, 28.
21. In Valeri, 177–78.
22. Dario Fo and Stuart Clink Hood, *The Tricks of the Trade* (New York: Routledge, 1991), 190.
23. In Valeri, 3.
24. *Le gai savoir de l'acteur*, 276–82.
25. d'Arcangeli, in Valeri, 161.
26. d'Arcangeli, in Valeri, 161.
27. In Valeri, 9.
28. See the references to Rame in Elin Diamond's article in Hart and Phelan's *Acting Out*, and in Elaine Aston's *Feminist Theater Practice: A Handbook* (New York: Routledge, 1999).
29. Gay Gibson Cima's article "Strategies for Subverting the Canon," in Elen Donkin and Clement, *Upstaging Big Daddy*.
30. In Hart and Phelan. See also Lizbeth Goodman's *Contemporary Feminist Theaters: To Each Her Own* (New York: Routledge, 1993).
31. Teresa de Lauretis, *Alice Doesn't: Feminism, Semiotics, Cinema* (Bloomington: Indiana University Press, 1984), 5–6.
32. Preface to *Récits de femmes*, 22–23.
33. In Valeri, 11.
34. In Valeri, 11.
35. This horrible event is mentioned by d'Arcangeli in Valeri, 169. Franca also speaks of it in the interview by Serena Anderlini, in her doctoral thesis entitled "Gender and Desire in Contemporary Drama: Lillian Hellman, Natalia Ginzburg, Franca Rame and Ntozake Shange" (University of California, Riverside, 1987). Franca turned this traumatic event into a dramatic piece called *The Rape*.
36. In Fo, *The Tricks of the Trade*, 191.
37. Quoted in d'Arcangeli, 159.
38. Both d'Arcangeli and Dario Fo himself have noted the debt of Franca's art to buffoons and clowns.
39. *Le gai savoir*, 277; translation mine.
40. In Valeri, 173.
41. In Farrell, 74.
42. In *Le gai savoir*, 282–84.
43. In Karen Laughlin and Catherine Schuler, *Theater and Feminist Aesthetics* (Madison, NJ: Fairleigh Dickinson University Press, 1995), 79.
44. Rame, in *Le gai savoir*, 292.
45. Translation mine, *Récits de femmes*, 17.
46. See Valeri's discussion of Rame's versatility in interacting with the audience, 3.
47. See Sue-Ellen Case, *Feminism and Theater* (New York: Methuen, 1988) 15.
48. Aristotle, *Poetics*. See the part about comedy.

49. See Margaret Miles, *Carnal Knowing: Female Nakedness and Religious Meaning in the Christian West* (Boston: Beacon Press, 1988), on the discussion of the female body as a deviant form of a male body and the grotesque representations of it in Western art. Mary Beth Rose also touches upon this issue.
50. See the article by Ron Jenkins in Valeri, 59. Jenkins worked very closely with Rame onstage as her personal interpreter, and he expresses his awe at Franca's impressive stage presence, improvisational abilities, and spontaneous humor.
51. See Gray, 28.
52. See Christine Miller, *Emily Dickinson, A Poet's Grammar* (Cambridge, MA: Harvard University Press, 1987), 178.
53. In Miller, 178–79.
54. Lizbeth Goodman, *Mythic Women/Real Women: Plays and Performance Pieces by Women* (London: Faber & Faber, 2000), x.
55. Goodman, 183, quoted in Cotino-Jones, in Valeri, 42.
56. Patti Gillespie in Laughlin and Schuler, *Theater and Feminist Aesthetics*.
57. In Morris, *American Women Humorists*, 155–68.
58. In Warhol and Herndl, *Feminisms*, 347.
59. In Warhol and Herndl, *Feminisms* 348.
60. In Morris, *American Women Humorists*, 23–30.
61. Kaufman, in Morris, *American Women Humorists* 32.
62. "Noi donne siamo fatte diversamente dagli uomini, anche come modo di pensare. Vediamo le cose in modo diverso dai maschi, anche per la condizione in cui viviamo. Ci sono cose a cui gli uomini non possono neanche arrivare." Translation mine. Anderlini, 261.
63. The interview with Franca in Anderlini, 258.
64. Serena D'Onofrio Anderlini's article on Franca Rame in Valeri.
65. In *Le Gai savoir*, 299–300.
66. Susan Glenn's book *Female Spectacle: The Theatrical Roots of Modern Feminism* (Cambridge, MA: Harvard University Press, 2000), 2.
67. Glenn, 3.
68. The entire text of *Sex? No, Thanks for Asking* is given in Valeri's collection, 83.
69. In Valeri, 81.
70. In Valeri, 81.
71. Gray, *Women and Laughter*, 6.
72. Elin Diamond in Hart and Phelan, 364.
73. Quoted in Shoshana Felman's article in Warhol and Herndl, *Feminisms*, 17.
74. See McGill, "Improvisatory Competence," 112.
75. See on improvisation Roberto Tessari, *La Commedia dell'Arte: La Maschera e l'Ombra*. (Milan: Mursia, 1981), 87–91.

76. Molinari, 37–47.

77. "Una efficace retorica della gestualità," 91.

78. Mario Appollonio, in *Quaderni*, 22, as described by Andrea Perucci in his *Dell'arte rappresentativa*.

79. McGill, "Improvisatory Competence," 111.

80. In "Attori ed Attrici," 183.

81. Rame, in *Sex? No, Thanks for Asking*, in Valeri, 105.

82. See Sylvie Jouanny, *L'actrice et ses doubles: figures et représentations de la femme de spectacle à la fin du XIXe siècle* (Génève: Droz, 2002).

83. See Albert Lord, *The Singer Resumes the Tale* (Ithaca, NY: Cornell University Press, 1995), 34.

84. Lord, *The Singer Resumes the Tale*, 62.

85. In *Le gai savoir*, 292.

86. Quoted in Pat Gillespie's article in Laughlin and Schuler, *Theater and Feminist Aesthetics*.

87. In Laughlin and Schuler, *Theater and Feminist Aesthetics*, 78–79.

88. In Valeri, 105.

89. In Warhol and Herndl, *Feminisms*, 361.

90. Cixous in Warhol and Herndl, 357.

91. In Warhol and Herndl, *Feminisms*, 20.

92. In Warhol and Herndl, *Feminisms*, 16.

93. Quoted in Felman, in Warhol and Herndl, *Feminisms*, 7.

94. In *Récits de femmes et autres histoires*, Trans. Valérie Tasca (Paris: Dramaturgie, 1986), 83. See also, in English translations, the following collections of plays and monologues by Franca Rame, in collaboration with Dario Fo: *Female Parts: One Woman Plays* (London: Pluto Press, 1981); *A Woman Alone and Other Plays* (London: Methuen, 1991); and, in Italian, the famous collection *Parliamo di donne: il teatro* (Milano: Kaos, 1992).

95. In *Récits de femmes*, 84.

96. Felman, in Warhol and Herndl, *Feminisms*, 16.

97. Ibid.

98. In *Récits de femmes*, 74.

99. Ibid, 79.

100. Fellman, in Warhol and Herndl, *Feminisms*, 16.

101. In *Récits de femmes*, 74, 78.

102. As when she vows vengeance in the name of all women, or as in the play where she mocks and punishes the reprehensible Marquis for the way in which he misuses his position as a spectator onstage, by indecently staring at women.

103. See Kathleen Rowe, *The Unruly Woman: Gender and the Genres of Laughter* (Austin: University of Texas Press, 1995). The book offers excellent discussions of the "carnivalesque" and the "unruly" woman who destabilizes established notions of femininity and gender roles in film and on television.

104. In Kathleen Rowe, *The Unruly Woman*, 31.

105. See Guerrilla Girls, *Bimbos, Bitches and Ballbreakers: The Guerrilla Girls' Illustrated Guide to Female Stereotypes* (New York: Penguin, 2003), especially the section on Barbie dolls.

106. Rowe, *The Unruly Woman*, 5.

107. Scuderi in Valeri, *A Woman on Stage*, 177.

108. See Scuderi's discussion of Franca's timing and talent for improvising in Valeri, *A Woman on Stage*, 178.

109. See McGill, "Improvisatory Competence," 119.

Chapter Four

1. Sue-Ellen Case, *Split Britches*, 2.

2. Case referenced in the collection co-edited by Ellen Mayock and Domnica Radulescu, *Feminist Activism in Academia: Essays on Personal, Political and Professional Change* (Jefferson, NC: McFarland, 2010), 104–05.

3. Which was the result of merging together for that conference passages from her play *Index to Idioms* and *O Yes I Will (I Will Remember the Spirit and Texture of This Conversation)*.

4. The quote from Lynda Hart is given in Dolan's *Utopia in Performance*, together with Dolan's comment that follows, on p. 59.

5. Her work has been reviewed in such journals and newspapers as *San Diego Gay News* (2003) and *Hawaii Tribune-Herald* (2002 and 2003), and she tours the country with her shows, which she performs largely (but not exclusively) for university audiences.

Chapter Five

1. As I mentioned earlier, Franca Rame is noted in passing as a performer who performs the mimesis mimicry of breaking up known feminine molds, in Elin Diamond's article in Hart and Phelan's *Acting Out* and in Elaine Aston's *Feminist Theater Practice*.

2. Aston, 63.

3. See Vivian Patraka, "Split Britches: Performing History, Vaudeville, and the Everyday," in Hart and Phelan.

4. See Duchartre's study on the commedia troupes and their mode of working.

5. See Patraka in Hart and Phelan, *Acting Out*, 220.

6. In Patraka's article, in Hart and Phelan, 221.

7. In Patraka's article, in Hart and Phelan, 223.

8. In Patraka's article, in Hart and Phelan, 223.

9. More often than not out of necessity, when finding myself with a class of mostly or all

women and deciding to produce plays with both male and female characters.

10. See Laughlin and Schuler's *Theater and Feminist Aesthetics*, Hart and Phelan's *Acting Out*, and Aston's *Feminist Theater Practice*.

11. In Valeri's *A Woman on Stage*, 3.

12. See the article by Julie Malnig and Judy C. Rosenthal, "The Women's Experimental Theatre: Transforming Family Stories into Feminist Questions," in Hart and Phelan, *Acting Out*.

13. See Joyce Devlin's article, "Siren Theatre Company: Politics in Performance," in Hart and Phelan, 184.

14. See Sabrina Hamilton's article, "Split Britches and the Alcestis Lesson: 'What Is This Albatross?,'" in Donkin and Clement, *Upstaging Big Daddy*, 135–37.

15. Both McGill and Taviani noted that before the inclusion of women in the troupes, neither improvisation nor collaborative creation were very developed and were rather rudimentary.

16. One of the actresses in Siren, quoted in Aston, *Feminist Theater Practice*, in 1997, 86.

17. Evidence of Franca's freedom in creating her shows and her role as creator, director and performer is to be found in Valeri's *A Woman on Stage*, Jenkins' *Artful Laughter*, and Farrell's *Harlequins of the Revolution*.

18. See Kathleen Lea's book *Italian Popular Comedy: A Study of the Commedia dell'Arte, 1560–1620* (Oxford: Clarendon Press, 1934), 386–87.

19. See Serena Anderlini's interview with Franca, in her doctoral thesis entitled *Gender and Desire in Contemporary Drama*.

20. Quoted in Aston, 35.

21. As in the studies of Aristotle or Reginald Blyth.

22. As already noted, such writers and performers as Blyth, Congreve, and Coquelin have maintained and expressed such views.

23. Recounted in Farrell, 27.

24. See Eugenio Barba and Nicola Savarese, *A Dictionary of Theater Anthropology: The Secret Art of the Performer*. Trans. Richard Fowler. (New York: Routledge, 2004), 7–8.

25. See Aston on disguise and cross-dressing, *Feminist Theater Practice*, 74.

26. See the seminal work by Sandra Gilbert and Susan Gubar, *The Madwoman in the Attic: The Woman Writer and the Nineteenth Century Literary Imagination* (New Haven: Yale University Press, 1984).

27. See Torril Moi's book *Sexual/Textual Politics: Feminist Literary Theory* (London: Methuen, 1985), 140.

28. See Anna Furse's *Augustine (Big Hysteria)* (Amsterdam: Harwood Academic Publishers, 1997).

29. Quoted in the doctoral dissertation by Maera Claudia, Carnivalesque Disruptions and Political Theater. Plays by Dario Fo, Franca Rame and Caryl Churchill (University of Reading, 1999), 717.

30. See Gordon's book about *lazzi*, quoted earlier.

31. See the article about Karen Finley in Hart and Phelan, *Acting Out*.

32. See the discussion of carnivalesque women and Roseanne Barr as such an example, in Rowe, *Unruly Women*.

33. See Judy Little's article "Humoring the Sentence," 157.

34. Quoted and given as an example of carnivalized dialogue, in Judy Little's article, "Humoring the Sentence," 158.

35. See Francine du Plessix Gray, *Rage and Fire* (New York: Simon and Schuster, 1994) and her discussions of the backlash against women in the nineteenth century, which followed their emancipation during the French Revolution.

36. See Teresa de Lauretis, *Alice Doesn't*.

37. McGill, "Improvisatory Competence," 114.

38. Ibid, 116.

39. See Les Essif, "A Workshop on the Re-creative Approach to Performing and Teaching," in Domnica Radulescu and Maria Stadter Fox, eds., *The Theater of Teaching and the Lessons of Theater* (Lanham, MD: Rowman and Littlefield, 2005).

40. See "Strategies for Subverting the Canon," in Donkin and Clement's *Upstaging Big Daddy*, 102.

Bibliography

Anderlini, Serena. Gender and Desire in Contemporary Drama: Lillian Hellman, Natalia Ginzburg, Franca Rame and Ntozake Shange. Dissertation. University of California, Riverside, 1987.

Andreini, Isabella. *Fragmenti di alcune scritture della Signora Isabella Andreini, comica gelosa, & academica intenta.* Venetia: Presso G.B. Combi, 1627.

_____. *Lettere della Signora Isabella Andreini Padovana comica gelosa, & Academica Intenta, Nominata l'Accesa.* Venetia: Alla Minerva, 1647.

_____. *La Mirtilla: A Pastoral.* Trans. Julie D. Campbell. Tempe, AZ: Arizona Center for Medieval and Renaissance Studies, 2002.

Andrews, Richard. *Scripts and Scenarios: The Performance of Comedy in Renaissance Italy.* Cambridge: Cambridge University Press, 1993.

Appollonio, Mario. *Teresio Olivelli.* Roma: Edizioni cinque lune, 1966.

Apte, Mahadev. *Humor and Laughter: An Anthropological Approach.* Ithaca, NY: Cornell University Press, 1985.

Aristotle. "Poetics." In *Classical Literary Criticism.* Trans. T.S. Dorsch. New York: Penguin, 1965.

Aston, Elaine. *Feminist Theater Practice: A Handbook.* New York: Routledge, 1999.

Attinger, Gustave. *L'Esprit de la commedia dell'arte dans le théâtre français.* Paris: Librairie théâtrale, 1950.

Auslander, Philip. "Brought to You by Fem Rage." In *Acting Out: Feminist Perfromance.* Lynda Hart and Peggy Phelan, eds. Ann Arbor: University of Michigan Press, 1993.

Bakhtin, Mikhail. *Rabelais and His World.* Trans. Hélène Iswolsky. Bloomington: Indiana University Press, 1984.

Barba, Eugenio. *On Directing and Dramaturgy: Burning the House.* Drama and Theater Studies series. New York: Routledge, 2009.

Barba, Eugenio, and Nicola Savarese. *A Dictionary of Theater Anthropology: The Secret Art of the Performer.* Trans. Richard Fowler. New York: Routledge, 2004.

Barbieri, Niccolò. *La Supplica, doscorso famigliare di Niccolò Barbieri detto Beltrame diretto a coloro che scrivendo o parlando trattano dee'comici trascurrando I meriti delle azzioni virtuose.* Venice: M. Ginammi, 1634.

Barreca, Regina. *Last Laughs: Perspectives on Women and Comedy.* New York: Gorgon and Breach, 1988.

Bauman, Richard. "Verbal Art as Performance." In *American Anthropologist 77* (1975).

Bergson, Henri. "Laughter." In *Comedy.* Wylie Sypher, ed. New York: Doubleday Anchor Books, 1956.

Bernardin, N.M. *La Comédie italienne en France et les théâtres de la foire et du boulevard (1570–1791)*. Paris: Editions de la revue bleue, 1902.

Blyth, Reginald. *Humor in English Literature: A Chronological Anthology*. Folcroft, PA: Folcroft Library Editions, 1959.

Boal, Augusto. *The Aesthetics of the Oppressed*. Trans. Adrian Jackson. London & New York: Routledge, 2006.

_____. *Theater of the Oppressed*. Trans. Charles A. Maria-Odilia Leal McBride. New York: Theater Communications Group, 1985.

Brown, Pamela Allen. *Better a Shrew Than a Sheep*. Ithaca, NY: Cornell University Press, 2003.

Burke, Peter. *Popular Culture in Early Modern Europe*. New York: Harper & Row, 1978.

Butler, Judith. *Gender Trouble*. New York: Routledge, 1999.

Case, Sue-Ellen. *Feminism and Theater*. New York: Methuen, 1988.

_____. *Split Britches: Lesbian Practice/Feminist Performance*. New York: Routledge, 1996.

Cima, Gay Gibson. "Strategies for Subverting the Canon." In *Upstaging Big Daddy*. Ellen Donkin and Susan Clement, eds. Ann Arbor: University of Michigan Press, 1993.

Cixous, Hélène. "The Laugh of the Medusa." In *New French Feminisms*. Elaine Marks and Isabelle de Courtivron, eds. Brighton: Harvester Press, 1981.

_____, and Catherine Clement. *The Newly Born Woman*. Trans. by Betsy Wing. Minneapolis: University of Minnesota Press, 1986.

Clubb, Louise. *Italian Drama in Shakespeare's Time*. New Haven: Yale University Press, 1989.

d'Amico, Silvio, and Sandro d'Amico. *Enciclopedia dello Spettacolo*. Rome: Casa Editrice le Maschere, 1975.

d'Arcangeli, Luciana. "Franca Rame Giullaressa." In *Franca Rame: A Woman on Stage*. Walter Valeri, ed. West Lafayette, IN: Bordignera, 2000.

de Lauretis, Teresa. *Alice Doesn't: Feminism, Semiotics, Cinema*. Bloomington: Indiana University Press, 1984.

De Visé, Donneau. *Le Mercure Galant*. October 1683.

Devlin, Joyce. "Siren Theatre Company: Politics in Performance." In *Acting Out: Feminist Performance*. Lynda Hart and Peggy Phelan, eds. Ann Arbor: University of Michigan, 1993.

Diamond, Elin. "Mimesis, Mimicry, and the 'True-Real.'" In *Acting Out: Feminist Performance*, Lynda Hart and Peggy Phelan, eds. Ann Arbor: University of Michigan Press, 1993.

Dollan, Jill. *The Feminist Spectator as Critic*. Ann Arbor: University of Michigan Press, 2009.

_____. "Geographies of Learning: Theatre Studies, Performance, and the 'Performative,'" *Theatre Journal* 45 (1993): 417–41.

_____. *Utopia in Performance. Finding Hope at the Theater*. Ann Arbor: University of Michigan Press, 2008.

Donkin, Ellen, and Susan Clement, eds. *Upstaging Big Daddy*. Ann Arbor: University of Michigan Press, 1993.

Duchartre, Pierre-Louis. *La Commedia dell'Arte*. Paris: Editions d'Art et Industrie, 1955.

du Plessix Gray, Francine. *Rage and Fire*. New York: Simon and Schuster, 1994.

Elam, Keir. *The Semiotics of Theatre and Drama*. London: Methuen, 1980.

Essif, Les. "A Workshop on the Re-creative Approach to Performing and Teaching." In *The Theater of Teaching and the Lessons of Theater*. Domnica Radulescu and Maria Stadter Fox, eds. Lanham, MD: Rowman and Littlefield, 2005.

Farrell, Joseph. *Dario Fo and Franca Rame: Harlequins of the Revolution*. London: Methuen, 2001.

Ferris, Lesley. *Crossing the Stage: Controversies on Cross-Dressing*. New York: Routledge, 1993.

Fo, Dario. *Le gai savoir de l'acteur.* Trans. Valerie Tasca. Paris: L'Arche, 1990.
_____, and Stuart Clink Hood. *The Tricks of the Trade.* New York: Routledge, 1991.
Foley, John Miles. *The Singer of Tales in Performance.* Bloomington: Indiana University Press, 1995.
Furse, Anna. *Augustine (Big Hysteria).* Amsterdam: Harwood Academic Publishers, 1997.
Gadol, Joan Kelly. "Did Women Have a Renaissance?" In *Feminism and Renaissance Studies.* Lorna Hutson, ed. Oxford: Oxford University Press, 1999.
Gambelli, Delia. *Arlecchino a Parigi: Dall'inferno alla corte del re sole.* Rome: Bulzoni Editore, 1993.
Garzoni, Tomasso. *La Piazza universale di tutte le professioni del mondo, nobili e ignobile.* Venice: Gio. Battista Somasco, 1585.
George, David J., Christopher J. Gossip. *Studies in the Commedia dell'Arte.* Cardiff: University of Wales Press, 1993.
Gilbert, Sandra, and Susan Gubar. *The Madwoman in the Attic: The Woman Writer and the Nineteenth Century Literary Imagination.* New Haven: Yale University Press, 1984.
Gillespie, Patti. "Feminist Theory of Theater: Revolution or Revival?" In *Theater and Feminist Aesthetics.* Karen Laughlin and Catherine Schuler, eds. Madison, NJ: Fairleigh Dickinson University Press, 1995.
Glenn, Susan. *Female Spectacle: The Theatrical Roots of Modern Feminism.* Cambridge, MA: Harvard University Press, 2000.
Goodman, Lizabeth. *Contemporary Feminist Theaters: To Each Her Own.* New York: Routledge, 1993.
_____. *Mythic Women/Real Women: Plays and Performance Pieces by Women.* London: Faber & Faber, 2000.
Gordon, Mel. *Lazzi:The Comic Routines of the Commedia dell'arte.* New York: Performing Arts Journal Publications, 1983.
Gray, Frances. *Women and Laughter.* Charlottesville: University of Virginia Press, 1994.
Griffiths, Bruce. "Sunset: from *Commedia dell'Arte* to Comédie Italienne." In *Studies in the Commedia dell'Arte.* David J. George and Christopher J. Gossip, eds. Cardiff: University of Wales Press, 1993.
Grotowski, Jerzy. *Towards a Poor Theater.* New York: Routledge, 2002.
Guerrilla Girls. *Bimbos, Bitches and Ballbreakers: The Guerrilla Girls' Illustrated Guide to Female Stereotypes.* New York: Penguin, 2003.
Hamilton, Sabrina. "Split Britches and the Alcestis Lesson: 'What Is This Albatross?'" In *Upstaging Big Daddy.* Ellen Donkin and Susan Clement, eds. Ann Arbor: University of Michigan Press, 1993.
Hart, Lynda, and Peggy Phelan, eds. *Acting Out: Feminist Performance.* Ann Arbor: University of Michigan, 1993.
Henke, Robert. *Performance and Literature in the Commedia dell'Arte.* Cambridge: Cambridge University Press, 2002.
Hobbes. "On Human Nature." In *The English Works of Thomas Hobbes*, Vol. IV. W. Molesworth, ed. Aalen: Scientia, 1840.
Howard, Jean. "Cross-Dressing, the Theater, and Gender Struggle in Early Modern England." In *Crossing the Stage: Controversies on Cross-Dressing.* Lesley Ferris, ed. New York: Routledge, 1993.
Howarth, William. *French Theater in the Neo-Classical Era, 1550–1789.* Cambridge: Cambridge University Press, 1997.
Hutner, Heidi, ed. *Rereading Aphra Behn: History, Theory, and Criticism.* Charlottesville: University of Virginia Press, 1993.
Irigaray, Luce. *Speculum of the Other Woman.* Ithaca, NY: Cornell University Press, 1985.
_____. *This Sex Which Is Not One.* Ithaca, NY: Cornell University Press, 1985.
Jenkins, Ronald Scott. *Dario Fo and Franca Rame: Artful Laughter.* New York: Aperture, 2001.

Joplin, Janice Kliendest. "The Voice of the Shuttle Is Ours." In *Rape and Representation*. Lynn A. Higgins and Brenda R. Silver, eds. New York: Columbia University Press, 1991.

Jordan, Constance. "Feminism and the Humanists: The Case for Sir Thomas Elyot's Defense of Good Women." In *Rewriting the Renaissance: The Discourses of Sexual Difference in Early Modern Europe*. Margaret Ferguson, Maureen Quilligan, and Nancy Vickers, eds. Chicago: University of Chicago Press, 1986.

Jouanny, Sylvie. *L'actrice et ses doubles: figures et représentations de la femme de spectacle à la fin du XIXe siècle*. Génève: Droz, 2002.

Kaufman, Gloria, ed. *In Stitches: A Patchwork of Feminist Humor and Satire*. Bloomington: Indiana University Press, 1991.

Kristeva, Julia. *Histoires d'amour*. Paris: Denoel, 1983.

Lakoff, Robin. *Language and Woman's Place*. New York: Octagon Books, 1976.

Laughlin, Karen, and Catherine Schuler. *Theater and Feminist Aesthetics*. Madison, NJ: Fairleigh Dickinson University Press, 1995.

Lea, Kathleen. *Italian Popular Comedy: A Study of the Commedia dell'Arte, 1560–1620*. Oxford: Clarendon Press, 1934.

Little, Judy. *Comedy and the Woman Writer*. Lincoln: University of Nebraska Press, 1983.

Lord, Albert Bates. *The Singer Resumes the Tale*. Ithaca, NY: Cornell University Press, 1995.

Lust, Annette. *From the Greek Mimes to Marcel Marceau and Beyond*. Lanham, MD: Scarecrow Press, 2000.

MacNeil, Anne. *Music and Women of the Commedia dell'Arte in the Late Sixteenth Century*. Oxford: Oxford University Press, 2003.

Maera, Claudia. Carnivalesque Disruptions and Political Theater: Plays by Dario Fo, Franca Rame and Caryl Churchill. Dissertation. University of Reading, 1999.

Malnig, Julie, and Judy C. Rosenthal. "The Women's Experimental Theatre: Transforming Family Stories into Feminist Questions." In *Acting Out: Feminist Performance*. Lynda Hart and Peggy Phelan, eds. Ann Arbor: University of Michigan, 1993.

Margolin, Deb. *Time Is the Mercy of Eternity*. London: Samuel French, 2007.

_____, and Lynda Hart. *Of All the Nerve: Deb Margolin Solo*. Critical Performances. New York: Cassell, 1999.

Marranca, Bonnie, Elinor Fuchs, and Gerald Rabkin. "The Politics of Representation: New York Theater Season, 1990–1991." In *Performing Arts Journal* 13:3 (1991).

Mattei, Pietro. *Histoire de France, et des choses mémorables, advenues aux provinces estrangères Durant sept années de paix. Du regne du Roy Henry IIII, Roy de France & Navarre. Divissé en sept livres*. Paris: Chez I. Metayer Imprimeur du Roy, and M. Guillemot, 1606.

Mayock, Ellen, and Domnica Radulescu. *Feminist Activism in Academia. Essays on Personal, Political and Professional Change*. Jefferson, NC, and London: McFarland, 2010.

Mazouer, Charles, ed. *Evaristo Gherardi: Le Théâtre italien*. Paris: Société des Textes Français Modernes, 1994.

McGill, Kathleen. "Improvisatory Competence and the Cueing of Performance: The Case of the Commedia dell'Arte." *Text and Performance Quarterly* 10 (1990).

_____. "Women and Performance: The Development of Improvisation by the Sixteenth-Century Commedia dell'Arte." *Theater Journal* 43 (1991).

Miles, Margaret. *Carnal Knowing: Female Nakedness and Religious Meaning in the Christian West*. Boston: Beacon Press, 1988.

Miller, Cristanne. *Emily Dickinson: A Poet's Grammar*. Cambridge, MA: Harvard University Press, 1987.

Moi, Torril. *Sexual/Textual Politics: Feminist Literary Theory*. London: Methuen, 1985.

Molinari, Cesare. "L'altra faccia del 1589: Isabella Andreini e la sua pazzia." In *Firenze et la Toscana dei Medici nel Europea del 500*. Florence: L.S. Olschki, 1983.

_____. *La Commedia dell'Arte*. Milano: Arnoldo Mondadori, 1985.

_____. *Theater Through the Ages.* Trans. Colin Hamer. New York: McGraw-Hill, 1972.

Morris, Linda. *American Women Humorists: Critical Essays.* New York: Garland, 1994.

Mouchembled, Robert. *Passions de femmes au temps de la Reine Margot 1553–1615.* Paris: Seuil, 2003.

Nicoll, Allardyce. *Masks, Mimes and Miracles: Studies in the Popular Theatre.* London: George G. Harrap, 1931.

Olender. "Aspects of Baubo." In *Before sexuality: The Construction of Erotic Experience in the Ancient Greek World.* David M. Halperin, John J. Winkler, and Froma I. Zeitlin, eds. Princeton, NJ: Princeton University Press, 1990.

Parfaict, François. *Histoire de l'ancien Théâatre Italien depuis son origine en France jusqu'à sa suppression en l'année 1697.* Paris, 1767.

Patraka, Vivian. "Split Britches: Performing History, Vaudeville, and the Everyday." In *Acting Out: Feminist Performance.* Lynda Hart and Peggy Phelan, eds. Ann Arbor: University of Michigan, 1993.

Pavoni, Giuseppe. Diario. *Delle feste celebrate nelle solennissime nozi delli serenissimi sposi, il sig. Don Ferdinando Medici, & la sig. Donna Christina di Loreno gran duchi di Toscana. Nel quale con brevità si esplica il torneo, la battaglia navale, la comedia con gli intermedii, & alter feste accorse di giorno in giorno per tutto il di di 15, Maggio, MDLXXXIX.* Bologna: Giovanni Rossi, 1589.

Pershing, Linda. "There's a Joker in the Menstrual Hut: A Performance Analysis of Comedian Kate Clinton." In *American Women Humorists.* Linda Morris, ed. New York: Garland, 1994.

Perucci, Andrea. *Dell'arte Rappresentativa Premeditata ed all'improviso.* Napoli: n.p., 1699.

Phillippy, Patricia. *Painting Women: Cosmetics, Canvases, and Early Modern Culture.* Baltimore: Johns Hopkins University Press, 2005.

Radulescu, Domnica. "Caterina's Colombina: The Birth of a Female Trickster in Seventeenth Century France." *Theater Journal,* March 2008.

_____. "Developing Feminist Theater Pedagogy with Undergraduate Students. Two Performances of Beckett's *Happy Days.*" In *Radical Acts: Teaching Feminisms, Theater and Transformation.* Ann Elizabeth Armstrong and Kathleen Juhl, eds. San Francisco: Aunt Lute's Press, 2007.

Radulescu, Domnica, and Maria Stadter Fox, eds. *The Theater of Teaching and the Lessons of Theater.* Lanham, MD: Rowman and Littlefield, 2005.

Rame, Franca, and Dario Fo. *Female Parts: One Woman Plays.* London: Pluto Press, 1981.

_____. *Parliamo di donne: il teatro.* Milano: Kaos, 1992.

_____. *Récits de femmes et autres histories.* Trans. Valerie Tasca. Paris: Dramaturgie, 1986.

_____. *A Woman Alone and Other Plays.* London: Methuen, 1991.

Rasi, Luigi. *I Comici Italiani: Biografia, bibliografia, iconografia.* Florence: Fratelli Bocca, 1897–1905.

Rose, Mary-Beth. *Women in the Middle Ages and the Renaissance:Literary and Historical Perspectives.* Syracuse, NY: Syracuse University Press, 1986.

Rosenthal, Margaret. *The Honest Courtesan.* Chicago: University of Chicago Press, 1992.

Rowe, Kathleen. *Unruly Women: Gender and the Genres of Laughter.* Austin: University of Texas Press, 1995.

Sajé, Natasha. "'Artful Artlessness': Reading the Coquette in *Roderick Hudson,*" *Henry James Review* 18, no. 2 (1997).

Scala, Flaminio. *Scenarios of the commedia dell'arte: Flaminio Scala's Il teatro delle favole rappresentative.* New York: New York University Press, 1967.

Scott, Virginia. *The Commedia dell'Arte in Paris. 1644–1697.* Charlottesville: University Press of Virginia, 1990.

Scuderi, Antonio. "Improvisation and Framing in the Fo-Rame Collaboration." In *Franca Rame: A Woman on Stage.* Walter Valeri, ed. West Lafayette, IN: Bordignera, 2000.

Shemek, Deanna. *Ladies Errant: Wayward Women and Social Order in Early Modern Italy.* Durham, NC: Duke University Press, 1998.

Smith, Winifred. *The Commedia dell'Arte: A Study in Italian Popular Comedy.* New York: Columbia University Press, 1912.

_____. *Italian Actors of the Renaissance.* New York: Benjamin Bloom, 1968.

Spelta, Antonio Maria. *La curiosa, et dilettevole aggionta del Sig. Ant. Maria Spelta, cittadino pavese, all'historia sua; nella quale oltra la vaghezza di molti cose che dall'anno 1596, fino al 1603, s'intendono, sono anco componimenti arguti, da quail non poco gli elevati spiriti potrano prendere.* Pavia: Pietro Bartoli, 1602.

Stortoni, Laura Anna, and Mary Prentice Lillie. *Women Poets of the Italian Renaissance: Courtly Ladies and Courtesans.* New York: Italica Press, 2008.

Tannen, Deborah. *You Just Don't Understand: Women and Men in Conversation.* New York: Morrow, 1990.

Taviani, Ferdinando. "Attori ed attrici della Commedia dell'arte." In *El teatre durant l'edat mitjana i el renaixement.* Ricard Salvat, ed. 177–205. Barcelona: Publications i edicions de la Universitat de Barcelona, 1986.

_____. "La fleur et le guerrier: Les actrices de la Commedia dell'Arte." Translated by Eliane-Deschamps-Pria. In B*ouffoneries: L'Energie de l'Acteur: Anthropologie Théâtrale.* No. 15/16 (1986).

_____, and Mirella Schino. *Il segreto della Commedia dell'Arte: la memoria delle compagnie italiane del XVI, XVII e XVIII secolo.* Firenze: La casa Usher, 1982.

Tessari, Roberto. *La Commedia dell'Arte: la Maschera e l'Ombra.* Milan: Mursia, 1981.

Tuttle, Lisa. *Encyclopedia of Feminism.* New York: Facts on File Publications, 1986.

Ubersfeld, Anne. *Lire le théâtre II. L'école du spectateur.* Paris: Belin, 1996.

Unterbrink, Mary. *Funny Women: American Comediennes 1860–1985.* Jefferson, NC: McFarland, 1987.

Valeri, Walter, and Franca Rame. *Franca Rame: A Woman on Stage.* West Lafayette, IN: Bordignera, 2000.

Vickery-Bareford, Melissa. *Isabella Andreini: Reimaging "Woman" in Early Modern Italy.* Dissertation. University of Missouri, Columbia, 2000.

Warholl, Robyn, and Diane Price Herndl. *Feminisms.* New Brunswick, NJ: Rutgers University Press, 1997.

Weaver, Elisa. "The Convent Muses: The Secular Writing of Italian Nuns." In *Women and Faith: Catholic Religious Life in Italy from Late Antiquity to the Present.* Lucetta Scaraffia and Gabriella Zarri, eds. Cambridge, MA: Harvard University Press, 1999.

_____. "The Convent Wall in Tuscan Convent Drama." In *The Crannied Wall: Women, Religion, and the Arts in Early Modern Europe.* Craig Monson, ed. Ann Arbor: University of Michigan Press, 1992.

Zeitlin, Froma. *Playing the Other: Gender and Society in Classical Greek Literature.* Chicago: University of Chicago Press, 1996.

Index

251

DATE DUE	RETURNED